*We Are Not a Vanishing People*

# *We Are Not a Vanishing People*

THE SOCIETY OF AMERICAN INDIANS, 1911–1923

THOMAS CONSTANTINE MAROUKIS

THE UNIVERSITY OF
ARIZONA PRESS
TUCSON

The University of Arizona Press
www.uapress.arizona.edu



ISBN-13: 978-0-8165-4227-7 (hardcover)
ISBN-13: 978-0-8165-4226-0 (paperback)

Cover design by Leigh McDonald
Cover illustration of the logo of the Society of American Indians, featuring an ancient stylized eagle. Designed by Angel De Cora. Photograph of SAI members at the first conference. First published in *The Columbus Dispatch*, Sunday edition, October 15, 1911, p. 10. All images courtesy of The Ohio State University Libraries.
Typeset by Sara Thaxton in 10/14 Warnock Pro (text), Bulmer MT Std, and Golden WF (display)

The proceeds from the sale of this book will be donated to the Dr. Thomas C. Maroukis Endowed Scholarship Fund for Native American Students.

Publication of this book is made possible in part by the proceeds of a permanent endowment created with the assistance of a Challenge Grant from the National Endowment for the Humanities, a federal agency.

Library of Congress Cataloging-in-Publication Data
Names: Maroukis, Thomas Constantine, 1938– author.
Title: We are not a vanishing people : the Society of American Indians, 1911–1923 / Thomas Constantine Maroukis.
Description: Tucson : The University of Arizona Press, 2021. | Includes bibliographical references and index.
Identifiers: LCCN 2020051223 | ISBN 9780816542277 (hardcover) | ISBN 9780816542260 (paperback)
Subjects: LCSH: Society of American Indians—History. | Indians of North America—Politics and government—20th century.
Classification: LCC E75 .M36 2021 | DDC 323.1197—dc23
LC record available at https://lccn.loc.gov/2020051223

Printed in the United States of America
♾ This paper meets the requirements of ANSI/NISO Z39.48-1992 (Permanence of Paper).

*To my dearest wife, Dr. Cassandra Tellier, "my best buddy," for her love and support during the time-consuming process of travel, research, and writing. This would have been impossible without her encouragement and assistance.*

# CONTENTS

# ILLUSTRATIONS

# ABBREVIATIONS

| | |
|---|---|
| *AIM* | *American Indian Magazine* |
| CM | Carlos Montezuma Papers |
| GPO | Government Printing Office |
| *NYT* | *New York Times* |
| OIA | Office of Indian Affairs (Bureau of Indian Affairs) |
| *QJ* | *Quarterly Journal of the Society of American Indians* |
| SAI | Society of American Indians |
| *WJ* | *Wassaja: Freedom's Signal for the Indians* |

# PREFACE

In the fall of 1911, a group of American Indians met in Columbus, Ohio, to establish a national organization. Although the resulting Society of American Indians had only a brief history (1911–1923), it had a long-range impact. While the historic significance of the Society has been recognized recently, there is an ongoing reassessment of its role in American Indian history. This study will analyze the Society's goals, policies, and strategies, placing them at the forefront of early-twentieth-century Native American protest and activism. It will also assess the Society's legacy as part of American Indian intellectual history and the development of political activism aimed at empowering American Indians to determine their own future.

While living and teaching in Columbus, I discovered that this major American Indian organization was founded here more than a century ago. By coincidence, while browsing at a garage sale, amid old books, maps, and magazines, I came across five original offprints of papers that were presented at the inaugural 1911 conference—on sale for fifty cents each. One was Arthur Parker's paper "The Philosophy of Indian Education"; another was Marie L. Baldwin's "Modern Home-Making and the Indian Woman." The caption on the papers' title pages states, "A paper read before the First Annual Conference of the American Indian Association [the original name of the Society], Ohio State University, Columbus, Ohio, October 12–15, 1911." Intrigued by this find, I began to research the Society's origins in Columbus and its conferences at The Ohio State University (OSU). I wrote a paper on the founding of the Society and presented it at the annual Ohio Academy of History conference in April 2011. This coincided with another event: the American Indian Studies Program at Ohio State was planning a centennial symposium to commemorate the founding of the Society.

My early interest in the SAI also stemmed from my studies on the Yankton Sioux and the history of the Peyote faith. In both studies, my research crossed paths with well-known author and Society member Gertrude Bonnin (aka Zitkala-Ša), who grew up on the Yankton Sioux Reservation in South Dakota. While researching the emergence of the Peyote faith among the Yankton, I discovered that Bonnin led an assault on peyote: she successfully lobbied the South Dakota legislature, as well as several other state legislatures, to outlaw its use and possession. In a later study on the history of the Peyote faith and the establishment of the Native American Church, I examined the federal government's attempt to criminalize its use and possession. In 1918, at the request of the Office of Indian Affairs, congressional hearings were held to debate and recommend the criminalization of peyote. Puzzled at first by the fact that SAI members testified on both sides of the issue, it became obvious that this controversy created turmoil that contributed to the demise of the Society. The debate was intense and acrimonious. Bonnin gave the most dramatic testimony opposing the use of peyote. I wrote an article on the impact of the peyote controversy on the SAI, which was published in an edited work on the Society of American Indians. This larger study followed.

Several other factors piqued my interest. I discovered the building that held the first two conferences at The Ohio State University was still in use as an office building and conference facility. Today it is the Frank W. Hale Jr. Black Cultural Center, housing the Office of Diversity and Inclusion. Also, the Hartman Hotel where the SAI attendees stayed in downtown Columbus is still in use. I was surprised that after more than one hundred years, the two facilities were still in existence. Although the hotel is now an office building with a new name, the original name, Hartman Hotel, is carved in a large granite block above the fourth-floor windows. I imagined that, at the time, fifty or so American Indians coming in and out of the building likely received puzzled glances from the local population. The present Frank Hale Center was the new student union building in 1911. It is now listed on the National Register of Historic Places. I walked through the building on several occasions, and as I wandered through the halls and up and down three stories of old oak staircases, admiring the original furniture in a reception area, I envisioned the conference participants walking through the building. I walked around the back of the building where the attendees posed for an iconic panoramic photograph (figure 5) that was published in the first issue of the Society's magazine and reprinted in the 2011 symposium program. I asked several people in the building if they knew of its historic import. No one knew about the 1911 and 1912 conferences or had even heard of the Society of American Indians. This, however, is changing due to recent publicity about the Society. In recent years, the staff of Ohio State's American Indian Studies Program hoped to acquire appropriate signage indicating the site's historic significance. The SAI members reflected fondly on their days at Ohio State, for throughout the organization's history, their official letterhead read "The Society of American Indians: A National Organization of Americans Organized at Ohio State University, April 1911."

As part of the celebration of the founding of the SAI, a three-day symposium titled "The Society of American Indians Centennial Symposium: 1911–2011" was hosted by The Ohio State University. It was a timely event, coming full circle, as the university had hosted the first two conferences and now, one hundred years later, the centennial symposium. As planned by the symposium organizers, there were many parallels between the 1911 conference and the 2011 event. Both were held in newly opened student union buildings; both featured welcoming addresses by the university president; both held banquets with speeches, entertainment, and academic presentations; both included visits to ancient American Indian mounds; and both featured an impressive array of Native scholars and activists.

At the centennial symposium, Sioux historian Philip J. Deloria noted that a group of scholars was gathering in Columbus to contemplate, consider, and celebrate the founding of the Society of American Indians. An air of poignancy was added as Deloria discussed his great-grandfather, also named Philip J. Deloria, who attended the first conference in 1911. Renya Ramirez (Ho-Chunk/Nebraska), from the University of California, Santa Cruz, co-chaired a roundtable discussion on SAI leaders, including Henry Roe Cloud, her grandfather, who was a member of the Society's original Executive Committee. The centennial symposium participants made presentations, held roundtable discussions, and on the last day, visited the two-thousand-year-old Octagon Earthworks at the Newark Earthworks site, about thirty-five miles east of Columbus. It was an exceptional conference, with present-day Native scholars assessing and reevaluating Native activists and intellectuals from one hundred years ago. Following the symposium, a variety of papers were submitted by the participants and others, published in 2013 as *The Society of American Indians and Its Legacies*, in a special combined issue of *Studies in American Indian Literatures* and *American Indian Quarterly*, edited by Chadwick Allen (former coordinator of the American Indian Studies Program at The Ohio State University, former editor of *SAIL: Studies in American Indian Literatures*, and presently associate provost for faculty advancement at the University of Washington) and Beth Piatote (associate professor of Native American studies at Stanford University). Professor Allen noted in his introductory chapter that their work on the SAI was in no way exhaustive or conclusive. He asked the question why "Native leaders, activists, and scholars who have come after the SAI, especially since the 1960s, have found its members and their ideas problematic or worse, irrelevant?" The symposium organizers challenged this perception, pointing out that the publications of the Society of American Indians were of great significance to "twentieth-century American Indian political, cultural, intellectual, and literary development." The 2011 symposium reflected and stimulated a renewed interest in the history of the SAI. The publication of some of the symposium papers added to this interest.

It took almost a century to initiate a reassessment of the SAI, recognizing its contributions to subsequent American Indian history. This study will demonstrate that the SAI had a significant impact, as it helped initiate a century of protest and activism, an essential step on the long road to self-determination.

# ACKNOWLEDGMENTS

I first want to thank the incredible staff at the University of Arizona Press. Kristen Buckles, editor-in-chief, made this all possible by arranging a smooth transition through the process of publication. Elizabeth Wilder, editorial assistant, provided insightful recommendations on the text and the arrangement of the images and captions. Her help was invaluable. Amanda Krause, editorial, design, and production manager, coordinated the production and editing process. Leigh McDonald, art director, assisted in preparing the images and designing the cover. I truly appreciate the friendliness of the staff and the immediate responses I received to my many emails and phone calls.

I thank Nick Spitulski of The Ohio State University Libraries for access to photographs. Thanks also go to Ohio History Connection (formerly the Ohio Historical Society) for assistance in accessing Society of American Indians publications.

I also want to recognize Chad Allen and Beth Piatote for organizing the "Society of American Indian Centennial Symposium, 1911–2011," at The Ohio State University, which I attended. At that time, I had already begun researching the origins of the Society in Columbus; however, the conference spurred me on to do a full history.

I also want to thank Richard Ashbrook, former provost at Capital University, for supporting my sabbatical, making this research and writing possible.

Also, thanks to my student assistant Caroline Hinders for her help with computer searches and typing.

Lastly, I must offer my appreciation to the late Lindsay Jones in the Department of Comparative Studies at The Ohio State University. We became friends about twenty-five years ago. He encouraged and supported me on several of my research ventures. He will be missed.

*We Are Not a Vanishing People*

# Introduction

The Society of American Indians was established in 1911 by a group of reform-minded Indians. It was the first influential national organization by and for American Indians. The possibility of establishing such an organization had been debated by several Native activists for more than a decade before it came to fruition at its first conference. The founding generation was a diverse group of highly motivated individuals who already had or would go on to have significant accomplishments as authors, teachers, clergy, public speakers, artists, doctors, and lawyers. They were a veritable who's who of Native intellectuals, professionals, and activists that cut across tribal and regional lines. Most were educated in government boarding schools, colleges, universities, and professional schools. Many had grown up on reservations. They were a dynamic collection of individuals, many with strong opinions and combative personalities.

A major impetus for establishing the organization was to try to solve the "Indian problem" or "Indian question" as it was sometimes called. The undefined legal status of American Indians was a major issue the SAI struggled with throughout its history. Were Native Americans citizens or wards of the state, taxpayers or not, voters or not, and how did one's status change from state to state? What about the sizable number of Native Americans who resided off the reservations? There were no simple answers. There were, however, a myriad of conflicting federal and state laws, policies, and regulations, in addition to the complicated issue of treaties and treaty rights. All this meant that Indian rights and responsibilities were unclear, as was the issue of individual or tribal control over one's physical and financial resources. The arbiters of the federal system were the Office of Indian Affairs, located within the Department of the Interior, along with Congress, which legislated administrative policies and budgetary priorities. It was a complex situation, with government officials and the general public largely ignorant about American Indians, who were in fact often referred to as a "vanishing race." In the late nineteenth and early twentieth centuries, the official position of the federal government was that Indians should be assimilated into American society and thus "disappear." The SAI founders believed that a national organization could address these issues and provoke change, leading to a defined legal status that included U.S. citizenship. It was a consistent policy, with strategies that were developed to lobby Congress and the executive branch to take action regarding the so-called Indian problem. One focus of this study is to trace the strategies of the SAI to acquire citizenship and to have the opportunity to function in a changing nation with the full panoply of rights and responsibilities. The SAI demanded many changes in federal Indian policies. They believed citizenship would provide the means to eliminate or reduce government control over American Indians' lives and help them achieve a degree of self-determination.

Arthur Parker (Seneca), longtime secretary-treasurer and editor of the *Quarterly Journal of the Society of American Indians*, described the everyday reality very succinctly in an essay on the "Indian problem." He cited as an example the complex legal status of SAI member Reverend Sherman Coolidge (Northern Arapaho). Coolidge was college educated, ordained in the Episcopal Church, a missionary, and a future Society president. Parker raised significant questions in his essay: What was Coolidge's legal status? Was he regarded by the federal government as a citizen, a ward of the state, or both? Did he have the right to vote in local and national elections? Was he required to pay federal taxes? How did his status vary from state to state, as he was allowed to vote when he lived in Minnesota but not when he lived in Wyoming. Parker also pointed out that one's status changed depending on whether one lived on or off a reservation or if one had allotted land or not. The background to this situation was the government's goal to break up the reservations. The passage of the General Allotment Act of 1887 (known as the Dawes Act) authorized the division of tribally held land into individual allotments to be held in trust for twenty-five years, leading to private ownership and citizenship. The so-called surplus land was to be sold to non-Indians. This was part of a broader plan to assimilate Native Americans by eliminating tribally held land. The situation became more complicated with the passage of the Burke Act of 1906. The secretary of the interior could now reinstate the full trust period, delaying citizenship or eliminating it, and award outright title to the land (fee-simple title). That individual could then be declared "competent" and become a citizen. The secretary of the interior had sole authority over the process. To inform the American public about this complex and uncertain reality, the SAI published a pamphlet in 1912, "Lo! The Poor Indian," by Dr. Fayette McKenzie, an Ohio State University professor, Associate member of the Society, and organizer of the first two conferences in Columbus. McKenzie was clear: "The political status of the Indian varies from state to state and from Indian to Indian in a way most demoralizing to the race and disastrous to the nation." The SAI drafted a resolution requesting Congress to pass a bill requiring the president of the United States to appoint an Indian Code Commission to codify all existing federal laws pertaining to American Indians. Parker wrote: "We have a perplexing problem on our hands called the 'Indian question.' It is hedged about by so many details, great and small, that the greatest minds are puzzled."[1]

In addition to the debate over legal status, or the so-called Indian problem, there were a variety of issues that affected the SAI throughout its history. Some were very contentious and divisive; some contributed to its later demise. For example, SAI members supported U.S. citizenship for all American Indians, yet there was a debate about how to accomplish it. Should they lobby for birthright citizenship, or should they advocate for a path to citizenship as was available for immigrants? In developing a strategy to further the case for citizenship, SAI leadership referred to American democratic principles in the main argument, although some feared that citizenship might abrogate treaty rights. In an insightful essay, anthropologist K. Tsianina Lomawaima (Muskogee/Creek) analyzed SAI leadership choices when it came to the Society's goals regarding citizenship, guardianship, tribal existence, and treaty rights. She postulated a theory of "layered citizenship," which implied an ambiguous status, such as the previously provided example of Reverend Coolidge. When it came to choices for the SAI, she concluded that citizenship and sovereignty were not mutually exclusive, as one could be a citizen and still be part of "tribal life." Or, as historian Paul Rosier wrote, the SAI wanted "to assert themselves in modern America, as citizens of the United States and of indigenous nations." Reflecting these ideas, the SAI fought for citizenship without guardianship, but not at the expense of treaty rights and claims against the federal government, implying that citizenship and sovereignty were indeed mutually compatible. The SAI did not want one at the expense of the other. This was a major disagreement with the Indian Office, which did not view U.S. citizenship and tribal membership as compatible. This major goal of the SAI became a reality later in the twentieth century.[2] As will be demonstrated, the SAI pursued full citizenship, without surrendering any legal rights inherent in the hundreds of treaties and other agreements with the government and without surrendering membership in an Indian nation. In this sense, the SAI was lighting a path to the future, which provides a window to better understand its long-range impact.

The debate over the relationship between the Office of Indian Affairs (OIA) and the Society of American Indians was another contentious issue. Some SAI members believed the OIA should be abolished, as its paternalistic policies, as well as its incompetence, were detrimental to American Indians. Others argued that abolishing the OIA would not be practical or even possible, but claimed that it needed to be reformed so that its primary goal would be the welfare of American Indians. A similar controversial issue involved several thousand Indian men and women who worked for the federal government. Some members believed anyone who worked for the government should be prohibited from holding SAI elected leadership positions, arguing that it was a potential conflict of interest. How could a federal employee put Indian interests first when working for a federal agency whose policies were detrimental to Indian interests? Some also argued that such a conflict of interest might provide the government with an opportunity to influence or control the SAI. On the other hand, it was argued that talented individuals might not join the SAI because of such a policy. Compromise was difficult. It was the same with the controversy over peyote. This divisive debate contributed to the SAI's demise, as some believed that the use and possession of peyote should be criminalized; others argued that it deserved First Amendment protection. These debates were intense, fueled by strong personalities who took challenges to their views very personally.

There were also other issues on the SAI's agenda. As American Indians did not have the right to file a claim in the U.S. Court of Claims without special congressional legislation, the SAI proposed legislation to allow such claims to be filed. They also wanted the government to address the terrible living conditions on most reservations: poor housing, poverty, unemployment, hunger, high infant mortality, and continued land loss. Infectious diseases such as tuberculosis, trachoma, and influenza were of epidemic proportions. The SAI protested the arbitrary power held by reservation superintendents and agents over people's daily lives. Those living on reservations were under constant pressure from reservation officials to change their ways, from giving up one's spiritual and cultural heritage to cutting one's hair, changing one's clothing style and wearing "citizen's clothing," and discouraging the use of Indigenous languages. The SAI also hoped to provide legal aid to reservation communities and to challenge the federal Indian boarding school system in order to improve the quality and scope of instruction. They also challenged the rhetoric of the "vanishing race" and sought to change the American public's stereotypic views of American Indians portrayed in Wild West shows, films, and dime novels.

To begin solving these problems, the SAI hoped to develop a corps of motivated American Indian intellectuals who would take a leadership role in the fight for freedom, equality, and justice: freedom from federal tutelage, equality of educational and occupational opportunity, and justice and equal status within America's legal system. As Indians at the beginning of the twentieth century did not generally consider themselves as one people or "race," as the term was then used, Parker stressed that these changes could only occur by developing a "race consciousness" and that unity among the various Indian peoples was of vital importance. His statements, however, did not preclude the importance of tribal identities. Parker and others believed it was essential to speak with one voice on crucial issues of legal status and citizenship. Although speaking with one voice would be difficult to achieve, the objective was clear, as described in the Society's "Statement of Purpose": "The primary aim of the organization is to develop and organize men and women of Indian blood as wise leaders of their race."[3]

The SAI had several broad strategies for achieving its goals: lobby Congress and the Indian Office, educate the public, and encourage American Indians to become active in their own liberation. The Society developed a variety of means to implement these goals. They held annual conferences, published a quarterly journal, printed and circulated numerous pamphlets, and mailed a continuous stream of circular and personal letters to Society members and government officials. They also sent letters and pamphlets to missionary and philanthropic organizations, the latter "friends of the Indian," who supported federal assimilation policies that they believed were in the best interest of American Indians. The SAI engaged in extensive lobbying; they met with presidents William H. Taft, Woodrow Wilson, and Warren Harding, as well as members of Congress and officials of the Department of the Interior. They corresponded with hundreds of American Indians, trying to elicit new memberships. They were prodigious letter writers, corresponding with elected officials, government administrators, and secular and religious leaders. (Thousands of these letters have survived.) They chose urban locations and university settings for their annual conferences, hoping for maximum public exposure. At almost every conference, the mayor of the city gave a welcoming address, and the conferences received support from the local community and professional organizations such as chambers of commerce and historical societies. By inviting reporters to attend these conferences, the SAI received considerable press coverage. Many of the Society's members were accomplished public speakers and spoke in churches and schools whenever possible. "Indian Sunday" was initiated in Columbus, Ohio, in 1911. On the last day of the annual conferences, many members spoke to local congregations. This continued throughout the Society's history, allowing the members to speak to thousands of churchgoers, hoping to educate the public on American Indian issues. Speaking in parishes and various organizations throughout the country for more than a decade was a form of resistance, as Society members spoke out against harsh federal policies and terrible reservation conditions.

Recent scholars examining the early twentieth century are reassessing Native resistance to settler colonialism, investigating American Indians' degree of agency and ability to manipulate the sociopolitical and cultural environment to benefit or protect themselves and their communities. Rosier argues that Native activists emerged early in the century to challenge the government as the SAI helped shape the conversation about Indians' status and place in America. Several other scholars have documented various forms of this resistance. For example, Beth Piatote's *Domestic Subjects* identifies the home and family, or what she calls the "intimate domestic," as the locus of resistance. She argues that the domestic is the primary site through which Indian families and nations have resisted assimilation. As she points out, the Indian wars were wars on Indian families. Clothing choice also can be described as a form of resistance—in particular, the wearing of traditional regalia in public while either speaking or performing. This attracted attention to one's message or performance, but also displayed identity and resistance to Anglo norms. This is further exemplified in an analysis of the many performances of the popular "Song of Hiawatha." It may have reinforced some stereotypes, yet according to religious studies scholar Michael McNally, it contains a continuity of Indigenous languages, music, and dance, and despite Longfellow's text, it was a source of Native agency. Michelle Patterson's "Real Indian Songs" also examines what she refers to as "pedagogical entertainment," particularly the SAI's use of song, dance, and stories in performances as a way to attract attention and display a positive image of American Indians to the public, while using Native culture to advance social and political goals. In a similar vein, anthropologist Linda McNenly, in *Native Performers*, argues that participation in Wild West performances was a form of resistance and a challenge to assimilation. Performing in the shows brought needed income that was not available on the reservation. Such performances strengthened family ties as families traveled together, wore traditional regalia, and performed dances and songs that represented their identity. During their travels, they were also able to escape the harsh realities of everyday life on the reservation. It is important to note that in analyzing these forms of agency, McNenly does not downplay the role of the Wild West shows in reinforcing stereotypes to the American public.[4] In a further analysis of forms of resistance, "The Sartorial Indian" is a study of the traditional attire that Gertrude Bonnin (Zitkala-Ša) wore in public appearances. Her attire attracted attention to her message, but it also displayed a public presentation of "Indianness." The same could be said of her name. In her public appearances and writing, she used the Lakota name Zitkala-Ša (Red Bird). Both her attire and her name can be considered forms of resistance against federal assimilation policies.

Kiara Vigil's *Indigenous Intellectuals* focuses on early-twentieth-century forms of resistance. It is a literary, cultural, and political analysis, a "collective cultural biography" as she calls it, of four intellectuals, three of whom were influential members of the SAI: Dr. Charles Eastman, Gertrude Bonnin, and Dr. Carlos Montezuma (Yavapai). The fourth, author and actor Luther Standing Bear (Lakota), was not affiliated with the SAI. These four were chosen for their numerous writings and public personas, but also because they have been criticized for advocating assimilation. With a careful analysis of their writings, Vigil has challenged that assumption and concluded their writings were part of the resistance, as they all had a "tribal-centered agenda." She also argues that all four were determined to change how non-Indians viewed Indians, and that their performance strategies and writings were meant to influence American society in order to improve the lives of American Indians. She also views the SAI as a precursor to the National Congress of American Indians (NCAI), founded in 1944, as it had similar membership guidelines, lobbied the government, proposed legislation, utilized and produced various media, and sought support from non-Indian organizations. The NCAI also learned from the SAI's mistakes, establishing connections with reservation communities and developing more efficient fund-raising efforts.[5] I would include the SAI within the same framework of resistance, as their continual opposition to federal Indian policies was a form of resistance as well as an early form of political activism.

Following the first conference in 1911, a letter was mailed to members and potential members outlining the Society's goals and strategies. The Executive Council invited Indians and non-Indians to join, as the primary goal was to bring together various tribes, nations, and groups of Indians to effect change, particularly pointing out to American Indians that the Society was devoted to "the race, its uplift, its development and its adjustment to the circumstances of [the] modern environment." Throughout the SAI's history, this theme reverberated: adjust to a changing world but do not change one's identity as an Indian, or as Dr. Carlos Montezuma titled one of his poems, "Changing Is Not Vanishing." This theme of adjustment is discussed throughout this text and offers a strong argument against seeing the SAI as an assimilationist organization. The reality as I see it, and as many SAI members have pointed out, was simply to adjust to a changing twentieth-century society. However, to make this adjustment, American Indians needed to not only talk or write back; they needed freedom and equality to compete in American society. In a four-page "General Statement" sent to members and others, the SAI stated its goals clearly: "Through this Society the red man may break the long silence and voice his opinion and beliefs. The future of the Indian is thus placed in the hands of the Indian himself."[6] One could argue that this statement was a forerunner of self-determination. It was part of a long-range goal to speak with one voice in order to influence federal Indian policies.

In examining the SAI's strategy and goals, one must consider its long-range impact on American Indian history, especially on the history of protest, activism, and intellectual history. A recent study on the Red Power movement challenged the idea that the movement began in the late 1960s and early 1970s with the occupation of Alcatraz, the founding of the American Indian Movement, the march on Washington, and the occupation at Wounded Knee on the Pine Ridge Reservation. Instead, Bradley Shreve, in his study *Red Power Rising*, locates the origins of the Red Power movement in the National Indian Youth Council (NIYC), founded in 1961. He argues that the NIYC combined protest, activism, and militancy, with a goal of self-determination, including the first use of the term "Red Power." Shreve does not see the National Congress of American Indians (NCAI) or the Society of American Indians as contributing much to the later Red Power movement. He argues that the NCAI engaged in lobbying and litigation, and advocated self-determination but "disavowed direct action and protest." Shreve also claims the Society of American Indians was a self-help, assimilationist organization. He concludes that neither organization prepared the groundwork for the Red Power movement.[7] On the other hand, one could draw a line from the SAI to the NIYC, by way of the NCAI. The latter's original 1944 constitution states that its goals are "to enlighten the public toward the better understanding of the Indian race; to preserve cultural values; to seek an equitable adjustment to tribal affairs; to secure and to preserve rights under Indian treaties with the United States; and to otherwise promote the common welfare of the American Indian." Also, the language of the NIYC's 1961 resolution states, "It is morally and legally right that the Indians have a voice in matters of jurisdiction" and that it "recognizes the inherent rights guaranteed all people in statutes of the United States." The same language appears in their present mission statement: "The NIYC has advocated diligently and continuously to ensure that all American Indians have equitable access to educational opportunity, health and social services, employment, human and civil rights." Note that SAI members could have written these statements.

I will argue against Shreve's analysis, demonstrating that the SAI was an activist organization focused on self-determination and was a forerunner of later political activism. For example, Daniel Cobb and Loretta Fowler see the "concentrated militancy" of the 1970s in the context of a century-long history of political activism. More recently, Cobb has defined activism "as politically purposeful acts rather than just militancy." As will be demonstrated, the SAI carried out a decade of politically purposeful acts. In this sense, one can argue that the SAI was a precursor of the NCAI, as Kiara Vigil also argues.

Several SAI members were part of NCAI's founding generation, particularly Arthur Parker, who was elected to the Executive Council. Vigil also considers D'Arcy McNickle (Flathead), an anthropologist, author, and founder of the NCAI, as a bridge. She writes that he "reflected the political history and intellectual traditions he had inherited from an earlier generation," specifically SAI leaders Carlos Montezuma, Gertrude Bonnin, and Charles Eastman.[8]

The assertion that the SAI was an assimilationist organization is no longer tenable, as historians and literary scholars have been reassessing the SAI and its place in American Indian history. The Society has often been referred to as an accommodationist or assimilationist organization, and from a 1970s–90s self-determination/sovereignty perspective, that was meant as critical commentary. For the most part, this interpretation has changed, and this study is part of that change. Up through the 1990s, with the exception of Hazel Hertzberg's work in the early 1970s on twentieth-century American Indian organizations, the SAI was not given any significant scholarly attention. In the past two decades, the SAI has been included in a variety of studies. One such example, Lucy Maddox's *Citizen Indians,* analyzes the role of the SAI in the struggle for full citizenship. She has a nuanced view of its successes and failures, taking into consideration its historic milieu, its constraints, and limited possibilities to effect change in federal policies. Maddox, like Vigil, is not assessing specific federal policy changes but using a broader platform, viewing the SAI as providing intellectual grounding for succeeding generations as they interjected Native issues into public discourse.

Some earlier authors and several recent scholars did not see the Society as successful or even relevant, as there were no specific accomplishments such as new legislation, improvement in reservations conditions, and changes in destructive federal Indian policies. Hertzberg and Joy Porter, Arthur Parker's biographer, regarded the SAI as an unsuccessful organization. Porter stated that its basic agenda was the final detribalization and absorption of Indians into American society as patriotic citizens. She references the preface of the *Proceedings* of the first SAI conference, but a careful reading of the preface reveals no such statement. The preface refers to Tecumseh's goal of creating Indian unity to fight colonization as a model. In a recent text, *First Americans,* the authors argue that SAI members believed accommodation and assimilation were essential. As another example, Leon Speroff, in his biography of Carlos Montezuma, claims that Montezuma "wanted to eliminate reservations and make Anglo-Saxons out of Indians, leaving no vestiges of tribal culture and heritage." Speroff, however, varies his argument in the epilogue, claiming Montezuma's identity as an American Indian "formed his life." Robert Warrior (Osage), who had a somewhat negative view of the SAI in the 1990s, wrote that the members "had lost all but minimal ties to Native culture." Adding that they were part of a generation that supported assimilation ideology, he referred to their writings as "Christian and secular assimilationist." However, Warrior added in a footnote that the period needed a thorough reexamination. Recently, he has modified his views and argued that the period needs contextualization, as the SAI was adjusting from an old world to a new one. He now credits the Society as contributing much more to the present than had previously been ascertained. He also pointed out that the SAI members, later in their lives, were reconnecting to their roots and were committed to a vision of "what was best for the Native world of the future."[9]

More recent scholars see the SAI in a positive light. For example, Philip Deloria recently asserted that what may appear as "elements of assimilation" or "apostles of further assimilation" now seems quaint, in that the SAI cohort "worked to preserve elements of Native cultures and societies from destruction." David Martínez takes a similar view in his anthology *The American Indian Intellectual Tradition*. He argues that it is time for a reassessment. He places the SAI within the long tradition of American Indian intellectual history. He describes them as the most important generation of Native intellectuals prior to the Red Power movement. Frederick Hoxie claims that the SAI founders "represent a remarkable generation of Native activists" and adds that the SAI was actually "part of the resistance to assimilation." Looking back on the preface to the *Proceedings* mentioned previously, it is clear that the SAI wanted Indian unity to fight for the elimination of the paternalism of the "Great White Father." I will attempt to demonstrate that SAI members were determined to preserve an Indian identity for themselves and others in all Indian communities. Their goal was to put tools in Indian hands to fight federal control and to function in contemporary society—and those tools were citizenship and education.[10]

The intertwined history of Native protest and activism has deep roots. I would argue that modern Indian political activism is part of a continuum that extends from early national organizations, such as the Society of American Indians, to the National Congress of American Indians, to the American Indian Youth Council, to the American Indian Movement, to the Red Power movement, and to subsequent struggles for self-determination. These organizations may have differed, but they all had several essential themes in common: the government should uphold all federal treaties, and Native people should have the power to determine their own futures. Was the SAI the first "modern" all-Indian organization? In the early twentieth century, there were other organizations, such as the Indian Memorial Association and the Brotherhood of North American Indians, but they were short-lived and far less influential. The SAI made an important contribution to twentieth-century Indian activism. Hoxie and Martínez also argue that the SAI is part of a continuum of both political activism and intellectual history. Most of the voices included in Hoxie's *Talking Back to Civilization* belong to SAI members. In Martínez's anthology, almost all of the selections from his chapter "Reservations to Reform" are from SAI members. Another recent anthology, edited by Daniel Cobb, on the history of politics and protest in Indigenous Americans from the late nineteenth century to the present, includes writings by Arthur Parker and Carlos Montezuma. The theme of the writings: "We are nations."[11]

It is also important to reassess the assertion of the Society as a so-called Pan-Indian organization. When Pan-Indianism is discussed, it is not unusual for the SAI to be mentioned as an example, as is the Native American Church. I would not support this characterization of the SAI, as the term *Pan-Indian* is contested and confusing. Most apt is Philip Deloria's description of the SAI as an "inter-Indian political and cultural lobbying organization," or D. Anthony Tyeeme Clark (Sac and Fox) describes it, an "emergent intertribal identity sometimes horribly expressed as 'Pan-Indian.'" These are not inaccurate descriptions, and they avoid the complexities of the term *Pan-Indian*. In addition, most Native scholars today eschew the term. An early definition of Pan-Indianism came from anthropologist James H. Howard, who argued in 1955 that Pan-Indianism was contributing to what some referred to as an "American Indian" ethnic group, helping create a nontribal Indian identity. I challenged this idea in a previous publication, citing that participation in a broad-based Native American Church does not diminish one's specific tribal identity. In the same way, I would argue that participation in the SAI did not diminish one's particular Indigenous identity to be replaced with a "generic" Indian identity, much less a "generic" Anglo American identity. If Pan-Indianism is defined as diverse individuals with regional and cultural differences working together toward common goals, such as self-determination, then there is no problem with the term.

Dr. Charles Eastman, a Society founder, as well as other SAI members, argued it was necessary to work together to achieve policy goals, not to change or alter one's identity. A contemporary example is the National Congress of American Indians, a national organization where diverse American Indian individuals and groups work together for the common good. They stress the need for unity and cooperation among Native governments. In their constitution and their "Policy Statement," they call for the preservation of Indigenous languages and free exercise of traditional practices. They would never be accused of being assimilationist or promoting a "generic Indian." In fact, they represent the opposite. They were founded "to speak with one voice to protect tribal sovereignty." The NCAI is an all-Indian organization, with non-Indians as nonvoting Associates, as was the case with the SAI, both encompassing groups of diverse American Indians attempting to work together for the benefit of all.[12] For example, did Dr. Charles Eastman become less of a Santee Dakota as an SAI member, Arthur Parker less of a Seneca, Carlos Montezuma less of a Yavapai, Gertrude Bonnin less of a Yankton Sioux, Thomas Sloan less of an Omaha, Sherman Coolidge less of an Arapaho, or Laura Cornelius Kellogg less of an Oneida? I think not. This study will demonstrate that SAI members did not forgo their roots. They clearly identified themselves as Indian, but not at the expense of tribal, band, or clan identities. Citizenship would not compromise one's Indigenous roots but would be a tool for functioning in twentieth-century America.

The Society's strategies and their focus on multiple issues were to give voice to the voiceless. They wanted to be heard; they wanted change. They began "talking back," sometimes loudly and certainly very often. Hoxie used the term "talking back" to describe those American Indians who challenged not only federal policies but the arrogance and smugness of those who were determined to impose those policies and who believed they represented a superior civilization. Some of the voices he used as examples of "talking back" challenged the idea that it was the Europeans who brought civilization to the Americas. They were "talking back" as the colonized subjects who were describing conditions, challenging policies, demanding change, and undermining settler colonialism. According to historian Norman Wilson, this suggests a strategy "capable of motivating people to create change." In terms of the SAI, the colonized used the voice of the colonizer to undermine the latter by using the colonizers' own arguments for citizenship rights based on freedom, liberty, and justice, as well as by using the basic tenets of

Christianity to demonstrate the hypocrisy of Christians who do not act like Christians. As discussed in chapter 5, during the Great War (World War I) era, Native activists used the language of democracy, as in President Wilson's "Make the World Safe for Democracy" speech, to insist on democracy for American Indians. In this context, the SAI attempted to undermine the Office of Indian Affairs, the Department of Interior, and federal Indian policies in general. The SAI can be assessed within this analytical framework. They can also be described as a generation of American Indian activists and intellectuals whose agenda was to provide American Indians with the political and economic power to determine their own future.[13]

## Sources

The primary sources for a study of the Society of American Indians are extensive. I have utilized the microfilm collections of the papers of the Society of American Indians and the papers of Carlos Montezuma (ten reels of SAI Papers and nine reels of Montezuma Papers).[14] The SAI Papers were collected from more than thirty-five repositories; they include thousands of letters between members and nonmembers, correspondence with the Office of Indian Affairs, constitutions and bylaws, Society publications, conference programs, speeches, resolutions, and election results. There are also financial documents, budget reports, membership applications, requests from reservation communities for assistance, and newspaper clippings mostly from the cities where annual conferences were held. The Montezuma Papers include the full run of his journal, *Wassaja: Freedom's Signal for the Indians*. In addition to the collected papers, the Society published a quarterly journal from 1913 to 1920, originally called the *Quarterly Journal of the Society of American Indians* and renamed *American Indian Magazine: A Journal of Race Ideals* in 1915 (not included in the microfilm). The magazine is a rich source for the history of the Society, as it includes many of the conference papers, editorials, Society news, as well as reprinted articles of interest to the membership. At first, it was distributed by subscription and later sent as part of membership dues. With four issues a year, some with hundreds of pages, it is a very extensive and valuable source. It was also distributed free of charge to libraries and historical societies. The magazine was published for public consumption, and as such, it did not always cover the internal turmoil of the Society. However, using the magazine in conjunction with documents and correspondence, as well as the newspaper accounts, makes it possible to produce a well-rounded analysis of the Society. The last years of the Society, particularly the conferences, were more difficult to reconstruct, as the magazine ceased publication and the level of correspondence declined after 1920. Some of the gaps can be filled by Montezuma's *Wassaja*, which provided significant information and commentary on the SAI, but it was not as comprehensive as the Society's official publication, as it usually was only four pages per issue. In addition, there are biographies of a number of SAI members who were active in the organization but who also had careers mostly of a professional nature. Many were prominent in their own right. These works are examined to help uncover the contributions of various individuals and their interactions within the SAI and with the outside world.[15]

## Organization

The narrative follows a chronological pattern interspersed with sections covering specific themes and topics, as mentioned earlier, such as citizenship, the Office of Indian Affairs, the peyote controversy, the Great War, the draft, and responses to the "vanishing Indian" rhetoric. There is also extensive analysis of the origins of the SAI, its demise, as well as its place in history. The twelve annual conferences (with 1917's conference canceled due to the war) are covered in each chapter, reviewing speakers, presentations, elections, resolutions, debates, and public performances, as well as assessing the significance of each conference.

Considerable attention is given in the first chapter to the founders of the Society in the years prior to 1911, when contacts were made, relationships were developed, correspondence was exchanged, and meetings were held to discuss the establishment of a new national organization. The first decade of the twentieth century was crucial, as American Indians from different regions were making connections with other activists. Chapter 2 covers the first two years of the Society in detail, as it was the foundational period and set the tone for the future. Membership criteria were established for Indians (who could vote) and non-Indians (who had voice but no vote), a constitution was ratified, officers were elected, and strategies and policies were established. Many problems emerged, due to insufficient membership, inadequate finances, and vigorous debates and clashes among members with strong opinions and personalities.

Chapter 3 analyzes the growth of the SAI and the establishment of a legislative agenda supported by considerable lobbying. The SAI also campaigned to change the American public's perceptions of American Indians, particularly attacking the negative imagery of Buffalo Bill Cody's Wild West shows and the stereotyping and negative portrayal of Indians in the new film industry. A controversy over the criminalization of peyote emerged and contributed to internal dissension with complex battle lines: among Indian members themselves, between some Indian members and non-Indian Associates, as well as complicated interactions with "friends of the Indian" groups, such as the Indian Rights Association and the Lake Mohonk Conference of Friends of the Indian. The latter group consisted of prominent non-Indians who wielded considerable influence on government officials to pursue assimilation policies.

Chapter 4 analyzes the dramatic speech of Dr. Montezuma, "Let My People Go." He attacked the reservation system and called for the abolition of the Office of Indian Affairs. He began publishing *Wassaja* in 1916 and used it to criticize the Society for being too moderate in its stand on federal policies. Gertrude Bonnin joined the SAI and played a major role, serving in a variety of capacities, particularly as editor of the Society's magazine. The SAI also initiated a concerted effort to establish a national Indian day.

As discussed in chapter 5, the Great War (1914–18) took up much of the Society's time and energy, raising the intertwined issues of citizenship, registering for the draft, and the draft itself. If one was not a citizen, what was one's responsibility in a wartime environment? Should one support the war on the home front? Should one register for the draft, as required, and serve in the military? Or, if drafted, should one serve without citizenship status?

The last chapter analyzes the slow demise of the SAI, symbolized by its decision to discontinue publishing the *American Indian Magazine*. It had been the lifeblood of the organization—a significant voice—maintaining connections with a wide variety of audiences, publicizing conference proceedings, fund-raising, and publishing policy decisions. The last issue appeared in 1920. The final years were marked by the departure of many of the stalwart members of the Society: Arthur Parker, Charles Eastman, Gertrude Bonnin, Henry Roe Cloud, and others. The new leadership created another divisive issue as they became involved in partisan politics, such as support for Warren G. Harding, the Republican nominee for president in 1920. Meanwhile, other organizations, such as the Tepee Order of America, emerged and competed for members and funds. In the end, it was an interplay of internal and external circumstances: declining membership, failure to connect with reservation communities, inconsistent leadership, lack of funds, controversial policies, and interpersonal conflicts that brought the SAI to an end. These problems occurred in an external sociopolitical environment that was not conducive to change, as the Indian Office was intransigent and determined to continue its assault on Indian resources, land, and culture. Nevertheless, as this study demonstrates, SAI members were determined to maintain their identity and heritage, reduce or eliminate federal guardianship, and acquire the tools to function in a modern changing society.

This study analyzes the SAI's goals, policies, and strategies, and its long-range impact on American Indian reform movements. I have attempted to stay true to the perspectives, words, and actions of the Society members and others who interacted with them, as reflected in the primary sources. Whenever feasible in the narrative, I use their words directly in order to elucidate and assess their purposes, views, and goals, and ultimately to assess their legacy—a legacy that has had a significant impact on twentieth-century and twenty-first-century American Indian history.

# CHAPTER 1

# The Society of American Indians

## *The Founders in a Changing World*

The Society of American Indians emerged in the early twentieth century as the result of several corresponding trends. The first, and most significant, involved a new generation of American Indian men and women who were "talking back to civilization," as described by Hoxie in the introduction to his book of the same name. Hoxie emphasized this theme by using a 1913 photograph on the cover of Blackfeet Indians "talking back," with Blackfeet spokesman pointing his index finger in the face of a very-well-dressed Anglo-looking man. This form of body language was and still is considered rude and challenging. Those who "talked back" were reacting to the unclear legal status of American Indians, the overbearing guardianship of the Indian Office, terrible reservation conditions, and the government's ongoing assault on traditional social and cultural practices. The founding generation of the Society of American Indians wanted to be heard. The Society was composed of a group of Native intellectuals who were committed to improving the lives of American Indians. They reacted to their status as so-called wards of the state without the rights of American citizenship. They reacted to high poverty rates and land loss on the reservations. They wanted American Indians to be free to control their own resources and free to pursue their own destinies. The SAI clearly articulated this view in its 1913 "General Statement": "Through this Society the red man may break the long silence and voice his opinions and beliefs. The future of the Indian is thus placed in the hands of the Indian himself."[1] This set the tone for subsequent agendas of the Society and was a significant early step toward self-determination.

An additional factor in the creation of the SAI was the growing collaboration among the eventual founders in the first decade of the twentieth century. Most of them already knew each other. These contacts were essential; they prepared the way for the initial meetings to establish the new organization. Once the founders began to organize, they realized they needed non-Indian support to succeed. An early goal was to gain one thousand non-Indian Associate members. These groups of non-Indians, who considered themselves "reformers" or "friends of the Indian," had roots in the Progressive movement and the Social Gospel movement. What they agreed upon was eventual citizenship for all American Indians. Where they differed from the SAI was regarding the end result. For SAI members, citizenship meant the right to self-determination and the right to remain "Indian." For non-Indian reformers, citizenship was the only way to save the American Indian, as it would lead to full assimilation into American society and the subsequent vanishing of American Indian cultures. These two views coexisted uncomfortably throughout the SAI's history. As the SAI matured and had more forceful views about the Office of Indian Affairs, many of their non-Indian "friends" drifted away.

The founding of the Society occurred at a time of rapid change. The early twentieth century was an era of economic, social, and cultural shifts stimulated by modernization, industrialization, immigration, the growth of cities, population growth, urban poverty, and corresponding tension and social dislocation. The pseudo-scientific theory of social Darwinism provided a philosophical basis to defend the status quo of an Anglo elite and the economic inequality in a corporate-controlled society. It was used in Europe and America as a rationalization for the subjugation of so-called inferior peoples, manipulating the Darwinian idea of the "survival of the fittest." There was an assumption that the races could be arranged from the highest to the lowest in terms of evolutionary development, with American Indians near the bottom. From the perspective of the "friends of the Indian" groups, it was the white man's burden to uplift the downtrodden, following the popular "savage to civilization" paradigm.

Reform, led by so-called progressives, was in the air. They wanted to change society by limiting corporate power, reforming politics, expanding workers' rights, supporting women's suffrage, and hoping to ameliorate the stresses of early-twentieth-century life. The Progressive Party emerged in 1912 as a third party with former president Teddy Roosevelt as their candidate. The Progressives, as an elite group of reformers, believed they could improve American society. They campaigned on a platform of civil liberties and economic reform. They believed America's problems were economic and structural, and that trusts and monopolies had to be regulated, as they contributed to the growing income inequality. Their goal was to reform the worst aspects of society, such as corrupt politics, endemic poverty, impoverished and overcrowded cities, unsafe working conditions, child labor, and public health, and to assimilate newly arrived immigrants from eastern and southern Europe. Many reformers also applied this idea of assimilation to American Indians, believing it was in their best interests to be "Americanized." SAI members disagreed with this, as they did not want to be "Americanized"; they wanted citizenship, civil rights, better education, and opportunities to compete in American society.

Despite a growing push for reform and the influence of several reform organizations, such as the National Association for the Advancement of Colored People (NAACP) and the National Urban League, contrary trends made it increasingly difficult to truly implement reform in the United States. Racial, ethnic, and religious prejudices were widespread. Discrimination was rampant. Jim Crow laws were in full swing. African Americans were segregated from the cradle to the grave. Segregation was supported by President Woodrow Wilson and reinforced by the popular film *Birth of a Nation* (1915). The Ku Klux Klan reemerged, and lynchings and anti-black race riots were commonplace. The NAACP was founded to combat racialized violence and help African Americans to exercise their citizenship rights. There was also a growing anti-immigrant sentiment and a movement to restrict the entry of Asians and southern and eastern Europeans, as a result of a growing Nativist movement. Madison Grant, president of the New York Zoological Society, published *The Passing of the Great White Race* (1916), which reinforced Nativist beliefs and helped create a climate of fear, stirring long-held anti-Semitism and anti-Catholicism. Many Americans still believed in social Darwinism, espousing that those of Anglo-Saxon Germanic descent were racially and culturally superior to all others, including American Indians. Many non-Indians referred to American Indians as the "vanishing race." This term was used in two different ways; some believed that the survival of American Indians was contingent on their full assimilation into American society and their disappearance as a distinct group or race; others believed Indians would literally disappear since they were incapable of becoming "civilized" and coping with the modern world. The "friends of the Indian" groups followed in the tradition of General Richard H. Pratt, the founder of the Carlisle Indian Industrial School, with its motto "Kill the Indian and Save the Man." He believed that American Indians could survive only if fully integrated into American society. He supported the establishment of the SAI, became an Associate member, and attended many of the conferences. As mentioned previously, non-Indian "reformers" and SAI members did not always have the same agenda. In fact, there was a disconnect. The SAI did not perceive assimilation in the same way as "reformers" such as Dr. Fayette McKenzie, professor at The Ohio State University, who wanted to eliminate virtually all vestiges of Native American culture; conversely, SAI members were determined to preserve their Indigenous identity and parts of their cultural heritage, although most believed it was essential to have the tools to compete in American society. Citizenship was widely believed to be such a tool.

Throughout the inaugural conference, the delegates expressed pride in being American Indians. This pride was reflected by Dr. Charles Eastman (Santee Dakota), one of the SAI founders, in his oft-quoted statement, "I am an Indian. . . . Nevertheless I am an American." The SAI leadership believed non-Indian "reformers" would be very useful as allies for their ultimate goals of acquiring citizenship and reducing or ending federal tutelage. This was clearly articulated by the Executive Council in the SAI's statement on federal Indian policy: "The paternal system of the federal Government which now exercises control over 300,000 native [*sic*] Americans has bred many gross evils, and the Indian of today as a result of that system finds himself unable to assert himself in any natural way. . . . He is allowed no voice in his destiny, for it is the paternal hand of the 'Great White Father' that assumes the right to guide him." SAI members considered themselves reformers. The press occasionally referred to them as "red progressives." The members often referred to themselves as progressives, but not with the same reform agenda as the so-called Progressive movement. In 1911 and 1912, SAI publications and correspondences to potential members used the term "progressive" in several ways—for instance, "To Progressive Indians of the Country," "To Indian Friends of Progress," or "Regarding Proposed Conference of Progressive Indians"—but these materials never included the adjective "red" before "progressive." Some also suggested naming the organization the Progressive Indian Association. Although many non-Indian progressives believed in assimilation, they were dealing with Native Americans who were determined to remain "Indian." As historian Tom Holm (Cherokee/Muskogee) has pointed out, this created a great deal of confusion, as it became clear by the 1910s and 1920s that American Indians were not about to disappear. Holm pointed to what he called "peoplehood," which he defined as language, place, ceremony, and sacred history. He argued that it provided power to Native cultural resilience and was a major factor in the failure of assimilation.[2]

Following the "Indian wars" of the nineteenth century, the establishment of the reservation system, the destruction of Indigenous economies, restrictions on Native spiritual and cultural practices, the reduction of communal ownership of land under the Dawes Act of 1887, and the horrid massacre at Wounded Knee in 1890, a group of American Indians, many who had attended government boarding schools and American colleges and universities, began to "talk back" and protest the status of American Indians as wards of the state under the control of the federal Office of Indian Affairs (OIA).[3] They also protested the denial of U.S. citizenship for many Native Americans, inadequate education, poverty, poor health conditions, exploitation and misappropriation of funds (i.e., graft) on the reservations, and the continuing negative stereotyping of Indians in the media and in the Wild West shows. Their goal was to improve life for American Indians with equal rights and equal opportunities, but without denying their cultural and spiritual heritage. Adjusting to the economic and social realities of the new century did not mean one had to surrender one's identity as a Native person. The two were not mutually exclusive. SAI members represented significant voices that were seeking the power to control their own destiny. Eastman was quite emphatic on this. He wrote: "It has been apparent to us that absolute distinctions cannot be maintained under the American flag. Yet we think each race should be allowed to retain its own religion and racial codes as far as it is compatible with the public good." Eastman never lost contact with his Santee Sioux roots.[4]

## The Founders

In the late nineteenth and early twentieth centuries, several American Indians began discussing the possibility of forming some type of national organization that could be used to benefit all Native Americans. Many of the founders of the SAI already knew each other. Several had attended or worked at the same boarding school. Montezuma and Francis La Flesche (Omaha) were corresponding as early as 1899. Eastman and Carlos Montezuma were already friends. Along with La Flesche, they were commencement speakers at Carlisle in 1899. Eastman also knew Charles Dagenett (Peoria), an Indian Office employee. They had traveled together briefly through New Jersey visiting "outing" students from the Carlisle Indian School, as Eastman was the outing agent for a year before he became the government physician at Crow Creek Reservation in South Dakota. Both became SAI founders. Although he was quite busy, Eastman published *Indian Boyhood* in 1902, the first of many books. It is also possible that the SAI founders were aware of Chief Simon Pokagon's (Potawatomi) challenge to those professing superior civilization at the World's Columbian Exposition in Chicago in 1893. Pokagon ended his speech with "we stand as upon the seashore, chained hand and foot, while the incoming tide of the great ocean of civilization rises slowly but surely to overwhelm us." Future SAI members wanted to break those chains. In 1899, in Washington, D.C., Eastman, his brother Reverend John Eastman, and Reverend Sherman Coolidge (Arapaho) had discussions about "establishing a national organization of progressive Indians." Eastman believed it was not the right time, since it might arouse the enmity of the Office of Indian Affairs as they were not accustomed to listening to Indian voices. He feared that "progressive" Indians who worked for the OIA would be in a difficult situation. Their jobs could be in jeopardy if they belonged to an organization that criticized government policies.[5] Around the same time, General Pratt and Dr. Montezuma were discussing the possibility of creating a new organization. Montezuma sent a copy of a constitution he had written for such an organization to Pratt, who did not like the idea. He criticized it, saying that such an organization would need a wealthy backer. He added that individual action might prove more effective than a "body of people congregating together." A decade later, Pratt changed his opinion and supported the SAI. Montezuma shared his thoughts on a new organization with Gertrude Bonnin (Zitkala-Ša), who was involved with Montezuma in a recently ended romantic relationship. He suggested a male-only organization funded by contributions. She totally opposed the male-only idea and did not think it should depend on white contributions, but she liked the idea of an organization in general. Montezuma and Eastman were also corresponding during this time. Eastman wrote about his job with the Indian Office, revising Sioux allotment rolls. He informed Montezuma that he lived in nearby St. Paul, Minnesota, hoping to move to Chicago soon. It was a very friendly letter, indicative of a long-standing friendship. Eastman asked Montezuma to pass his greetings along "to your fancy lady friend [Gertrude Bonnin] who went with us to church last winter."[6]

For more than a decade, a network of relationships developed that led directly to the founding of the SAI in 1911. These individuals came from a variety of backgrounds but had one common goal: to ameliorate the conditions of American Indians by advocating an end to federal control. Scholars have debated the origin of the idea for a national organization. Some see it as the logical outcome of several ephemeral Indian organizations, such as the Indian Memorial Association (1909) and the Brotherhood of North American Indians (1911). Some early scholars credited McKenzie with founding the SAI; however, recent scholars see it as emerging from the friendships that developed in boarding schools, especially the Carlisle Indian School and Hampton Institute. It was the beginning of a Native American intellectual network. McKenzie's ideas fit into what was a significant trend, as more and more Indian activists believed the time had come to form a national organization.[7] At the same time, another web of relationships was developing throughout the west among members of the Peyote faith. Prominent leaders such as Oliver Lamere (Ho-Chunk, Wisconsin), Albert Hensley (Ho-Chunk, Wisconsin), attorney Thomas L. Sloan (Omaha), and Judge Hiram Chase (Omaha) were traveling widely and making contacts with Peyotists. All four became members of the SAI and attended the first conference in Columbus. They hoped to end the federal assault on the Peyote faith. Anthropologist Omer Stewart pointed out that the Peyote faith had been spread by connections and friendships that developed in government boarding schools.[8] These interpersonal contacts were significant in the emergence of the SAI. Equally important was the ability of the founders and future members to travel and communicate with each other and potential new members. By the second decade of the twentieth century, rail lines crisscrossed the nation. Travel was relatively easy between Washington, Philadelphia, New York City, Albany, and Boston. Travel westward was facilitated with direct rail lines to Columbus, Chicago, Omaha, and Denver. Also, the U.S. Postal Service, telephones, and telegraphs made communication more viable, along with trolley lines and automobiles. The mass production of letters, announcements, pamphlets, and journals also made it easier to ship large volumes of printed material to members and potential members. The growing ease of communication facilitated the rise of the Society.

Professor McKenzie, determined to ameliorate the plight of American Indians, encouraged the establishment of a national organization and provided the impetus to hold a convention in Columbus. In 1904, when he was teaching on the Wind River Indian Reservation in Wyoming, he wrote a letter to W. E. B. Du Bois, seeking his opinion about the "advancement" of the Indian "race." In 1905, Du Bois, a prominent African American scholar and activist, helped found the Niagara movement, leading a direct assault on racial discrimination. Followed by the establishment of the NAACP in 1909, Du Bois was in contact with several SAI members. McKenzie was concerned about the young American Indians who returned to the reservation after attending boarding school. He feared they would return to the "old life." To avoid this, he proposed the establishment of an organization of "50 to 100 or 200 Indians," forming an association that stood for unity and solidarity, with the goal of encouraging leaders to "guide the whole race to a higher level of civilization." He suggested hosting a convention to get the organization started. McKenzie also drew up a pledge that members would recite on joining what he called the "Fraternity of American Indians":

> Membership open to all Indians who can speak English, who are recommended by some reputable school, who will take the following -Pledge-
>
> I believe that the Indian has certain inalienable rights, among which is that of freeing himself from the bondage of ignorance, superstition, poverty, by education, religion, and self-support.
>
> I believe that by united efforts he can become an independent American citizen, and free himself from all injustice, which ignorance or cupidity has imposed upon him. I, therefore pledge myself to further all efforts for the advancement of my race in education, morality, and civic rights, to discourage and oppose all backward tendencies, all immorality, and all crime, and to work for the time when all red men shall be brothers in love and purpose, proud of their people, and influential among the united tribes and races of America.[9]

Du Bois replied to McKenzie, "I think your plan most excellent and would be glad to aid in any way. The uplift must always come from the top and the training and unification of leaders is the great thing." Du Bois's response fits with his belief described in the "The Talented Tenth," an essay published in 1903 that a 10 percent intellectual elite should provide leadership for the African American community. The follow-up between Du Bois and McKenzie is unclear. McKenzie's pledge does not appear in any official SAI publications or papers. In addition, the pledge is extremely paternalistic—indeed, it is hard to imagine anyone reciting it. McKenzie did follow through, however, on helping to plan for a new organization and conference. In 1911, Du Bois became an Associate member of the SAI at least for a year, but it is unclear whether this was in response to McKenzie. It is more likely because of his acquaintance with Charles Eastman. Why McKenzie wrote to Du Bois is uncertain; possibly McKenzie had read his essay "The Talented Tenth." McKenzie and Du Bois had similar views on the role of leadership; however, there is quite a difference between the philosophical basis and cultural assumptions of Du Bois on African American culture and McKenzie's views on American Indian culture. For example, in *Souls of Black Folks,* Du Bois articulated a double consciousness, hoping "to make it possible for a man to be both a Negro and an American." McKenzie did not advocate a double consciousness of being an Indian and an American, only the latter. According to General Pratt, he and McKenzie began corresponding in early 1905. It is unclear about the content of the exchange, but given McKenzie's recent letter to Du Bois, it was probably about leadership and developing an organization.

The emergence of the NAACP and the SAI at more or less the same time cannot be a coincidence. Both were responding to the negative racial climate and the absence of having a meaningful voice in society. Both used the term "race" in a similar way, using it to create unity, uplift, and foster leadership. They both labeled their situations as the "Negro problem" and the "Indian problem," and both were determined to influence public opinion. They referred to themselves as the "New Negro" and the "New Indian." Although both organizations emerged in a similar historical milieu of the Progressive Era and had some parallel goals, such as fighting colonialism, poverty, racism, and obtaining equal rights and equal education. However, there are limits to the comparison. Both wanted non-Indian memberships but differed on the issues of leadership and voting. The NAACP included whites in leadership positions, including the presidency; the SAI had an all-Indian leadership. The NAACP afforded full voting rights to non–African Americans; the SAI only allowed Indian members to vote. There is no evidence that the establishment of the NAACP directly influenced the founding of the SAI, though they knew of each other's existence. The impetus to establish an organization like the SAI predates the NAACP by almost a decade. Even though Du Bois was an Associate member and knew Charles Eastman, he had no other known contacts. It is unclear why he did not renew his membership. The organizations did not work together. With few exceptions, neither organization mentions the other in their publications. Several SAI members are mentioned in the NAACP journal the *Crisis*, including a reference to the American Indian opera *The Sun Dance* by Zitkala-Ša, but the article contained no mention of her SAI affiliation. The *Crisis* also mentioned the upcoming second SAI conference and published a photo of Charles Eastman. It also mentioned that Gabe Parker (Choctaw) was appointed registrar of the Treasury, but again there was no specific mention of his SAI membership. Part of the problem was that certain SAI members believed it was in their interest to distance themselves from African Americans, expressing this publicly. One of the most obvious instances of conflict was when the SAI tried to dissuade American Indian students from attending Hampton Institute, a predominantly African American institution. At least one SAI member did not want the Indian Office to hire African Americans. Several SAI members accepted the negative racial stereotypes of African Americans held by the white public. They did not want white hostility toward African Americans directed at them and did not want the public to associate the two groups by casting them in a similar racial mold. Any potential for collaboration went unrealized.[10]

## The First Conference: Background

Professor McKenzie played a major role in holding the first conference at The Ohio State University. He had a background in Native studies. In 1906, McKenzie completed his doctoral dissertation, "The American Indian in Relationship to the White Population," at the University of Pennsylvania. He believed strongly in the role of education for "progress," which to him meant lifting "less civilized" groups up the ladder of civilization. He believed federal Indian policies were inadequate for this task. He wrote that the tribal spirit was not "compatible with the white man's life and civilization." As in his 1904 letter to Du Bois, he reiterated his belief that an organization of "progressive" Indians could help accomplish this goal. McKenzie belonged to a group of reformers who considered themselves "friends of the Indian." He believed the Indian "race" could be saved through a transfer of culture. He put it rather bluntly: "In all these matters the Indian must accept the forms set by the Caucasian." He believed the answer was in schooling and leadership. He advocated the closing of government boarding schools and on-reservation schools, along with sending American Indian children to public schools and then on to "white" colleges, precluding the possibility of separate Indian institutions. With strong public support and the development of Indian leaders, he believed an organization could effectively bring about change.[11] There may have been an additional influence on McKenzie's views. Charles Kealear (Yankton Sioux), who joined the SAI in 1912, told Parker that he and his wife "worked hard till we got McKenzie to take up the work and finally advocated [to him] the need of an organization by the Indians." The conference in Columbus was the result. Kealear added that he sent letters to many individuals explaining how the evil forces on the reservations can only be corrected by the "combined forces of the Redmen themselves." It was after McKenzie left the Wind River Reservation and returned to The Ohio State University that he began planning for a new organization. Kealear must have known McKenzie, and they must have discussed the possibility of an organization. Since 1896, Kealear was employed by the Office of Indian Affairs on the same reservation at the same time with McKenzie. Kealear told Arthur Parker that he got into trouble when he protested against local conditions. The Indian Office responded by transferring him. Kealear refused, resigned his government post, and opened a general merchandise store in the nearby town of Arapahoe, Wyoming. He remained a member of the SAI until its demise, serving on the Advisory Board from 1917 to 1921. He had planned to attend the first conference in Columbus and is listed on the program to make a presentation titled "Land History," but given a problem with his business, he did not attend. Parker responded by saying it was a "pleasure to learn that you are one of the prime movers of the organization." Kealear also knew Reverend Coolidge, as he mentioned Coolidge's removal from the reservation for protesting the treatment of his fellow Arapaho. It is clear that Kealear, McKenzie, and Coolidge all knew each other prior to the 1908 meeting in Columbus.[12]

In November 1908, McKenzie invited Eastman, Montezuma, and Coolidge to Columbus. They agreed to give a series of lectures at OSU in connection with a course of study on American Indians. Their lectures were covered by local newspapers, with some publications included front-page photos of Coolidge and Montezuma. They also spoke at other venues—mostly churches. Eastman gave two talks: one on his recent book, *Indian Boyhood*, another on the "Custer Massacre." Coolidge spoke at the Social Workers' Club, The Ohio State University chapel, and several churches, on the topic of "What Is Christianity Doing for the Indian?" He may have been to Columbus previously, as his foster grandfather, John Neil, was a Columbus resident. Whenever Coolidge spoke, the press retold his life story. As a seven-year-old, Runs-On-Top, his Arapaho name, and his brother were captured during a raid on his village by Bannocks and Shoshones. The boys ended up with American troops and were given to white families. Runs-On-Top was given the name William Tecumseh Sherman. Later, he was officially adopted by Captain Charles A. Coolidge and renamed Sherman Coolidge. He did not attend a government boarding school but a public school in New York City. He then attended Shattuck Military School in Minnesota and later went to Seabury Divinity School as he contemplated a career as a missionary. He received a bachelors of divinity degree in 1884 and continued his education at Hobart College in New York and eventual ordination as a priest in the Episcopal Church. On several occasions, he returned home to minister to the Arapahos and Shoshones, on the Wind River Reservation, where he saw firsthand the poverty, poor health, inadequate education, and insufficient food and supplies. In the early 1890s, he worked as an interpreter for ethnologist James Mooney, who was studying the Ghost Dance movement. In 1911, Coolidge became the director of the Indian Protestant Episcopal mission in western Oklahoma. He was an excellent public speaker and had an impressive presence, wearing his clerical collar in public. He was one of the most notable founders of the SAI and a future president of the organization. Carlos Montezuma, the so-called witty Apache, was the most controversial speaker of the group. He delivered a speech, "On the Future of the Indian," in which he referred to reservations as prisons and called for their breakup, along with the closing of reservation schools and placement of Indian children in public schools. He blamed the government for creating the present problems on the reservations by stifling opportunity and fostering dependency. He said, "To civilize the Indian, he must be removed from the reservation, where he is surrounded by sloth, vice and idleness." He added that Indians should be given the same opportunity that new immigrants receive. His was a hard-hitting talk that received considerable press coverage.[13]

In Columbus, Eastman, Montezuma, and Coolidge consulted with McKenzie about establishing an all-Indian organization. Further correspondence followed as McKenzie wrote to Eastman, saying it was now time to establish a new organization. He also began a regular correspondence with Montezuma and others, discussing the possibility of forming an organization and holding a conference. By September 1909, plans were underway for both. McKenzie sought support from the Indian Office, writing to Robert Valentine, commissioner of Indian affairs, that the problem was that the public did not believe the Indian was capable of "education, culture, or high morality." He hoped a conference of "educated and progressive Indians" would help dispel such beliefs. He asked Valentine for his approval and cooperation and added that we need a "Mohonk by Indians," not a "Mohonk for Indians." This was a reference to the Lake Mohonk Conference of Friends of the Indians, a very influential group of mostly Protestant clergy and self-appointed "humanitarians," who supported policies to Christianize and "civilize" American Indians. Most had a deeply religious conviction of their righteousness. They considered themselves reformers whose goal was to save American Indians by supporting the government's assimilation programs. The Lake Mohonk group, founded in 1883, met annually at Lake Mohonk in New York. They issued position papers, lobbied Congress, passed resolutions, and attempted to influence public opinion. They specifically believed it was essential to eliminate the social and cultural practices that existed from the pre-reservation era. Some of the Mohonk group, such as General Pratt, were also Associate members and attended SAI conferences, and some of the Active members, such as Arthur Parker and Henry Roe Cloud (Ho-Chunk, Wisconsin), participated in their conferences. This relationship was significant, as Parker and other SAI leaders wanted support from the Mohonk group and on occasion tried to align SAI policies with Mohonk policies, specifically regarding the peyote issue (as discussed later).

As plans were progressing for a new organization and a conference, the possibility of a competing organization emerged. A number of Native Americans proposed the establishment of a new organization called the Indian Memorial Association. It included some of the same individuals who had been planning for almost a decade to establish a national organization, such as the Eastman brothers, Thomas Sloan, and Carlos Montezuma. Walter Battice (Sac and Fox) from Oklahoma, an Indian Office employee, was instrumental in trying to establish the new group. He and Montezuma were in regular correspondence throughout 1909. They planned a meeting at Haskell Institute, a federal boarding school for Indian youth in Lawrence, Kansas. They choose Thomas Sloan as president and drafted a set of resolutions calling for a change of administration in Washington and the removal of Francis Leupp, the commissioner of Indian affairs. Meanwhile, those planning a conference in Columbus became concerned about the conflict. McKenzie, hoping to get support from the Indian Office for the Columbus conference, wrote to Commissioner Valentine mentioning the uncertain situation, as the Indian Memorial Association was proposing a similar conference. However, McKenzie pointed out that their plan for a conference was abandoned and went ahead with the Columbus conference. McKenzie heard about another possible conference in Muskogee, Oklahoma, but apparently little came of it. The IMA never materialized into a formal organization, but as with other early groups, its importance, as pointed out by D. Anthony Tyeemep Clark (Sac and Fox), was that it contributed to the growing contacts among American Indians from different parts of the country, which made the development of future organizations possible.[14]

Following the correspondence with Commissioner Valentine, McKenzie mailed out announcements for the upcoming Columbus conference. In late 1909, Montezuma invited McKenzie to Chicago to continue planning for a new organization. McKenzie also wrote to Charles Dagenett (Peoria), the supervisor for employment in the Indian Office, informing him of plans for a conference. Dagenett was the highest-ranking American Indian working for the Indian Office. In November 1909, he informed Commissioner Valentine of the proposed conference. Dagenett wrote that this was in line with "your idea of having something done for Indians by Indians." Dagenett wanted to know if Valentine sanctioned the idea. It seemed as if Dagenett was seeking the approval of his boss for the conference. Dagenett followed with a letter to McKenzie, telling him that by getting Valentine's approval, there would be a better chance of success.[15] Valentine was supportive but informed Dagenett that because the Indian Office was accused of paternalism, he would not give financial or moral support. Valentine then informed Charles Norton, secretary to President Taft, that a new organization was being established. He took some of the credit himself, writing that "one of the movements I am trying to get started is to get them to take responsibility for their own industrial and moral progress." He said he was willing to help with information and accept criticisms of federal policies, but it must be kept independent. Valentine must have assumed such an organization of "progressives" would support government policies of assimilation. McKenzie wrote again to Valentine, identifying twenty-five Indians (appendix A) who expressed approval of the conference, this time asking for his sanction and the names of "worthy and competent" Indians. Valentine responded that he would cooperate and that he would send a memorandum to his people in the field asking for names of "other progressive Indians," but reaffirmed that the Indian Office would not be involved, nor would it help with expenses. Meanwhile, McKenzie sent out invitations for a conference to be held at The Ohio State University in the fall. He addressed the letter "To the Progressive Indians of the Country," asking for their participation. He said the conference would be about education, religion, industry, and government relations. He included a blank form requesting a response to his invitation.[16] As the fall of 1910 was quickly approaching, the conference was postponed until the following year.

In early 1911, a circular letter was sent from the Temporary Executive Committee "To the Indian Friends of Progress," informing them that McKenzie had asked them to serve as a temporary committee to ensure that the conference was by Indians for Indians. The issue was stated directly: Are you for "Death or Progress"? The answer was *progress* defined by Indian means and leadership. The circular added that the responsibility for the "red brothers" rested upon "ourselves." In April 1911, six "distinguished Indians" now functioning as the Temporary Executive Committee came to Columbus to plan for the new organization. In addition to Eastman, Montezuma, Sloan, and Dagenett, Laura M. Cornelius Kellogg (nee Kellogg; Oneida, Wisconsin) and Henry Standing Bear (Lakota) joined the Executive Committee in Columbus. Arthur Parker was invited by McKenzie to join this group but backed out after a fire burned part of the American Indian collection at the State Museum in Albany. He was added later to the Executive Committee. These seven, plus Reverend Sherman Coolidge and Rosa La Flesche (Ho-Chunk, Wisconsin), should be considered the true founders of the SAI. These individuals, along with Dr. McKenzie, actively planned for the organization and helped launch its inaugural conference in October 1911. The original six "distinguished Indians" were hosted by the Columbus Chamber of Commerce. Eastman, introduced by Mayor George S. Marshall, gave a public address in the Chamber's auditorium. The other five were invited to give brief remarks. Eastman spoke on "The Real Indian." He focused on spirituality as a way to challenge stereotypes of American Indians. He said the essence of "native spirituality" is generosity and simplicity, based on prayer. He also challenged the "squaw" image of Native women and the stereotypes it engendered. The Executive Committee also met with city officials to plan the conference. In all, they met for two days in the office of the Columbus Chamber of Commerce, where they developed a structure for a new organization and a preliminary platform. They set up committees to coordinate the conference and discussed strategies to get delegates from all reservations. They divided the country into districts and assigned each committee member responsibility to seek delegates from their areas. The most significant action of the committee was establishing criteria for membership. They declared that "membership be confined to those of Indian blood." This clearly established an Indian-only organization. They also established a nonvoting honorary membership for non-Indians (later called *Associate members*) and a junior member category, with two-dollar annual dues for all. They debated a name for the organization. Suggestions included the Progressive Indian Association and the First American National Forward Movement. Both were rejected in favor of the American Indian Association, which was later changed to the Society of American Indians. They changed the name to

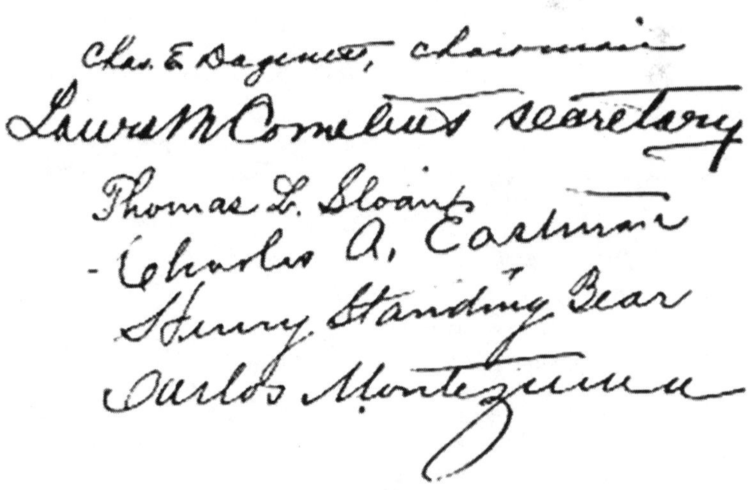


**Figure 1** Signatures of the six founders on thank-you letter sent to W. O. Thompson, The Ohio State University president, for the kind welcome they received while in Columbus, April 4, 1911. Papers of the Society of American Indians, microfilm edition, Reel 7.

make it clear that it was an American Indian organization with only Indian members having the vote. While in Columbus, the committee wrote to General Pratt asking for his support and for his spirit to be with them. They also thanked the mayor of Columbus, the YMCA, the State Historical and Archeological Association, and the principals of Columbus high schools for the hospitality shown to them.[17] The founders also signed a thank-you note to the president of The Ohio State University.

Dagenett was elected provisional chair; Laura Cornelius was the secretary. Rosa B. La Flesche was added as the eighth member of the Executive Committee, as recording secretary and treasurer. The executives drew up a "Statement of Purpose" (written by Eastman), which became the basis for the constitution. (The SAI officially adopted a constitution in 1912; see appendix B).

1. To promote the good citizenship of the Indians of this country. To help in all progressive movements to this end, and to emulate the sturdy characteristics of the North American Indian, especially his honesty and patriotism.
2. To promote all efforts looking to the advancement of the Indian in enlightenment which leaves him free as a man to develop according to the natural laws of the social evolution.
3. To exercise the right to oppose any movement which appears detrimental to the race.
4. In all conferences and meetings of this Association, there shall be broad, free discussion of all subjects bearing upon the welfare of the race.
5. This Association will direct its energies exclusively to general principles and universal interests, and will not allow itself to be used for any personal or private interests. The honor of the race and the good of the country will always be paramount.
6. It is the sense of this Committee that every member of the Association should exert his influence in every legitimate way to bring before each member of the race the necessity of promoting good citizenship and of contributing their individual and united effort for race betterment.[18]

Professor McKenzie requested the assistance of William O. Thompson, president of The Ohio State University, to help secure facilities, funds, and the involvement of local and national officials. Thompson wrote Commissioner Valentine, inviting him to Columbus. Valentine accepted and attended the first part of the conference. Thompson also wrote to Charles D. Hilles, secretary to President Taft, inviting him to the conference. Taft declined, citing a planned visit to Oregon. A resolution inviting General Pratt to head the list of Associate members was also passed.[19] In June, four members of the Temporary Executive Committee and McKenzie met at Laura Cornelius's home in Wisconsin to finalize the proposed program prepared by Dr. Eastman. A committee was appointed to draw up a constitution that would be presented to the delegates at the upcoming conference. Invitations to attend the conference and join the SAI were mailed to four thousand "Dear Fellow Indians." A small, seven-page, three-by-five-inch pamphlet that described the new organization and a copy of the above "Statement of Purpose" was sent with the letter. The invitation included the following text:

> What is to be the future of the American Indian? Is he to continue to be a creature of outside forces? Every Indian says, No! We earnestly believe the time has come when the American Indian should take the initiative in the struggle for race betterment. . . .
>
> This will be the first association of its kind, and it is hoped that every person of Indian blood will take pride in assisting to make it one of the leading and most beneficial associations in the United States. Its primary object will be to serve in every way possible the best interests of the race. You alone, as an Indian, can realize what an immense advantage will come to you personally by whatever gains the Association shall secure for our race. Personal freedom and personal advancement are dependent upon racial rights and racial achievement.[20]

The pamphlet that was sent with the letter was developed as a recruiting tool. It described the two years of correspondence among the group of Indians who met in Columbus in April 1911 to establish an organization "of Indians by Indians." It described the organization's proposed platform and objectives, listing the six temporary executive committee members, outlining a committee system and membership criteria. It was hoped that all tribal groups would send delegates to the inaugural conference.[21]

McKenzie wrote a letter to non-Indian supporters, asking for their help. He also wrote an article on the upcoming conference for the *Red Man*, a Carlisle Indian School publication. He invited one and all to attend the

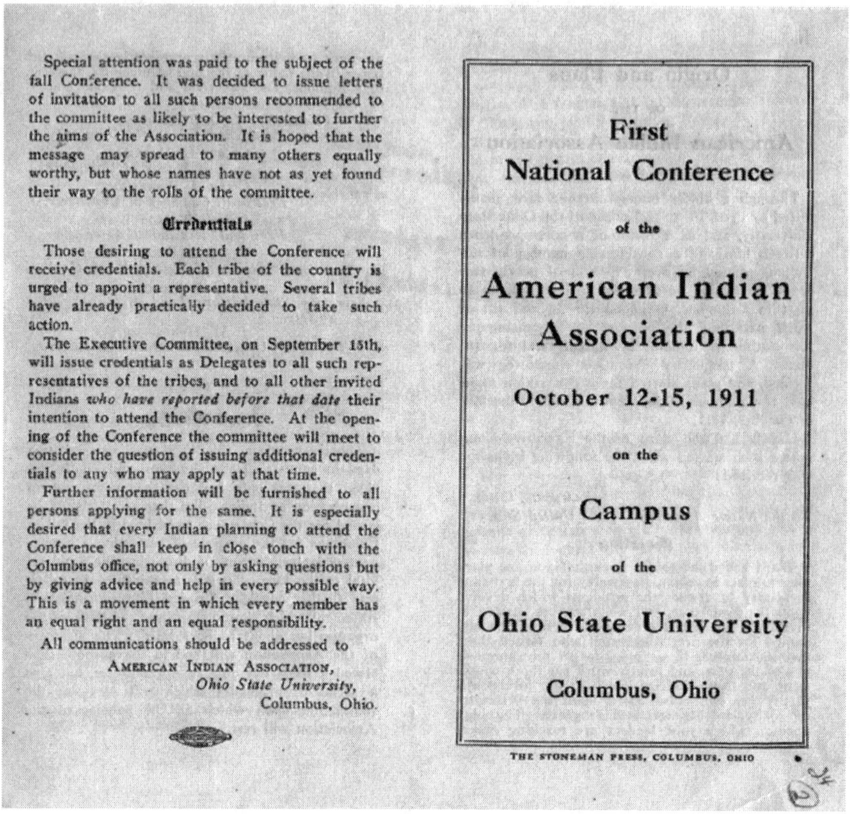

Special attention was paid to the subject of the fall Conference. It was decided to issue letters of invitation to all such persons recommended to the committee as likely to be interested to further the aims of the Association. It is hoped that the message may spread to many others equally worthy, but whose names have not as yet found their way to the rolls of the committee.

**Credentials**

Those desiring to attend the Conference will receive credentials. Each tribe of the country is urged to appoint a representative. Several tribes have already practically decided to take such action.

The Executive Committee, on September 15th, will issue credentials as Delegates to all such representatives of the tribes, and to all other invited Indians *who have reported before that date* their intention to attend the Conference. At the opening of the Conference the committee will meet to consider the question of issuing additional credentials to any who may apply at that time.

Further information will be furnished to all persons applying for the same. It is especially desired that every Indian planning to attend the Conference shall keep in close touch with the Columbus office, not only by asking questions but by giving advice and help in every possible way. This is a movement in which every member has an equal right and an equal responsibility.

All communications should be addressed to

AMERICAN INDIAN ASSOCIATION,
*Ohio State University,*
Columbus, Ohio.

First
National Conference
of the
American Indian
Association
October 12-15, 1911
on the
Campus
of the
Ohio State University
Columbus, Ohio

THE STONEMAN PRESS, COLUMBUS, OHIO

**FIGURE 2** Announcement of the First National Conference of the American Indian Association, using the SAI's original name. Courtesy of The Ohio State University Libraries.

conference and to meet together to "help save the native race of America." The cost of the conference became a concern. The two-dollar membership fee was insufficient for funding the planned activities. To help defray expenses, they planned an evening of entertainment that would be open to the public at a minimal cost.[22]

A new letterhead was designed, listing the officers and new members of the Temporary Executive Committee. As mentioned previously, it included Dagenett as chair, Laura Cornelius as secretary, and Rosa La Flesche as secretary-treasurer. Committee members included Henry Roe Cloud; Emma D. Johnson; Charles Eastman; Carlos Montezuma; the Honorable Charles D. Curtis

(Kaw-Osage), lawyer, Republican congressman and senator from Kansas, and later vice president under Herbert Hoover; John M. Oskison (Cherokee), an author and editor at *Collier's Weekly*; attorney Marie L. Baldwin (Ojibwe); and others. The committee, which included four women, now numbered twenty, plus McKenzie as a local representative. During the summer, McKenzie and La Flesche made arrangements for the conference. They set up local committees to help with the planning. La Flesche stayed in Columbus for the summer and was given office space at The Ohio State University, which formally agreed to host the conference. By early summer, La Flesche, with help from McKenzie, established local arrangement committees to plan the daily activities. They arranged for tickets to be printed for events, arranged for delegates to speak at local churches on what was dubbed "Indian Sunday," contacted local teachers, and set up an Honorary Reception Committee. They also helped plan for new members. La Flesche read the letter that had recently been sent out, although she said it went to three thousand individuals, not four thousand.[23]

When it was clear that President Taft could not attend the conference, it was suggested that former president Teddy Roosevelt be invited. McKenzie wrote to Lawrence Abbott, president of the *Outlook*, a New York–based popular journal, who was friends with Roosevelt. Abbott suggested that McKenzie write a formal letter to Roosevelt, accompanied by a letter from Commissioner Valentine supporting the request. Valentine agreed and encouraged Roosevelt to attend the conference. He added, "It would be of the greatest help in the first real effort I know to create an Indian public opinion about the affairs of the Indians. It marks an epoch."[24] The plan failed, as Roosevelt could not attend, but it was significant that many people in prominent positions now heard about the new organization.

The early meetings seemed to go smoothly, aside from some clashes between Montezuma and several Temporary Executive Committee members over the future of the Indian Office. Since 1908, Montezuma was very involved in the discussions and planning. He had been one of the early advocates of such an organization. Montezuma had an exceptional life story, which he frequently shared while on the lecture circuit. He was born in the 1860s in Arizona to Yavapai parents. The Yavapai were also known as Mohave-Apache, and thus Montezuma became known as an Apache in the public eye and often referred to himself as an Apache. It was the Yavapai association with their Apache neighbors that led to the confusion and the

Mohave-Apache name (today they are the Fort McDowell Yavapai Nation). As Peter Iverson has pointed out, he was not an Apache. His parents named him Wassaja, or "signaling" or "beckoning" in English. In 1871, during a series of skirmishes with the Pima, he and his two sisters were captured. The Pima and Yavapai competed over scarce resources, brought about by the intrusion of many American settlers and miners in the region. The Pima sold the boy for thirty dollars to Carlos Gentile, an Italian immigrant. Gentile was a miner and also a professional photographer and artist. He had the boy baptized on November 17, 1871, and renamed him Carlos Montezuma. Gentile, a bachelor, moved to Illinois and later to Brooklyn, where the young Carlos attended public school. As Gentile's business failed, he could no longer care for the boy. Montezuma ended up in Urbana, Illinois, with Reverend William Steadman, a Baptist minister, as his guardian. In 1880, after two years in prep school, at age fourteen, he entered the University of Illinois, College of Natural Science, School of Chemistry. He graduated in 1884 with a bachelor of science in chemistry and went on to the Chicago Medical College (today Northwestern University School of Medicine), becoming an MD in 1889 at age twenty-three. After he received his medical license, he established a private practice in Chicago but had difficulty getting patients. Meanwhile, he began corresponding with Colonel Pratt of the Carlisle Indian School. Pratt was a mentor and friend, and over the years they exchanged many letters.[25]

With Pratt's help, Montezuma sought work with the Office of Indian Affairs as a reservation physician. For the next seven years, he served at four locations—three on reservations in the west and one as the school physician at the Carlisle Indian School. At this point in his life, he longed for more than being a physician. He began a lifelong commitment to Native people and an equal commitment to demonstrate to the American public that, given the opportunity, the American Indian could succeed in any walk of life. He said, "I can set them a good example." After leaving Carlisle in 1896, he again established a private practice in Chicago, specializing in gastrointestinal conditions. He was determined to prove that an Indian could be an accomplished professional, yet he never forgot his past. In 1901, for the first time, he returned to Arizona to learn more about the fate of his parents and to visit the site of his capture. He corresponded regularly with two cousins who lived on the San Carlos Reservation and asked for their help. He wrote to Pratt, telling him that his father died a mile from the agency headquarters and that his mother was found dead alongside a trail, shot by Indian police.

Montezuma was shocked by the deplorable conditions he saw and attributed them to alcohol abuse. He wrote: "Put an angel on a reservation, the angel will not be an angel very long. . . . It is not natural to cage my people." He traveled to Phoenix to visit the church where he had been baptized and found his name in the records. This visit helped further his commitment to improving the lives of American Indians. It was to this end that he helped plan for a new organization. Iverson pointed out that he maintained an Indian identity while striving for the betterment of the Yavapai people living in Fort McDowell, Arizona. Iverson added that Montezuma did not believe in the renunciation of one's Indian heritage.[26] By 1908, he was determined to help establish an Indian organization that would work to change federal Indian policy and remove Indians from guardianship into full citizenship. He threw his support to the upcoming conference in Columbus.

Montezuma attended most of the preliminary meetings for the new organization but clashed with others over various issues. His clashes went beyond the Indian Office, as he also argued that federal employees should not be part of the leadership of the new organization. Rosa La Flesche described Montezuma as "obstreperous." Montezuma advocated the immediate abolition of the Indian Office and the termination of the reservation system, a view he had been espousing since the 1890s. He often used inflammatory language, such as in an earlier letter to Pratt, where he suggested "bombard[ing] all the reservations into oblivion."[27] He was very adamant and very outspoken, or "fiery" as some said, on this issue. He was not quick to compromise. Several years later in an article in the New York *Daily Tribune,* he again called for the abolition of the reservation system and made it clear that the American Indian "is not content to remain silent."[28] Others believed Montezuma was too hasty and instead wanted to reform the Indian Office, specifically to help the many impoverished Indians on the reservations. Montezuma believed the SAI should be totally free from any governmental connections if it was to be successful in accomplishing its goals. Rumors surfaced that the Indian Office was behind the scenes manipulating the new organization. In June, he wrote to Pratt that he feared OIA influence on the new organization. As a result, Montezuma became suspicious because Dagenett, recently elected as provisional chair, was a federal employee in the Indian Office. Montezuma wondered how the SAI could be truly independent with federal employees in leadership positions. Equally concerning to him was McKenzie's appointment to work for the U.S. Census Bureau on the

American Indian population. This was unrelated to the Indian Office, but nevertheless, Montezuma considered McKenzie a federal employee; thus he could not be trusted in his involvement with the SAI. He believed the rumors about the SAI being controlled by the Indian Office. He cited a *Los Angeles Times* article about the SAI that he believed was planted by the Indian Office. Writing after the first conference, McKenzie said rumors were everywhere that the government secretly controlled the Society and that there also was a rumor that the government would have spies at the conference. Montezuma was so concerned that he decided against attending the conference and told Dagenett that he was resigning from the SAI and regretted that he had any part in its establishment. The Executive Committee immediately sent him a telegram requesting that he reconsider.[29] The idea of federal employees becoming SAI officers created tension and set the tone for future dissension. This issue haunted the Society throughout its existence.

Arthur Parker, a well-known author, ethnologist, historian, archeologist, and museum administrator, was one of the key founders of the Society. He was born on the Cattaraugus Seneca Reservation in New York. He did not have birthright membership in a clan. His father was Seneca, but his mother was white, and being a matrilineal society, Parker was not considered a full member. In 1903, however, he was adopted into the Bear Clan of the Tonawanda Band of Senecas, which gave him full membership. He was given the ceremonial name Gàwasowaneh, which he often used in his correspondence. In his youth, his family moved from the reservation to White Plains, New York, where he attended public school, and then to Dickinson Seminary in Pennsylvania for three years. He became interested in archaeology, spending time at the Museum of Natural History in New York City, where he befriended Frederick W. Putnam, a well-known anthropologist who later became an Associate member of the SAI. In 1906, Parker was hired as an archaeologist for the state of New York, eventually becoming the state archaeologist. He had a long and distinguished career, committing himself to empowering American Indians. He was an incredibly hard worker, keeping his state job while working many hours for the SAI. He wrote thousands of letters, hundreds of articles, and several books. He was also involved in many organizations and fraternal societies. In 1935, he became the first president of the Society of American Archeologists. He was active with the Freemasons for most of his adult life. In 1923, he was inducted into the thirty-third degree, their highest rank. In the mid-1920s, he was appointed chair of the Indian Office's Com-

**Figure 3** Arthur C. Parker, secretary-treasurer, 1911–18; editor of the *Quarterly Journal of the Society of American Indians* and *American Indian Magazine*, 1913–18; and prominent Iroquois studies scholar. Photograph from *American Indian Freemasonry* (1919).

mittee of One Hundred, which was working on recommendations to reform federal Indian policies. He was a complex person with shifting views while trying to please diverse audiences, including federal officials, "friends of the Indian groups," reservation leaders, and the SAI membership. There was one certainty, as pointed out by his biographer Joy Porter. His goal was "to retain an Indian identity while constantly striving toward full integration within American society." He was proud of his Seneca/Iroquois heritage but wanted to be judged on his individual merits. Archeologist Colwell-Chanthaphonh, in a biography of Parker's career as an archeologist, also argued that Parker believed Indians should have a "deep pride in cultures and histories." He was also proud of his great-uncle, Ely S. Parker (Seneca), who was General Grant's adjutant during the Civil War. Grant later appointed him as commissioner of Indian affairs. The success of his great-uncle was especially important to Parker, as some early twentieth-century scholars argued that miscegenation led to inferior offspring. In response, he argued that it was environment, not blood, that counted. In a June 1911 speech in Buffalo, New York, he said, "Good Indian blood and good white blood have produced some of the finest Americans . . . it is manhood, the character, the willingness of men that counts. It is environment that determines his conservatism or progress, and not his racial blood."[30] He wanted to improve the social, educational, and economic environment for Native people.

Parker was unable to attend the preliminary meetings of the SAI but played an important role in publicizing the new organization through correspondence, press releases, and opinion columns in the *New York Times*, and helping to develop its constitution and bylaws. He attended the two conferences in Columbus and had major leadership positions in the SAI, eventually becoming its president. He was elected secretary-treasurer in 1912 and was responsible for corresponding with the membership and the outside world on behalf of the SAI and was general editor of the *Quarterly Journal of the Society of American Indians*. He knew the success of the SAI depended on the recruitment of members, including non-Indians and "friends of the Indian" organizations, whose support he believed was essential. Throughout most of the organization's history, Parker carried the majority of the daily workload that kept the Society functioning.

In July 1911, just several months before the first SAI conference, Eastman traveled to London, England, as the only American Indian representative at the First Universal Races Congress. The purpose was to bring people together from around the world in order to improve international goodwill by bettering race relations between "white peoples" and "colored peoples," with a view of fostering a "hearty cooperation." Among the more than a thousand attendees, from "fifty races," were prominent Americans such as Jane Addams, Franz Boas, John Dewey, and W. E. B. Du Bois, who was elected co-secretary of the American delegation. As it turned out, Eastman and Du Bois were on the same panel giving similar papers on the present state of their respective communities. Since the NAACP had been established two years earlier, and the SAI was soon to have its initial conference, it is hard to imagine they did not share ideas. Eastman probably invited Du Bois to become

**FIGURE 4** Dr. Charles A. Eastman, an SAI founder, 1917 president, and prominent author. Courtesy of Minnesota Historical Society.

an Associate member. Eastman's paper, "The North American Indian," is the same paper he intended to read in Columbus. Apparently, Eastman got into a heated debate between Christian and non-Christian delegates over the use of the word *Christianity* in the Congress's platform. Eastman resolved the debate by proposing "universal brotherhood." Du Bois, as editor of the NAACP journal the *Crisis*, reported on the Congress and published a photo of Dr. Eastman with the byline "The American Indian."[31]

By the summer, after many letters between the SAI founders, preparations were complete for the inaugural conference. The mood among the leadership on the eve of the conference was guarded optimism, with a number of concerns. Most of the concerns were discussed by Rosa La Flesche, the secretary-treasurer, who had access to the correspondence, as much of it went through her office. Several American Indians criticized the platform of the SAI; according to La Flesche, some of it stemmed from jealousy from those not in leadership positions.[32] There was worry about memberships, dues, and donations. Could the SAI attract non-Indians? La Flesche asked for the names and addresses of potential members. She claimed that she had already sent out five thousand letters; she was also worried about the conference program, as it was set up hastily. However, in the end, she predicted the conference would be a great success. Nevertheless, Parker, worried about attendance, sent out a last-minute plea to come to Columbus to help inaugurate the all-Indian organization.

# CHAPTER 2

# "We Are All Indian Brothers"

## *The Early Years, 1911–1912*

Given the negative present-day attitudes toward Columbus Day, it is ironic that the Society of American Indians held its inaugural conference in Columbus, Ohio, with its opening-day ceremony on Columbus Day, October 12, 1911. The conference received considerable notoriety in the city, as it was well covered by the local press and drew great interest from the general public when several SAI delegates spoke in local churches. The conference was sponsored by The Ohio State University and held on campus and in several other sites in Columbus. The invitation to the SAI to hold its inaugural conference in Columbus was signed by quite an impressive group: George S. Marshall, the mayor of Columbus; William O. Thompson, the president of OSU; and E. O. Randall, the director of the Ohio Historical Society. The invitation was also signed by the presidents of the Columbus Chamber of Commerce, Columbus Ministerial Association, Columbus Federation of Labor, as well as Dr. Fayette A. McKenzie, the OSU professor who was responsible for initiating the idea of such conference in Columbus. Federal officials, such as Robert A. Valentine, the commissioner of Indian affairs, also attended and gave the keynote address.

On the opening day of the conference, the front-page headline of the *Columbus Dispatch* announced that "Tribal Delegates Meet to Discuss Problems of the American Indian." The paper outlined the conference program and included brief biographies and photographs of the main delegates. The reportage was positive and upbeat, mentioning the accomplishments of several delegates, such as Omaha attorney Thomas Sloan, who had exposed Indian land fraud schemes. On occasion, the reporters were patronizing, saying the Indians were as educated and as polished as any white man or mentioning that DeWitt Hare (Yankton Sioux), although brought up as a "savage," is now the legal representative of the Yankton. Since the opening of the conference was on Columbus Day, it shared front-page headlines with Italian Americans who held a large parade. (Ohio declared Columbus Day a state holiday in 1910). The *Ohio State Journal* had a catchy headline: "Indians Polite but Don't Bow Humbly," followed by "[They] Kindly Rebuke the White Man's Assumption That He Brought Civilization." The paper also pointed out the absence of feathers, wampum, war paint, and tomahawks. The SAI's executive committee did not spend much time discussing Columbus Day, except to imply that it represented a new beginning. It was city officials in their invitation that first mentioned Columbus, writing, "Light the camp-fire in the city named for the first white man who visited these shores."[1]

Forty-four Active members and forty-nine Associates attended the conference. (The names and addresses were listed in the official *Proceedings*.) They stayed at the luxurious Hartman Hotel. There had been considerable advanced planning, such as press releases, printing tickets for a concert, taking out advertisements in Columbus's three newspapers, hiring the Capitol News Bureau (a newspaper-clipping service), and publishing an eight-page pamphlet on the background of the SAI, the provisional platform, and the SAI's mission statement. These annual conferences were the lifeblood of the SAI. They were the only opportunity to gather as a group to develop policies and agendas and influence public opinion. On the first day of the conference, the *Ohio State Journal* featured a front-page cartoon welcoming the delegates. The top half, depicting Christopher Columbus, read "Columbus Discovers the Indians, 1492"; the bottom read "The Indians Discover Columbus," with a cartoonish-looking Columbus shaking hands with the delegates. The conference opened that night in Memorial Hall in downtown Columbus. That afternoon, a telegram arrived from President William H. Taft, sending best wishes for the success of the conference and apologizing for not being able to attend. President Thompson of Ohio State, who was invited to serve as chair of the conference, presided over the official opening. Many other dignitaries, such as Governor Harmon and Columbus mayor George

Marshall, were in attendance, as were representatives of the Indian Rights Association, the National Indian Association, and individuals from various missionary groups. It was quite an impressive crowd, as the hall was almost full. Mayor Marshall gave a brief welcoming address and in a semi-humorous tone recalled that some of his ancestors had been killed by Indians, adding that in those days, they had called it "murder." Some delegates took offense at this remark and pointed out that they went into battle to defend their homeland. Commissioner Valentine gave the opening address, beginning with a series of platitudes referring to the delegates as "my friends," with constant references to all the work that needed to be done on the basis of friendship and ethical standards. He did not say much that was disagreeable to the conferees. For example, he recommended more Indian children in school and more cooperation between reservations and the government. He asked the delegates to broaden their membership so they could develop an "all-Indian public opinion." He did not offer to pursue citizenship for all American Indians.[2] It should be noted that while Commissioner Valentine was offering friendship, the Indian Office was engaged in the sale of "Indian land" throughout the west. The availability of the "surplus" land was widely advertised under the signature of the commissioner.

Beginning Friday morning, all conference sessions were held in the newly built Ohio State Union and were open to students, faculty, and the general public. The sessions were run like an academic conference, with formal presentations; follow-up remarks by the delegates; and when time permitted, discussion from the floor. The morning session on "Industrial Problems" featured four papers, as did the afternoon session on "Education Problems." J. E. Shields and Marvin Jack delivered the first papers. Both emphasized that the good old days were gone and the open road leads to the future. Shields focused on how the Cheyenne and Arapaho were adjusting to an agricultural lifestyle through the mechanism of agricultural fairs sponsored by the Indian Office. Cash prizes were awarded to encourage farming and animal husbandry for the men and good homemaking skills for the women. The fairs were designed as part of the government's assimilation agenda. Marvin Jack pointed out that in upstate New York, Indians had farmed since time immemorial but were now having difficulty developing farming as a business, especially with dwindling parcels of land and credit virtually impossible to arrange. He added that the Indian, as a noncitizen, could not compete with non-Indian neighbors.[3]

Laura Cornelius Kellogg followed with the most challenging paper of the conference: "Industrial Organization for the Indian." She made a proposal for the survival of reservation land, but not under federal control. She had been very active as a founder. She attended the original planning meeting in Columbus in April 1911, served as secretary to the Temporary Executive Committee, and served as vice president for education, 1911–13. She was quite an accomplished person. She was fluent in Oneida, Mohawk, and English, and was considered one of the finest orators of her day. Born on the Oneida Reservation in Wisconsin, she was proud of her Oneida heritage and valued the knowledge of the elders. She did not attend a government boarding school; however, she attended an Episcopal boarding school for girls and went on to study at Stanford University, Cornell University, Barnard College, and the University of Wisconsin to study anthropology. A constant critic of the Indian Office for its paternalism, she spent many years battling the federal government on behalf of the Oneida people. As pointed out by several scholars, she came from a long line of strong Iroquois women.[4]

Her paper received a prominent headline in a local paper: "Solution to Indian Problem Proposed." The problem she described was dependency and paternalism. She proposed ending the federal reservation system and transforming reservation land into self-governing, independent "industrial villages," with communal economic activity in line with local resources and labor. The idea was to develop jobs to keep residents on the land and to provide opportunities for returning boarding school students. With industrial villages using modern business methods, Indian communities could be maintained and a reservation land base could be kept intact by developing a local economy that would lead to self-sufficiency and independence. She argued that this was the only way out of the present situation and added that this would be much better than life in the big cities, especially considering the desperate lives of factory workers, where "the average man in the white labor market lives a miserable existence to-day." Later that morning, she made one of the most memorable comments of the conference during the open discussion. She attacked the idea that there was a "new" Indian, claiming, "I am not the new Indian; I am the old Indian adjusted to new conditions." She drew loud applause. In her role as vice president for education, she wrote a highly critical analysis of Indian education. There were still nine thousand children without access to school. She claimed boarding schools were not adequate, since children were required to work half a day and attend classes half a day, thus only getting 50 percent of the education children were getting in public schools. She was also critical of medical care at the schools and the amount of graft by school officials. Her conclusion was that Indian children were better off in public schools, where they would receive a full day of classes.[5]

Kellogg's stint with the SAI was brief. She was outspoken, blunt, very direct, and at times contentious. In 1913, she and her husband, an attorney, were arrested in Oklahoma and charged with fraud for questionable fund-raising and impersonating a federal officer. They claimed they were raising money to cover legal costs for land claims cases. They were exonerated, but it was enough to damage her reputation. Some members believed the SAI would be better off without her, claiming she was a detriment to their image. Parker felt that any negative publicity was harmful to the SAI. Kellogg did not attend the 1913 conference in Denver. She was removed as a vice president and subsequently had little to do with the SAI. However, she continued her work, being outspoken, "talking back" on behalf of Oneida land claims in Wisconsin and New York, and continued to advocate for quality education for Indian youth. She committed her career to protecting Native-held land and in doing so protected social and cultural traditions.[6]

Later that afternoon, Marie L. Baldwin, an attorney, who served on the Executive Committee and as the SAI treasurer, presented "Modern Home-Making and the Indian Women," an analysis of contemporary Indian women. One significant aspect of the conference, and throughout the SAI's history, was the active involvement of women who held leadership positions, made formal presentations during the conferences, and had full voting rights, something women in American society did not have, as one Columbus newspaper editorial pointed out. Baldwin's paper focused on the essential role of women in traditional Indian societies, particularly in the many tribes where women were an "absolute equal" to men. Her paper was quite a remarkable essay on the role and status of women in Indian societies, particularly their role in religion. She attacked the stereotype of Indian women as "slaves" or "drudges" to men. She added, however, that in the twentieth century, Indian people were no longer independent and self-governing, and the "old ways" were not suited for a new situation. Therefore, old ways needed to be adapted, changed, or discarded in order to survive in the new environment. Her theme was to respect and honor the past, but adjust and change for the future, especially through education—a consistent theme throughout the conference. Baldwin also played another less-than-savory role in the SAI. She voiced very negative opinions against African Americans, going so far as to protest the employment of African Americans by the Indian Office to work on reservations.[7]

The first order of business in the afternoon was the appointment of a committee to draft a constitution, followed by a series of four papers, including "Higher Education for Indians," "Preservation of Native Indian Art," and "Indians in the Professions." The most highly anticipated paper was Arthur Parker's "The Philosophy of Indian Education." Parker was an accomplished scholar with more than one hundred publications in his lifetime and an activist for American Indian causes. He publicized the SAI conferences and issues in letters to the editor in the *New York Times*. He played a major role in the founding of the SAI and continued in leadership roles through most of its history. He began by saying that "ethnologically, so-called civilization of the whites was a distinct advance," describing some levels of civilization as "barbarian," "savage," taking a "stages of cultural evolution" perspective, not unusual for anthropologists at the time. However, he did not mean that American Indians were inferior—just on a lower level of culture, and with the right environment, they could be the equals of white civilization. He was not talking about the capacity to learn but the *opportunity* to learn. This reflected his philosophy of education. He advocated that under present conditions, with gradual adjustment through education and regeneration on reservations, the gap could be closed. He proposed "social betterment stations" that could teach hygiene and industry, along with how to grow better vegetables and breed better cattle. The problem, according to Parker, was that the dependent status of the Indian hindered improvement. He said, "To survive at all he must become as other men, a contributing, self-sustaining member of society." It might be easy to label Parker as an assimilationist like General Pratt, but his views were complex and multilayered, and sometimes depended on the audience. He argued that the goal was not to turn Indians into white men, nor to give up one's identity as an Indian, but for education to teach the Indian to adapt to modern circumstances. Parker was not advocating an Anglicized assimilation model. He said we must maintain an Indian identity but function in American society. He did not mention tribes or tribal affiliation in this paper—only individualism and "the race." However, throughout his life, he maintained a strong sense of pride in his Seneca heritage while arguing for Iroquois treaty rights (see chapter 5). He was not only speaking to the conference attendees but to the Indian Office. This was one of the themes of the conference and a broad goal of the SAI: to convince the federal government and the general public that there were no limits on what American Indians could accomplish—only limits on opportunity. Parker and other SAI members were constantly frustrated by the negative stereotypes held by government officials and the American public.[8]

Later that afternoon, Angel De Cora Dietz (Winnebago/Nebraska), who joined the SAI in 1911 and served on the Advisory Board from 1913 to 1915, argued for "The Preservation of Native Indian Art." De Cora, a painter and well-known illustrator, attended Hampton Institute, Smith College, and Drexel Institute of Art. Her reputation grew as the illustrator for Natalie Curtis's *The Indian Book* and Zitkala-Ša's *Old Indian Legends*. In 1906, she was appointed to the faculty at the Carlisle Indian School to teach in the Indian Arts Department, now named Leupp Indian Art Studio. She remained at Carlisle as the head of the art department until 1915. She married William "Lone Star" Dietz, an artist, student, and football player at Carlisle, who was of dubious Indian descent but claimed Lakota heritage. He played on the famous 1911 Carlisle team with Jim Thorpe. Both were selected All-Americans. Dietz went on to play professional football and coach in the National Football League with the so-called Boston Redskins, which later became the Washington Redskins. De Cora said she was concerned about the appropriation of Indian art, especially the decorative arts by American businesses with no recognition or compensation, noting that all too often, art education was unrelated to the culture of the students. She transformed art instruction at Carlisle from a European-style art curriculum to one that focused on Indigenous motifs. She explained how they used traditional Indian symbols and designs in art classes. Looking toward the future, she believed that with more training, young Indian men and women could make careers in design. She said, "Indians in native dress is a thing of the past, but his art that is inborn shall endure." Interjecting disagreement into the discussion, Horton G. Elm (Oneida), felt her talk implied too much separatism, in that Indians should not identify with "the racial life" but with American life. General Pratt and other Associate members agreed with Elm, whose remarks offer some insight into the underlying tension among the delegates over the issues of culture and education. Conference delegates were in total agreement, however, that Americans did not recognize the abilities of Indian people. Emma D. Johnson said that "the Caucasian race of the United States does not recognize the ability of the Indian to compete in society."[9] The afternoon session ended with a motion from the floor to request that the Indian Office and the U.S. Congress provide proper educational facilities for the nine thousand Indian children without access to schools (mentioned earlier by Commissioner Valentine in his speech). The motion passed unanimously.

The delegates looked forward to the Friday evening concert, hoping for a good crowd and admission fees, but also knowing that such entertainment could make a good impression on the city and open a wider audience to the SAI's agenda. Before the concert, a reception for the delegates was held at the luxurious Hartman Hotel in downtown Columbus. The delegates were greeted by Dr. Sam Hartman, the wealthy owner who lived in the hotel and used part of it as a medical facility for his practice. He was famous for his bottled patent medicine that supposedly cured all ailments. (It was mostly alcohol and opium and sold for a dollar.) His elixir was available to hotel guests and his patients; it was not mentioned by any of the delegates.[10] Following the reception, the delegates went to Memorial Hall for the concert. The program featured the Carlisle Indian School Quartette, who opened and closed the concert. Except for the quartette, all the performers were SAI members. There were about six hundred people in the audience, who applauded loudly. The concert was so successful that it was repeated on Sunday. The newspapers gave the concert positive reviews, although one reporter said the music was "unfamiliar, almost weird, but beautiful." With the success of these concerts, it was decided to hold similar events at subsequent conferences.[11]

The SAI received front-page coverage in the local papers during the first two days of the conference. By Saturday, the third day, the conference competed for coverage with the opening of the World Series between the New York Giants and the Philadelphia Athletics, but with an interesting twist to the coverage. It was not lost on the delegates or the newspapers that while this major Indian conference was going on, the Giants and the A's each had an American Indian star on their team. It drew considerable attention. Future hall of famer and Carlisle alumnus "Chief" Charles Bender was the star pitcher for the A's. He had won seventeen games in 1911 and 212 major league games in his career. "Chief" John Meyers, the star catcher for the Giants, batted .332 in 1911. The *Columbus Citizen* printed large photographs of both players wearing eagle-feather headdresses. The papers called both "chief" and referred to them as "redskins." Bender pitched in three games, losing 2–1 to Christy Mathewson but winning in games four and six, giving the A's the series, 4–2.[12]

Saturday's presentations covered significant topics that would be debated throughout the rest of the SAI's history. They included "Reservation System-Administration," "Land-Holding," "Trust Funds and Their Management," "The Law and the Indian in the United States," and "Citizenship for the Indian." Thomas Sloan, Hampton graduate, attorney, twice SAI president, and the first American Indian to argue before the U.S. Supreme Court, delivered the first paper on reservation administration. He was one of the members who vigorously defended the right to use peyote as a sacrament in what later became the Native American Church. Sloan's presentation on the reservation system pulled no punches. He listed a litany of abuses, from the refusal of the federal government to honor treaties, to stolen water rights, to the United States' general failure to uphold its moral and legal obligations to American Indians. What was so upsetting to him was the arbitrary and capricious behavior of many reservation superintendents, who could control one's daily life. He added that the government never respected the sovereign rights of Native people and always assumed that it knew what was best for the American Indian. Sometimes, he said, Indians were treated "as arbitrarily as subjects of the Czar of Russia."[13]

The commentary that followed was intense. Delegates shared their own horror stories about capricious government agents, inconsistent application of regulations, and a system meant to perpetuate dependency. Worse yet were those agents who held the purse strings and could arbitrarily decide who could or could not receive their funds held in trust or withholding annuities to force compliance with local officials. Delegates also demanded clarification on the legal status of American Indians. In a later paper, Judge Hiram Chase, elected to the first SAI Executive Committee, said Supreme Court Justice John Marshall's decisions were correct, that treaty land was sovereign, and thus the allotment system could not be constitutional since treaties were supreme. Clearly, Chase supported the continuation of reservation land but with treaty rights, not as dependencies of the government. Chase also added a historiographical comment that when whites win a struggle with Indians, it is interpreted as a battle (e.g., "Battle of Wounded Knee"), but when Indians win a battle, it is interpreted as a massacre (e.g., "the Custer Massacre"). Eastman followed with a poignant statement from one of his books that was also relevant to the role of Christianity in SAI discourse:

> There is no Christian civilization; that Christianity and modern civilization are direct opposites; direct opposites, irreconcilables. There are people who individually are Christian; there are families who are Christians; I have no fault with Christianity. One of the most beautiful things the white man has is Christianity, when he lives up to it. But modern civilization is so materialistic and has gone so far—why even the ministers in this State sell their votes if the papers are to be believed! I have stated in one of my public addresses . . . [that] every public official is a slave to your system. You have been developing a superb civilization; along these lines you have developed a magnificent civilization material, brilliant—but in it you have lost all spirituality.[14]

On Saturday, Eastman planned to read "The North American Indian" in the university chapel. It was the paper that he had read earlier at the First Universal Races Congress in London. Eastman painted the historical and sociological development of American Indian cultures in broad strokes, including a controversial theory that the archeological objects found in North America were not produced by American Indians but by some early mythological race. As for the present, he advocated the need to incorporate education and opportunity for American Indians to enter into American society. He condemned the federal government's paternalism yet praised the work of his longtime friend Richard Pratt.[15]

Sunday's Columbus newspapers reported on all the anti-government talk from Saturday's sessions. Headlines read: "Uncle Sam Is Scolded" and "American Indians Are on the Warpath Against Uncle Sam." The *Columbus Dispatch* reported that some of the delegates believed that the federal government was opposed to the establishment of the SAI. In these articles, the reporters used racist language, such as "redskins," but did summarize the proceedings from Saturday, in particular the demand to end government paternalism. The *Ohio State Journal* also published a formal photograph of all the delegates posed in the back of the Ohio State Student Union.[16] Sunday was dubbed "Indian Sunday" as delegates spoke at Columbus churches in the morning and evening and held a concert in the afternoon. Sunday's papers listed the speakers and the churches—for example, Eastman spoke at the First Congregational Church, and Arthur Parker visited the Northminster Presbyterian Church in the morning and the Indianola Presbyterian Church in the evening. Thomas Sloan spoke at the State School for the Blind. One paper reported that two thousand people attended the afternoon concert, which was swelled by the

**FIGURE 5** Photograph of SAI members at the first conference. Front row, left to right: President W. O. Thompson, P. J. Deloria, Hiram Chase, William H. Holmes, Laura M. Cornelius, Wallace Denny, Nellie R. Denny, Martin D. Archiquette, Elsie L. Elm, Thomas L. Sloan, Rosa B. LaFlesche, Charles Doxon, Nora McFarland, Arthur C. Parker, Henry Standingbear, Joseph Griffis, Sadie Wall, J. M. Oskison, Esther M. Dagenett, Mary E. Finn, Emma D. Johnson, J. E. Shields, Marie L. B. Baldwin, Angel DeCora Deitz, Jane M. Butler. Back row, left to right: John Goslin, Joseph R. Sequiechie, Clement Hill, James Mumblehead, Mack Setima, Michael V. Wolfe, Abe Colonahaski, DeWitt Hare, Sherman Coolidge, Horton G. Elm, Charles E. Dagenett, Albert Hensley, Oliver La Mere, Henry Roe Cloud, Charles A. Eastman. The Ohio State University Student Union, 1911, *Report of the Executive Council on the Proceedings of the First Annual Conference of the Society of American Indians* (Washington, D.C., 1912). First published in the *Columbus Dispatch*, Sunday edition, October 15, 1911, p. 10. Courtesy of The Ohio State University Libraries.

National Farmers Congress, which was also meeting in Columbus. They canceled their afternoon meetings to attend the concert. In addition to musical selections, some of the SAI members gave brief talks on present-day moral and religious problems. Everyone proclaimed "Indian Sunday" a success. It was estimated that ten thousand Columbus residents heard SAI delegates speak in churches and at concerts, fulfilling an SAI goal: engaging public opinion.[17]

On the last day of the conference, the delegates gathered in The Ohio State University Union for a long business meeting that was closed to the media and the public. The major agenda items included ratifying a constitution and establishing a permanent organization by electing an official Executive Committee, which was expanded to twenty, including McKenzie. Resolutions were proposed, debated, and voted upon. Several crucial issues, such as criteria for holding office, the wording of the constitution, and how strong the language should be in condemning the government's policies, were debated. Twenty-seven resolutions were presented. Some were perfunctory, thanking people such as President Thompson. The delegates also appointed a committee of three to develop a logo. They were instructed to choose something "typically American Indian." Angel De Cora chaired the committee with Parker and John Oskison (Cherokee). Parker recommended some type of sun symbol or a copper eagle pattern used by mound builders. He suggested an ancient copper eagle, which he called a thunderbird, a mythological creature, as a model for the logo. The copper figure was in the Smithsonian (they called it a "copper eagle") and had been discovered in an Indian mound in Peoria, Illinois, by James Wesley Powell. A photograph of the "sheet copper eagle" was published in the *Handbook of American Indians*. Parker made a drawing of it and sent it to the committee, writing that "it may have been made by the tribal ancestors of any one of us." De Cora used the drawing to develop the logo. They agreed on the eagle motif, since it was a spiritual symbol among many American Indian groups. John Hewitt, SAI member and employee of the Bureau of American Ethnology, wrote to Parker, insisting that it be called an eagle. According to the SAI minutes, the new logo would serve as a symbol of the "reawakened activity of the race" that would then proceed with wisdom, courage, and foresight. The logo appeared on the publications of the SAI.[18]

Other resolutions were more controversial. The delegates voted to table the adoption of the bylaws and constitution. The proposed constitution pro-

**FIGURE 6** The logo of the Society of American Indians, featuring an ancient stylized eagle. Designed by Angel De Cora. Courtesy of The Ohio State University Libraries.

hibited SAI members from holding office if they held a salaried job with the federal government, such as Dagenett held. This debate over leadership was contentious and continued to create hard feelings throughout the SAI's history. Several delegates argued that those on the reservations would be skeptical of federal employees holding office in the Society. It would appear to be a conflict of interest since the government could hold an employee's job over his or her head. It was not a personal attack on Dagenett or any other member but a question of how it would appear to outsiders. At all costs, the SAI wanted to be seen as an autonomous organization of Indian-only voting members. Despite this debate, Dagenett was reelected as chair of the Executive Committee, but citing the need for harmony, he resigned as chair. Thomas Sloan, Charles Eastman, and Reverend Coolidge were all nominated for the chair. In the ensuing vote, Sloan was elected. Dagenett was elected secretary-treasurer; Arthur Parker, Henry Standing Bear, Laura Cornelius, Reverend Coolidge, and Hiram Chase were elected as a temporary subcommittee. The tabling of the bylaws and constitution meant that the SAI was not a duly constituted organization and only had temporary elected officers.

Following the elections, the discussion focused on establishing a national headquarters. Washington, D.C., was chosen for its proximity to the government, where the Executive Committee could have easy access to the Indian Office and Congress. Another subcommittee drafted a statement of purpose for the SAI. The statement was virtually the same as that drafted in April 1911. One of the last resolutions was to request that Congress require the U.S. president to appoint a three-person Indian Code Commission to codify Indian law and determine the status of each Indian tribe and to "define more exactly the privileges and disabilities of the several classes of Indians." In January 1912, U.S. Representative Charles D. Carter (Chickasaw) of Oklahoma introduced the bill (HR 18334) to establish an Indian Code Commission.[19] This was the SAI's first attempt to initiate legislation, but it was not successful. Parker wrote to President William Taft, Vice President Sherman, former president Teddy Roosevelt, and many others, asking for their support. The delegates also established membership criteria: Active members, Indian Associate members, and Associate members. The first two had to be "persons of Indian blood." The Active members were the official voting members; the Indian Associate members were Indians from other parts of the country who could participate when issues of concern to them were being considered. The Associates were non-Indians, such as McKenzie, who were interested in Indian affairs with voice but no voting rights in the Society. The conference adjourned until the next Executive Committee meeting in January.[20]

The *Proceedings* were published in 1912, but they do not relate the full intensity of the debate in the business meeting. For example, resolutions that were proposed but voted down were not included. However, after the conference, a number of the delegates spoke with the press, giving some frank opinions that led reporters to claim that the SAI failed in its purpose. For example, the *Columbus Citizen* reported "Indian Congress Fails in Purpose: Braves Disagree," pointing out that because they had not ratified a constitution, they were not an official organization. The headline in the *Ohio State Journal* read, "Indian Conference Splits on Politics." It pointed out that no permanent officers were elected and that charges and countercharges flew among the delegates. The followers of Thomas Sloan blamed Charles Eastman; his followers blamed Sloan. It was also reported that Laura Cornelius threatened to resign if Dagenett was elected chair of the Executive Committee. According to Parker, it did not help when Dagenett "characterized the members of the constitutional committee as uneducated and the document the work of children." The constitution that had been tabled included a provision barring federal employees from holding an SAI office, and it was Eastman who had proposed the tabling. This created additional dissent and concern about moving forward without a constitution, which was frustrating because the Executive Committee did not accomplish what it had planned. It also left feelings of mistrust, as it seemed that factions and personal enmity were emerging. This did not bode well for the future.[21]

After the business meeting, the members were invited to a luncheon by the Improved Order of Red Men, a fraternal organization of non-Indians and its women's auxiliary, the Daughters of Pocahontas. They claimed to support American Indians in general and the SAI specifically. Both groups helped the SAI with conference logistics; however, they were white-only organizations that did not allow American Indians to become members. After the luncheon, some of the SAI members were taken on an automobile trip around Columbus. They visited Pope Farm along Dublin Pike to see a sizable Indian mound. According to the *Ohio State Journal*, a local newspaper, they visited a "Prehistoric Mound Near City":

> Following the dinner [lunch], the party took an automobile ride around the city [Columbus], led by Congressman Taylor. Then they were taken to Pope farm, on the Dublin Pike, where there is an Indian mound of considerable size. This was examined with much interest by the delegates. Before leaving the Indians gathered on top of the mound and sang "America," and following that the younger Indians gave an impromptu war dance at the same elevation.

The other Columbus newspapers did not mention the mound visit, and it is not mentioned in the *Proceedings*, except for McKenzie writing that there was an automobile trip after lunch. They did not go to the Newark Earthworks as some scholars have surmised, as they returned shortly to Ohio State to complete the business meeting, which lasted into the evening. They were gone just a few hours; a trip to Newark, Ohio, from Columbus and a return would have been an all-day trip. Several scholars, knowing they had visited a mound, assumed they visited the Newark Earthworks, being unaware that a large mound also existed near Columbus. There is no mention in the press, the SAI *Proceedings*, or elsewhere of a trip to the Newark Earthworks. The mound they actually visited was located along the Scioto River, in what is now the town of Grandview Heights, about five miles from The Ohio State University. It was an Adena era (500 BCE–100 CE) mound that was 30 feet high and 165 feet in diameter on a 3.5-acre site, which in 1911 was located on property owned by W. A. Pope. The story of what happened to the mound is very unfortunate but not unusual for American Indian burial mounds. Pope died in the 1930s, but his wife kept the land until 1947, when she sold it to Joseph Toepfner. Toepfner wanted to commercialize the area and renamed the site Toepfner Mound. He hired a company to bulldoze the mound, but a group of local citizens and the Ohio Historical Society (now the Ohio History Connection) protested. The mound had not been excavated, as the Pope family had protected it. After a seven-year struggle, Toepfner gave the historical society the right to excavate it. Preserving the mound was out of the question, as the historical society claimed it did not have the funds to purchase it. It was a sacrilege and a desecration beyond words. The top twenty-some feet were bulldozed, assuming the burials and artifacts were on the bottom, but these assertions quickly proved wrong. The bulldozer turned up human remains throughout—eighty-five individuals in all. After the excavation by archeologists, what was left of the mound was destroyed and a car dealership was built on the site. The human remains and the artifacts that were recovered are presently in the Ohio History Connection (formerly the Ohio Historical Society). It is too sad to contemplate, especially in light of the joy the Society members must have felt as they stood on the top of the mound and paid homage to their ancestors of yesteryear.[22]

After the conference, a lively exchange of letters ensued. Sloan wondered if he should resign, as he had been accused of earlier legal improprieties. He feared his past problems would affect the organization. Parker suggested he resign as chair since the organization was small and weak and needed to be above reproach. Sloan did not resign as chair at this point, but would soon do so. To make it more complicated, Rosa La Flesche, the secretary-treasurer, wanted Dagenett back as chair. She said she had total faith in him, as they had been friends for twenty years. She added, "So there things are. Muddle, is a very mild name for the state of affairs." Parker expressed great concern as Emma Johnson Goulette (Potawatomi), a member of the Advisory Board and later vice president for education, vehemently opposed closing the Indian Office and strongly supported Dagenett, while Laura Cornelius was "bitterly" opposed to him. Conflicts also arose regarding opinions about the future of the Indian Office. Montezuma wanted it closed; Goulette wrote to Parker that "to overthrow the Indian Bureau (if we could) would be the greatest disaster we could bring upon our race."[23] Parker wrote to Dagenett that he had received two types of criticism. One was a suspicion of government control over the SAI and the other was that the Society may be too "pagan" in its sympathy toward the "mescal-peyote element." He explained that Sloan was feared by some, especially the missionaries, for his sympathy toward the "mescal [peyote] eaters." Specifically, this criticism came from two Presbyterian ministers, A. L. Riggs and Thomas C. Moffett. They were engaged in the fight against Peyotism and accused Sloan of sympathizing with the "mescal eaters." Parker feared that the antagonism toward Sloan would have a negative effect on the SAI. Parker sent a similar letter to Coolidge, pointing out that we are accused of having supporters of the "mescal [peyote] religion" among us. Parker also wrote to Henry Roe Cloud that "many Indians it appears have shown a lack of confidence in us through fear of federal domination."[24] This flurry of correspondence is essential to understanding the future difficulties of the SAI. Four issues emerged: (1) Should federal employees have leadership positions in the SAI? (2) What should be done about the suspicion of government dominance? (3) What policies should the SAI pursue regarding the Indian Office and the reservation system? (4) And, finally, what stance should be taken about the rapidly growing Peyote faith? The latter was an especially difficult issue, as the membership was split. There was no middle ground—either peyote should be criminalized or it should receive constitutional protection. These issues plagued the SAI throughout the next decade.[25]

The months after the first conference were difficult. The future of the SAI was uncertain. There was no constitution, leadership was in flux, funds were short, and there was continual tension between some of the members. For example, Dennison Wheelock (Oneida-Wisconsin) made a severe personal attack on Laurel Cornelius.[26] This was important, as Wheelock played a major leadership role in the SAI. His opinion on Cornelius carried weight with some of the other members. He was vice president for legislation in the early years and served on the Advisory Board. A graduate of Carlisle, he became the bandmaster at Carlisle and later at Haskell, and was an accomplished musician, composer, conductor, and cornet soloist. The high point of his musical career was leading the U.S. Indian Band in its performance at

Carnegie Hall in 1900. In addition to his musical career, he became a lawyer, passing the bar in Wisconsin in 1910. He was close to General Pratt and shared his view that the reservation system should be terminated and the Indian Office should be abolished—both controversial issues that created tension among the members. Amid the turmoil, both Parker and Rosa La Flesche must be given credit for persevering and holding the small membership together. Parker worked at publicizing the new organization through his writings, including in letters to the *New York Times*. They both spent considerable time corresponding with a wide range of people, hoping to put the Society on firm footing.[27]

The new SAI office in the Metropolitan Bank Building in Washington, D.C., opened in November 1911. La Flesche agreed to staff the office in her position as secretary-treasurer for sixty dollars a month. In January 1912, the Executive Committee, including Sloan, Parker, and Coolidge, met in the new headquarters. They approved the constitution without a clause prohibiting federal employees from becoming SAI officers. It was now ready for a vote by the full membership at the next conference. At this meeting, both Sloan and Dagenett resigned as Executive Committee officers. It was a relief to some, including Parker, not just because of Sloan's reputation or Dagenett's reputed conflict of interest, but because of the growing animosity between them. This cleared the way for Reverend Coolidge to be elected chair of the Executive Committee and Parker as the secretary-treasurer. Eastman, who not present, was elected as a vice president but declined the position. At this point, Eastman was backing away from the SAI, much to everyone's regret. Part of the reason was the "Eastman incident," as referred to by John Hewitt. Hewitt was asked to assess the paper Eastman planned to deliver in Columbus, but he strongly disagreed with Eastman's theory that North American Indians did not produce the archaeological objects held in the Smithsonian and elsewhere. Hewitt insisted they were produced by North American Indians. Parker supported Hewitt, saying he was "scientifically" correct. Parker decided to forewarn Eastman, since Hewitt's rebuttal was to be read after Eastman delivered his paper. Hewitt was not in attendance but had an advanced copy (it had already been read in London) of Eastman's paper and asked Marie Baldwin if she would read his commentary. Eastman became very upset and did not read his paper—hence no rebuttal. Eastman took offense at Parker's comments. Parker wrote to McKenzie explaining the situation. He also wrote to Hewitt, telling him of his conversation with

Eastman and pointing out that they were now at odds and that Eastman was criticizing him in public and accusing him of being just an "ethnologist," not capable of understanding the Indian. It would be several years before Eastman resumed active involvement with the Society, although he remained a member. The Executive Committee also selected an eleven-member General Committee (later called the Advisory Board), which included some very prominent individuals: John Oskison, Marie Baldwin, Rosa La Flesche, Dennison Wheelock, as well as Sloan and Dagenett. They also established a Legal Aid Division, producing a twelve-page pamphlet, to carry out legal work for individuals and tribes unable to collect on claims against the government. They also printed five hundred copies of the new constitution and one thousand copies of the *Proceedings* and mailed them to members and others. The Executive Committee met again in February in New York City to discuss the upcoming conference; they voted to meet again in Columbus.[28]

After the January and February meetings, La Flesche, Parker, and Coolidge campaigned to increase the membership, asking present members to solicit new members. They also requested donations and loans. In order to facilitate a new membership campaign, they prepared a circular letter stating the SAI's purposes and aims and sent it to everyone on their mailing lists. They also published a pamphlet by Fayette McKenzie, "The Indian and Citizenship." A thousand copies were printed and distributed. In the pamphlet, McKenzie analyzed the complexities of citizenship with "Indians taxed" and "Indians not taxed." He supported the Indian Code Commission bill to bring order out of the chaotic situation of the legal status of American Indians, the so-called Indian problem, but he did not call for full citizenship. He also included U.S. Census data, mostly on health and mortality, and concluded that American Indians were not a "vanishing race."[29]

## The "Vanishing Indian" Myth and the Society of American Indians

As described in the introduction, the SAI spent considerable time and energy battling stereotypes. By the late nineteenth century, the idea that American Indians were vanishing had been developing for several decades. After centuries of destruction by America's westward expansion and an all-out assault on American Indian cultures by the federal government, many believed Indians were a "doomed" race. This belief was held by many anthropologists, biologists, and historians, as well as the general public, as the imagery of a vanishing people pervaded popular culture. There were several interpretations of how this "vanishing" was occurring. One view was that the assimilation programs of the government would work and American Indians would adopt Anglo American values and lifestyles and disappear into the mass society. Others argued that Native Americans were not capable of civilization, had limited cranial capacity, and could not cope with modern life and would literally vanish. The latter view was reinforced by U.S. Census figures for 1900 and 1910 listing approximately a quarter of a million Indians. In either case, Indians were portrayed as part of America's past, not part of a new, twentieth-century America. Anthropologists and ethnologists, mostly from the Smithsonian's Bureau of American Ethnology, contributed to this narrative by initiating fieldwork to preserve the remnants of what they claimed were dying cultures, or what has become known as salvage anthropology. Meanwhile, photographer Edward S. Curtis was continuing his decades-long quest to photograph Indians as he perceived them to be in the past, sometimes artificially creating photographic tableaus of an almost-forgotten era. Curtis's work, as excellent as it was from a photographic perspective, contributed to the belief that Indians were part of the past, not part of the future. In the midst of the vanishing imagery in popular culture, his photographs reinforced the vanishing narrative, particularly the one famous photo he titled "The Vanishing Race," with Navaho (Diné) men on horseback riding single file into the darkness, as in retreat. He wrote, "The thought which this picture is meant to convey is that the Indians as a race, already shorn of their tribal strength and stripped of their primitive dress, are passing into the darkness of an unknown future." This vanishing image became the lead photo in Curtis's first volume of photos and was featured in a photographic opera in a 1913 performance at Carnegie Hall in New York City titled *The Story of a Vanishing Race.* Even a sports magazine writing about Jim Thorpe and two other American Indians leaving for the 1912 Olympics in Sweden referred to them as "three champions of a vanishing race." It was the same with the Wild West shows. All the SAI members, Active and Associates, were opposed to Wild West shows and wanted to make sure the Society was not associated with them. These shows were developed and popularized by Buffalo Bill Cody and performed throughout America and Europe. His show featured a parade of Indians on horses wearing "Indian" regalia. The most striking part of the show featured "wild" Indians with war paint, feathers, and "whooping," attacking white settlements and wagon trails, with Buffalo Bill and the U.S. Cavalry coming to the rescue. The show included a "reenactment" of the defeat of Custer and the Seventh Cavalry at Little Big Horn, portraying it as a massacre, not a battle. Most of the participants (approximately two hundred) were American Indians who were in desperate need of work. For many, it was the only possibility for employment. Nevertheless, the actors were portrayed as savages and contributed to the negative stereotyping of Native people, once brave and proud but now doomed, unable to adjust to the modern world.[30]

In addition, there were books and comics, especially dime novels, that elicited the same message: a noble yet uncivilized race doomed to extinction in the face of American progress. Titles appeared such as *Tribute to a Vanishing Race* (1913) and Joseph K. Dixon's *The Vanishing Race: The Last Great Indian Council* (1913). Rodman Wanamaker (son of Philadelphia department store magnate John Wanamaker) wrote in the preface to Dixon's book that he wanted to build a memorial "in memory of a noble, though vanishing race." Dixon portrayed Indians marching proudly but sadly into the western evening sky and vanishing, repeating the common metaphor of Indians marching into darkness. Since 1909, Dixon, a publicist for the Wanamaker businesses, had been promoting the idea of a monument to the "vanishing race." Wanamaker proposed a 165-foot-high bronze statue of an Indian on Staten Island. It was to face the ocean with an outstretched welcoming hand. In order to further his plans, Wanamaker established the National American Indian Memorial Association to raise funds for the statue.[31] The U.S. Congress sanctioned the project by approving its construction on public land. In 1913, Wanamaker and Dixon held an elaborate ground-breaking ceremony, attended by President Taft and other government officials. During the ceremony, the new Indian head nickel, with a buffalo on the reverse, was released. It may have seemed ironic to some to have the vanishing Indian and the vanishing buffalo portrayed together on a coin at the site of a proposed memorial to a vanishing race. SAI members thought this was all ridiculous. The so-called memorial was connected to three Wannamaker expeditions (1908, 1909, 1913) led by Dixon to record the last vestiges of a "dying race," including hundreds of photographs portraying "traditional" Indians. On his second trip, he gathered a group of American Indians for what he called the last great Indian council, the subtitle of his book. After the ground-breaking ceremony for the memorial, Dixon left for his third trip, which he called

"Expedition of Citizenship." Lucy Maddox has pointed out that Dixon never reconciled his memorial to a "doomed race" with his expedition to prepare Indians for citizenship. She also claimed that Dixon's real goal was publicity for the Wanamaker enterprises. Trachtenberg argues that the proposed statue was meant to memorialize the Indian's defeat and loss of land, and was a signal of "national white power" to the non-Anglo-Saxon immigrants pouring into the country. Dixon continued pushing for the bronze statue for several years but was not able to raise the necessary funds. With the beginning of the First World War, the idea died and the memorial was not built, but Dixon and Wanamaker contributed greatly to the public's perception of the "vanishing Indian."[32]

Warren C. Moorhead, a well-known anthropologist, SAI Associate member, and a member of the Board of Indian Commissioners, included in his popular history of American Indians artwork by the young Wanamaker that depicted vanishing imagery with such captions as "The Last Arrow" and "The Fading Sunset." Several years later, Zane Grey's novel *The Vanishing American* appeared. One Indian character says, "The sun of the Indian's day is setting . . . we are a vanishing race." Perhaps the best known and certainly the most widely reproduced of these images was James E. Fraser's larger-than-life white marble public sculpture, *The End of the Trail.* Originally displayed in 1915 at the San Francisco Panama-Pacific Exposition, it was a sad, depressing image of an Indian on horseback, with all the elements of the sculpture focusing downward. The horse's head and body are drooping; the rider's body is slouching downward, signifying defeat; and the spear he is carrying faces downward. When the sculpture was exhibited, the guidebook read, "Before you is the end of the Indian race. The poor Indian, following a long trail, has at last come to the end. The worn horse and its rider tell a long pathetic story." The full sculpture epitomizes defeat: the end of the trail. Reproductions of the horse and rider flooded the nation, making it the most conspicuous public image of the "vanishing race." Clearly, all these images and more reinforced the idea that these were the dying days of the American Indian.[33]

The sad story of Ishi played into the vanishing narrative. In August 1911, Ishi, a starving and exhausted California Indian, wandered into a California town. He was the last surviving member of the Yahi people. All had died or been killed as part of the massive extermination of California Indians. He was dubbed "America's Last Wild Indian." He was housed in the Museum of Anthropology in San Francisco, where he was put on exhibit for the public and studied by a number of anthropologists. Ishi lived in the museum until he died of tuberculosis in 1916. Although against his wishes, an autopsy was performed and his brain was sent to the Smithsonian, where it was stored with thousands of other American Indian remains. In the 1990s, his brain was discovered in storage and returned to California to be united with his other remains. The widely publicized story of Ishi reinforced the narrative of the vanishing Indian.[34]

The vanishing imagery was anathema to SAI members. It energized the membership to do all that was possible to challenge the negative images. Parker took on the issue in a letter to the *New York Times*. He indicated that the leaders of the SAI denied that they were part of a vanishing race. Just because an Indian puts away his buckskin shirt and dons a tailored suit does not mean he disappeared: "It's just adjusting to the modern environment." He wrote that among the leaders were highly educated, well-known men and women: senators, congressmen, physicians, clergy, teachers, artists, and lawyers. He wrote about the Columbus conference, where leaders "proclaimed their Indian ancestry as the highest honor." Parker also took the opportunity to publicize the upcoming conference, writing that the SAI was seeking "the rights and destiny of the race as Americans in America." The *New York Times* editorial in response to Parker's letter indicates the scope of the problem the SAI faced. The *Times* wrote: "They [SAI members] are the nobler red men, without the blood thirstiness of their sires," predicting that members of the Society would lose their "racial identity."[35]

## Competing Organizations

The SAI was concerned about the emergence of potentially competitive organizations, such as the Indian Memorial Association (IMA) and the Brotherhood of North American Indians. The short-lived IMA (not to be confused with the Dixon / Wanamaker National American Indian Memorial Association) emerged after a series of letters was exchanged among Indian professionals and Indian office employees, suggesting a new organization. Walter Battice (Sac and Fox) a federal employee, seems to have initiated the correspondence. Many of those involved were future SAI members. They included Carlos Montezuma, Thomas Sloan, Dennison Wheelock, Henry Standing Bear, and Ohio State Professor Fayette McKenzie. This group and others met in Lawrence, Kansas, in June 1909. They drafted a series of resolutions attacking federal control and electing Sloan as president and Battice as secretary. The attempt did not last long. Within months they became divided, according to American studies scholar D. Anthony Tyeeme Clark (Sac and Fox), into moderates and militants, and progressives and separatists. However, personal connections were established, which aided the emergence of the Society of American Indians.[36]

The Brotherhood was established in December 1911 by Richard C. Adams (Delaware/Lenape), an activist and author from Oklahoma. He was the Delaware's legal representative in Washington, challenging control by the Department of the Interior over Delaware land. The Brotherhood opened a headquarters in Washington, wrote a constitution, and began recruiting members. They claimed to be a fraternal and cultural organization with full membership for American Indians and honorary membership for others, but Rosa La Flesche, who attended some of their meetings, believed they were a political organization. They also planned to establish local Brotherhoods in other cities. It was feared that the Brotherhood would compete for funds and take away potential SAI members. For example, they tried to convince Montezuma to join the Brotherhood.[37] Parker was quite concerned. He believed they were a threat, knowing that a broad-based unity was essential for the SAI to succeed. He did not want Brotherhood leaders to become SAI members, and he rejected any suggestion of an affiliation. He had nothing good to say about the Brotherhood and recommended that Society members not join other organizations. He was also concerned that Commissioner Valentine spoke at their recent convention. As it turned out, the Brotherhood was not a threat, but at the time no one could be sure, especially as rumors spread that industrial magnate Andrew Carnegie was donating $750,000 to the Brotherhood to erect an office building. Their conferences were somewhat chaotic, with personal struggles and accusations of authoritarian leadership under Richard Adams, who had the title "The Great Sachem." They withered away within two years. Other groups also emerged, such as the Grand Council of American Indians, but they were also short-lived.[38]

## Return to Columbus: The Second Conference

In the spring of 1912, Parker felt more confident about the future of the Society, yet he had concerns. The conference *Proceedings* were published and the leadership turmoil was resolved, at least for now. With Dagenett's resignation, there were no Indian Office employees on the Executive Council. Parker was concerned, however, about the poor financial condition of the Society, the need for more members, and the need to maintain unity among the present members. He wrote, "The tribal lines are taken away with us, *we are all Indian brothers* [italics added] fighting together for freedom and justice." He was also determined to get Montezuma to renew his membership and wrote that "we need the true Indian spirit and I think that the distinguished Apache has it." Parker was worried that he had insufficient time to do all the necessary work, as he was still employed by the state of New York. He complained to McKenzie that he was not getting enough support from the members. The answer was an all-out effort to increase memberships. Parker sent letters to the Active members. McKenzie did the same with the Associates. In fact, McKenzie put great effort into recruiting non-Indians as members and potential donors. Parker ordered 2,500 copies of the letters. The Executive Committee also sent out another "Dear Fellow Indian" letter to everyone on their mailing list, followed by another "Dear Friend" letter from Henry Roe Cloud, the vice president for membership, seeking new members. The goal was 1,000 new members in 1912.[39]

By the summer, plans for the second conference were in place. The first conference had set an agenda for the future, and Montezuma was back in the fold, having renewed his membership. Despite policy differences and intrapersonal tensions, there was a common core of essential beliefs and goals supported by almost all of the members. They advocated for cooperation among tribes and unity of purpose among American Indians. They believed in "racial" uplift, with many references to "the race"—similar to Du Bois and the NAACP's use of the term "the Negro race." The term and the concept of race as a distinct group were commonly used by SAI members in their speeches and documents. In the original statement of purpose and the constitution, phrases such as "welfare of the race," "honor of the race," "for race betterment," or "true history of the race" were used. References to "the race" were common throughout the SAI's history. This language was used to indicate the need for a broad-based unity, or as Parker said, so that the SAI could benefit "the whole race." It did not imply a disregard for tribal identity.

Another point of agreement was to work together to challenge and eliminate the American public's stereotypes of American Indians. Negative visual representations abounded, especially in advertisements for tobacco products,

Make remittance by Draft, Money Order or Check, payable to Arthur C. Parker, Secretary-Treasurer, and send to Albany, N. Y.

THE SOCIETY OF AMERICAN INDIANS

No 7....... ACTIVE MEMBERSHIP

Washington, D. C., August 27, .....1912

Received of Mr. Carlos Montezuma............

Annual Dues. 1912-13..................... $2.00

Donation, 1912..................................----

Total.......................... $ 2.00

Thank You !

Arthur C. Parker.

Secretary-Treasurer

**FIGURE 7** Dr. Carlos Montezuma's SAI membership card. Courtesy of the University of Arizona Special Collections.

in popular literature, and with the advent of the "cigar-store" Indian. The obnoxious "vanishing Indian" imagery was again condemned. The SAI wanted to convince the public that American Indians had the same capabilities and capacities as other Americans. The Society was proof that Indians were not vanishing. They just needed opportunities such as meaningful education. Virtually all the Active members agreed that reservations were awful places, as many had firsthand experiences with reservation life. The problem was that they disagreed about solutions. For example, there was total agreement that the Indian Office was not operating in the best interests of Native people, but it was unclear how this could be resolved. Many members believed the SAI should lobby Congress to change various laws and for the Indian Office to change some of its policies. There was also unanimous support to end federal guardianship and move toward full citizenship without giving up treaty rights or any claims that individuals or tribes had against the government. There is no indication that SAI members assumed that citizenship would preclude self-determination; in fact, they argued that citizenship would provide a basis for self-determination and the protection of treaty rights. Despite many differences, there was a basic agreement on certain issues.

As the second conference approached, there was an air of optimism among the leadership despite the uncertainties for the future. Invitations were sent out, the program was set, and facility arrangements were in place. The Columbus Chamber of Commerce welcomed the SAI. As with the first conference, the Society also had the support of the local chapter of the Improved Order of

Red Men and financial support from the Columbus Indian Hospitality Association, with a $1,000 donation to help with hotel bills. All three Columbus newspapers covered the conference. One paper included front-page photographs of four prominent women delegates: Marie Baldwin, Angel DeCora, Laura Cornelius Kellogg, and Emma Johnson Goulette. To help publicize the conference, several motioned to invite recent Olympic gold medal winner Jim Thorpe (Sac and Fox) to the conference. A Carlisle official said that this would not be possible, but they agreed to send Thorpe's Olympic medals and other trophies to be put on display, including a bronze model of a Viking ship presented to Thorpe by the czar of Russia, who was at the Olympics, and the gold medal for the pentathlon presented by King Gustav V of Sweden, who said, "Sir, you are the greatest athlete in the world." These were exhibited in Memorial Hall during the evening concert. The Society hoped to draw a large crowd and use the ticket sales to finance the conference. The story of Thorpe's medals was in all the Columbus newspapers. It was reported that 1,500–2,000 people attended the concert, netting $700. The display was so popular that the items were put on display at the Chamber of Commerce the next day. (The Thorpe medals were returned to the Amateur Athletic Association in 1913.) It was even suggested that Carlisle play Ohio State in a football game. The Ohio State athletic director took it under advisement but turned it down as impractical since the regular season was about to begin and the schedule was set.[40] (Or maybe the real reason was that in 1904 Ohio State played Carlisle at home on Thanksgiving Day and lost 23–0.)

The second conference was similar to the first in terms of its organization and structure. Papers were read, speeches were made, and debates were held among the attendees. A Friday-evening concert was held, which was repeated on Indian Sunday, and delegates conducted business meetings and elected officers. Attendance was better than at the first conference. Parker had to juggle the requests to speak, as there were only so many available time slots. The attendees included many of the same prominent American Indians, along with prominent non-Indians such as General Pratt, as well as government representatives and members of various "friends of the Indian" groups, such as the Indian Rights Association and the Lake Mohonk Conference of Friends of the Indian. On the first evening, Society members went to the First Congregational Church to hear Reverend Washington Gladden of Columbus, an Associate member, well-known progressive, and social gospel advocate, give the opening sermon. His theme was to uplift, unify, awaken race consciousness, and make progress and change, using "friends of the Indian" language, focusing on the oneness of humanity, but with distinct, separate races. He did not, however, equate race and culture.[41]

Earlier that day, fifteen SAI members attended a ceremony at the Logan Elm Memorial, located about forty miles south of Columbus. Local county officials ceded the deed to the tree and five surrounding acres as a memorial to Chief Logan (Cayuga/Mingo) to the Ohio Historical Society. It was under this tree in 1774 that a treaty was signed with the British. Logan refused to attend, but he reportedly sent his famous speech, sometimes called "Logan's Lament," which today is inscribed on the Logan monument. Supposedly the speech was given to an envoy of Lord Dunsmore of Virginia, who read it at the treaty signing. The SAI members were photographed under the Logan Elm with other dignitaries. It was mostly the women members who attended, including Emma Johnson, Angel De Cora, and Rosa La Flesche. Charles Dagenett was also with the group and gave a lengthy speech on the history of Chief Logan. At the end, he thanked all for the "tribute to Logan—to the Indian race" for the events at the Logan Elm.[42] Today the site is the Logan Elm State Memorial. The tree survived until 1965. As with the visit to the Pope (Toefener) Indian Mound during the previous conference, this was a celebration of Indian heritage.

President Coolidge officially opened the conference with a call for unity and harmony. He urged participants to come together as Indians and that it is "too weak a proposition in this, *our country* [italics added], to relinquish our land and then vanish." Combatting the "vanishing" stereotype was a constant theme during the conference. At the second session, Arthur Parker gave a major address that set the agenda for the conference and by extension the SAI. He emphasized that the theme and purpose of the conference and the Society overall was to uplift the people and destiny of a race; beyond just complaining or lamenting, the conference would attempt to right what was wrong and offer ways to correct injustices. He added that the conference sought to give Indians a voice to help stop abuses and to enlighten and awaken the "white race." We have been silent too long, he said. We want them to know we can govern ourselves; it is up to us to choose our lives. His was a dramatic speech full of strong language and expressive phrases, such as referring to exploiters as those who turn drops of blood into gold.[43] Attempting to enlighten the American public with such rhetoric was an essential part of almost all SAI gatherings.

Coolidge and Parker set the tone for a successful conference, given the uncertainties of the past year. At the business meeting, a constitution was approved (appendix B), as were a platform and resolutions for the conference. Delegates voted to publish a quarterly journal, hold annual conferences in a university setting, and send a petition to President Taft requesting that a new commissioner of Indian affairs be appointed without regard to political affiliation. Elections were held that were less rancorous than previous ones. Coolidge was reelected president; Parker secretary-treasurer; Sloan first vice president; and three vice presidents were appointed, with Kellogg on education, Dennison Wheelock on legislation, and Dagenett on membership. They elected a fifteen-person Advisory Board of Active members, with Henry Roe Cloud as the chair. During the nominations, Dagenett made a dramatic plea to not exclude Indian Office employees from becoming SAI officers. He said: "If the Society declares themselves against Indians in the Indian Service it is going to drive a good many Indians from the Society and cause them to lose interest. . . . There are hundreds of progressive honest men and women in that service who are loyal to their race first of all." His argument won the day: federal employees were not prohibited from holding SAI offices. With the election of officers, they were now an official organization. The platform and resolutions posed a major dilemma for the Society. The platform covered major policies, while the resolutions involved specific cases for action. This was a constant source of pressure for the SAI. Was it an organization dedicated to uplifting the "race" and influencing federal policies, or dedicated to helping local communities deal with their problems? This dilemma was never resolved, especially with limited financial resources. For example, Parker advocated influencing public opinion, lobbying Congress and the Indian Office, while Eastman pushed for local projects. He wrote, "We must do intensive work among our people." These differences made it difficult for leadership to maintain a consistent vision and focus. Again, they requested Congress to pass legislation requiring the president to establish an Indian Code Commission, and urged the commissioner of Indian affairs to put Indian welfare first, safeguard health, encourage the Indian Office to hire Indians, and establish an annual American Indian day. Other resolutions asked the American people to right several wrongs, specifically against the Jicarilla Apache, the Pueblo, the Mescalero Apache, the Turtle Mountain Band in North Dakota, the Cayuga in New York, and denounced the law enforcement's failure to solve the murder of Desota Tiger, a Seminole from Palm Beach County, Florida.[44]

On Friday evening, Reverend Coolidge delivered the official presidential address. He said the SAI was organized for the "uplift and adjustment of the Indian race" and "to awaken and deepen race consciousness." It was a call to unity and action, a war, but the new weapons were "the plow, the ballot, the pen," with the goal of terminating the Indian Office, ending federal guardianship, and implementing full unrestricted citizenship. He also referred to Christian citizenship in a Christian nation, as a way of encouraging Americans to act like Christians and provide good churches, schools, hospitals, clean cities, and clean industries. The struggle would be difficult, he added, facing deceit, greed, cruelty, ambition, and self-interest. His goal was for all Indians to be able to say "*Civis Americanus sum*" (I am an American citizen).[45] This also indicated the manner in which many SAI members used Christianity to encourage Americans to treat American Indians humanely. It was a strong message outlining future goals.

The Saturday evening session at the Chamber of Commerce featured Dr. Montezuma and General Pratt. Both were certain to draw media attention. Montezuma opened his talk with a challenge to stereotypical views. He quoted Senator Marcus A. Smith of Arizona, who had once proclaimed, "There is more hope of educating the rattlesnake, than of educating the Apache." Montezuma added, "I am an Apache." He had already set the tone the day before with remarks from the floor: "So I say the object of the meeting of the Society of American Indians is not to discuss the inside of the prison walls . . . but to consider how to beat down those walls, to destroy them all." The *Columbus Dispatch* called him "the wit of the conference." After his "I am an Apache" comment, he had the audience's attention. He went on to describe his capture as a child; being sold; attending public schools, college, and medical school; and becoming a physician. When he told his story, as he often did, he used dramatic intonation and much gesticulation. He also described his years on several reservations as a physician, where he witnessed wretched conditions and excessive government control firsthand. He used his life story to inspire others. He said he had an opportunity for education, which he would not have had if he was a "reservation Indian." He added that "colonization, segregation and reservations are the most damnable creations of men." He believed the only true solution to the "Indian problem" was closing the reservations and allowing free association with the "paleface." A dramatic, uncompromising speech, it was a total assault on the Indian Office and the reservation system and set the pattern for his future activism.[46]

Montezuma and Pratt, longtime friends, were allies on several issues. Pratt is an example of the role of Associate members in the SAI. In the early years, they outnumbered the Active members, but that changed later as the SAI advocated more aggressive policies. The SAI leadership, especially Parker and Montezuma, paid significant attention to the Associate members. Their annual dues and donations were important, but more so, high profile Associates such as Pratt and Gladden, federal officials from the Indian Office, and church leaders such as Father William Ketcham of the Bureau of Catholic Indian Missions gave the Society, according to Parker, prestige and creditability. Parker publicized Pratt's statement that this "is the most momentous event in all Indian history." The Associates could also help counter the American public's negative stereotypes, such as by opposing Wild West shows, as well as lobby the Indian Office and Congress on behalf of American Indians. On the other hand, there was a state of tension over the role of citizenship in the future of American Indians as the Associate members supported assimilation campaigns.[47]

Modern scholars have not been kind to General Pratt, yet most SAI members considered him an ally, even if they did not always agree with his opinions. He repeatedly attacked the Indian Office, its educational policies, the reservation system, and the failure to move rapidly toward full citizenship for American Indians. His speech included ideas he had been espousing since his removal as superintendent of the Carlisle School in 1904. His premise, like Montezuma's, was that reservations were prisons and one could not develop into an independent, functioning individual within a dependent status on a reservation. The reservation, he said, was a "manhood-destroying prison system the government adopted for their universal control." His answer was education in public schools, colleges, and universities. He used Montezuma as an example. He frequently extolled Montezuma as a role model for American Indians. Pratt believed education would lead to equal ability, which would lead to equal rights. Indian Office policies were a hindrance, as they segregated Indians and prevented integration into American life. His role inside SAI was important, but more so outside. He spoke to many groups. He also self-published and distributed some of his speeches. His Columbus speech was reprinted as a pamphlet and distributed along with another speech he gave two weeks later to the Military Order of the Loyal Legion in Philadelphia: "American Indians: Chained and Unchained." In this speech, he explained how the U.S. government had chained the Indians and now had the responsibility to unchain them by ending the reservation system. Citizenship was one of the most frequently discussed topics by Active and Associate members. There was one contentious issue: some claimed citizenship should be earned; others advocated birthright citizenship. Dennison Wheelock, a product of Carlisle, wanted Indian children to be taught to cultivate the land, and when they developed ambitions, they would become prosperous and competent Indians and take their place among "civilized" people. He opposed reservation day schools because they segregated the children and did not provide an adequate training ground for them to become "competent citizens." Father Ketcham of the Catholic Indian Mission argued that Indians could only become "civilized" by religion and education but nevertheless should be given citizenship as soon as possible, since the only preparation for citizenship is the practice of citizenship. It was not unusual to hear Associate members equate being "civilized" and "competent" with citizenship, using "civilized" from the now-discredited social evolution theory of a natural progression of culture in a series of stages from barbarism to civilization. Some argued that Christianity could contribute to this so-called evolutionary process. Asa Hill (Mohawk), Henry Roe Cloud, and Charles Kealear argued that the gospel and the words of Jesus should be disseminated widely.[48] As mentioned previously, this was a continuing strategy of SAI members to develop support from Christian organizations.

Many other papers were delivered, followed by commentary from the floor; however, when Parker was preparing the first issue of the *Quarterly* (January–April 1913), he decided to publish only what he thought were the seminal papers. He felt it would be great publicity to have the most important papers by Indian members out in general circulation as soon as possible. Except for Gladden's opening address, only American Indian presentations were published. The Associate members made a number of presentations, but they were not reprinted in the first issue of the *Quarterly*. The full conference proceedings were published in the second issue.

After two years in existence and two conferences, what did the SAI accomplish? Despite major differences, the members had enough in common to build upon, such as ending dependency, settling the confusion over citizenship, struggling against poverty and reservation mismanagement, improving health care, expressing outrage over the injustices of the past, and attacking the use of alcohol. It was agreed that some of these issues could be resolved by reforming or abolishing the Indian Office, the reservation system, and the boarding schools. All agreed on one point: public sentiment needed to be awakened. In hindsight, it is difficult to pinpoint the specific accomplishments of the SAI. The Indian Office was not moving toward reform, the superintendents on the reservations were not being reined in, and there was little movement toward full citizenship or improving reservation life. The government was still taking reservation land or allowing it to be sold or leased to private interests. Parker visited President Taft and gave him the Executive Council's petition concerning the selection of a new commissioner of Indian affairs. He spent an hour and a half with the president discussing possible candidates.[49] Parker pondered some of these same questions in his introductory editorial in the *Quarterly*. He concluded that the first two years were mostly spent building a membership base, slowly but solidly, by getting out the word and creating positive publicity. Parker believed that SAI's most important accomplishment to this point was to awaken the public to the "Indian problem." He also made it clear that the purpose of the SAI was for "the uplift and adjustment of the Indian race." He added, "No, we are not a 'vanishing people' because we have sought adjustment to the environment." The agenda was to create "race leaders" who could inspire and give hope, convincing American Indians that their individual actions would benefit all. Parker was seeking legitimacy for the Society, listing prominent members, and hoping to deflate concerns and negative publicity, all the while battling heavy odds in trying to move a federal government that was not about to be moved.[50]

The published *Proceedings* of the second conference did not include much negative commentary from the floor. There was negative commentary, but Parker chose not to include it. The first conference had received considerable negative coverage from the local press for the squabbles and disagreements among the delegates. This was not the case in the second conference. Parker released a statement to the press, citing the need for positive publicity:

> We have seized the attention not only of Indian sympathizers, but of educators and legislators. . . . It has long been recognized that the Indian race is a downtrodden and exploited one. It is in the power of the Indian agents to absolutely ruin the Indian on the reservation, and heretofore he has had

> no redress whatsoever. He has been held in continual fear of the agent and has not dared to air his grievances. These evil practices may well flourish in the dark, but when subjected to publicity can never stand. It is the purpose of our organization to furnish this necessary publicity. We believe that the Indian is the intellectual equal of the white. All that he needs is the opportunity and this opportunity can only come through publicity.[51]

By the end of 1912, the SAI boasted 220 Active members and 401 Associates. However, this increase in membership did not help finances. The Columbus Hospitality Association paid $997 in expenses and donated an additional $469. Dues and other donations totaled $1,028, and after expenditures, there was a small deficit of $54.[52] As the third conference approached, finances and memberships became a top priority. Parker realized that a smooth-functioning, well-financed organization was essential to success; however, so far, success was limited. The question remained: Had the Society laid a firm foundation for the future?

# CHAPTER 3

# We Are "The Indians of Today"

*Mid-Years, 1913–1914*

As the Society of American Indians entered its third year, there were still concerns about what actually could be accomplished in terms of Indian policy reform. The SAI office in Washington was still maintained with Alice H. Denomie (Ojibwe) as a full-time assistant secretary. The same issues remained: harmony among the members, financial stability, the recruitment of new members, influencing public opinion, Congress, and the Office of Indian Affairs. Parker believed the second conference was a success, and now with "renewed strength," he planned a major membership drive. He mailed two letters and Society literature to the members, asking each to recruit twenty individuals. He also asked for donations, subscriptions to the new journal, and support for his effort to create a national American Indian holiday. Dagenett, the vice president for membership, sent out a recruitment letter.[1] Attendance at the conferences was a concern. Some members who disagreed with certain policies responded by not attending. Eastman, for example, believed the SAI was not truly a representative body and backed away from participation. He felt there was too much emphasis on governmental issues and not enough emphasis on meeting the needs of those living on reservations. Aside from personality clashes, there were policy issues. President Sherman Coolidge tried to mediate but with little success. The debate on abolishing the Indian Office and the reservation system became more intense. Almost all agreed that the reservations were the root cause of most problems, as they fostered dependency and stifled initiative, but ideas on what to do about it ranged from immediate abolition, to gradual transformation leading to closure, to maintaining the present land base without federal oversight. There was no simple answer about what to do about the impoverished individuals living on the reservations. The controversy over peyote would soon create a serious strain among the members. There was also continuing debate on what type of schools and what type of curriculum was best for young people. Some advocated including American Indian subject matter, such as John Hewitt, who advocated teaching American Indian ethnology; some opposed any such teaching, such as Chauncey Yellow Robe (Lakota), who said, "The idea of teaching Indian music in the Indian schools is unprogressive—un-American."[2]

After the second conference, planning began for the third. A decision was not made immediately, but Parker considered traveling out west to encourage more Indians to attend the conferences and join the Society. The city of Columbus invited the SAI back, but a major flood in March 1913 made that impossible, with parts of the downtown area severely damaged. The

**Figure 8** Reverend Sherman E. Coolidge, SAI president, 1911–13, 1916. Advisory Board, 1913–21. Courtesy of the National Anthropological Archives at the Smithsonian Institution.

Colorado Publicity League and the Denver Convention Association had been trying to lure the SAI to Denver, offering the Society $2,000 for hotels and other expenses. But there was another reason why Denver wanted the SAI. The city was planning a huge world's fair–type pageant for 1915 and wanted the support and participation of the SAI. They dubbed it the Grand Council of North American Indians and planned to have Buffalo Bill's Wild West show as their centerpiece, with some of their ideas based on Dixon's book *The Vanishing Race* as the theme. They billed it as "The Last Farewell Meeting of the Only Real, True American—The North American Indian," a theme that focused on the vanishing narrative. By having the SAI in Denver in 1913, they hoped to gain their support and return in 1915 for the pageant. The Convention Association sent a formal invitation to the 1915 event, renamed "The Last Grand Council of Red Men." The invitation included a poem, "Ye Nations. Come! Behold It!" with the following excerpt:

> Soon the Whole Wide World Will Tell
> Of The White Man's Western Triumph,
> And The Red Man's Grand Farewell. . . .
> Come, Ye Nations, To The Red Rocks!
> To The Playground of the Sky!
> Come! Come Up, To Colorado!
> Here [*sic*] The Red Man—Say—GOOD BYE.

This self-righteous, arrogant poem, an ode to manifest destiny, was followed by a formal invitation to the SAI from the governor of Colorado and a defense of the pageant by J. R. Maling, an official of the Colorado Publicity League. Maling claimed that the purpose of the event was to honor American Indians. He said it was the grand farewell to all that "hampered and held him back." He also suggested something spectacular: a reenactment of the Battle of Little Big Horn. Parker politely answered the governor. He congratulated him for referring to it as a pageant, rather than the last grand council. Parker added, "[We are] *the coming race,* not the vanishing one, we however feel that our men and women . . . are Indians still, in blood, in loyalty" (italics in the original). He listed all the prominent professions of American Indians, from politicians, doctors, lawyers, journalists, government employees, judges, teachers, to clergy. He added, "[We are] red men still, even though we have plucked the feathers from our war bonnets and are using them for pens." Parker did not give a direct answer at this point. He said that the SAI needed to get together for some serious consideration.[3]

This situation became complicated, as many SAI members wanted nothing to do with the pageant. It became more problematic when Charles Dagenett, an SAI vice president, was in Denver to plan the 1913 conference. He met with Denver officials and seemed to approve of the 1915 pageant. He was quoted as saying, "The pageant would be a great thing." When General Pratt received clippings from a Denver newspaper, he became furious and fired off angry letters to Parker, Montezuma, and Franklin K. Lane, the secretary of the interior, criticizing the pageant and Dagenett. He said he would resign if the SAI was involved and threatened to write 1,800 letters to his former Carlisle students, telling them to have nothing to do with the Society. He added that he would also withdraw all the positive things he said about the Society. He wrote to Dagenett, telling him that support for the pageant would be disastrous for the SAI. He said he had fought Wild West shows all the years he was at Carlisle, since they reinforced stereotypes and showed Indians in a poor light, stressing to Dagenett, "You are the only man who can rise to the emergency and contradict it properly."[4] To the SAI leadership, these were not idle threats. They feared that Pratt could hurt them. Parker shared these concerns with McKenzie. "I understand from persons who know General Pratt intimately that he has become extremely sensitive and inclined to sudden fits of unaccountable anger. . . . I shall do all I can however to conciliate him and bring him again into sympathy with our work."[5]

Parker, Coolidge, and Montezuma all agreed with Pratt that the Society should not support such an event. Parker sent letters to the governor of Colorado, the mayor of Denver, and the president of the Chamber of Commerce, telling them that the dignity of the American Indian must be upheld and "not be forced to become a cigar store sign to attract customers." Coolidge, who was a member of the Colorado Publicity League, resigned. The SAI went ahead and met in Denver in 1913, but would not participate in the 1915 pageant. Pratt resigned over the issue, but Parker invited him to the conference anyway. He did not attend.[6] While Parker and the SAI were protesting Denver's proposed pageant, Joseph Dixon was undertaking his third western expedition. He planned to visit many Indian reservations on what he called the "Expedition for Citizenship." The plan was to present each reservation with an American flag and have residents recite an oath of allegiance to the United States, meanwhile taking photographs of people in "traditional garb" and settings.[7]

The SAI saw Dixon as an enemy. Parker was furious. He sent a scathing five-page letter to Secretary Lane, protesting government involvement, wondering why the U.S. president, the secretary of the interior, and the commissioner of Indian affairs supported Dixon's expedition. Parker challenged the expedition, questioning its value. He regarded the photographs as ethnographically and historically useless, posed and retouched in the "white man's ideas." He considered the expedition to be nothing more than theatrical sensationalism and fakery. He also took the opportunity to criticize the planned monument in New York City harbor and Dixon's ideas for a "Last Grand Indian Council."[8]

As if this situation was not taxing enough, Parker had to deal with personality clashes and accusations among SAI members in the weeks before the Denver conference. John Hewitt sent Parker a long letter complaining about the general activities of the Society and attacking most members of the Executive Council. Hewitt, born on the Tuscarora Reservation, was employed by the Bureau of American Ethnology for most of his adult life. He was a respected anthropologist specializing in linguists and Iroquois society and culture. He had authored seventy-five articles for the *Handbook of American Indians North of Mexico*, including most of the articles on the Iroquois.[9] At the 1912 conference, Hewitt argued that Indian schools should teach American Indian culture and advocated the publication of a school text on American Indian ethnology. He believed knowledge of the past was essential to growth in the future and that the American Indian should not be ashamed about anything in the past.[10] He also criticized the Society's decision to hold its conferences on university campuses. He believed they should be held on reservations in order to engage the local population. Hewitt was a sometime friend of Parker, a sometime critic of Parker's writings on the Iroquois, and a sometime competitor in Iroquois studies. He wrote very frank letters to Parker, highly critical of many things, but also complimentary to Parker for his work in the Society. His criticisms of SAI policies were sincere and reasoned, but his criticisms of the Executive Council were severe and accusatory. His targets were Wheelock, Kellogg, Dagenett, and Sloan. He asked if they could possibly be "more inharmonious, more inimical, and more invidiously antagonistic and repellant one to another." He wanted the Advisory Board to know that the "discord, disunion, deceit and envy" was paralyzing the Executive Committee. He believed this was why the energy of the SAI was dormant and stagnant, accomplishing very little. He referred to President Coolidge as a "microbe of inertia" and blamed him for the situation and what he considered to be a lack of accomplishments. He followed with a recitation of rumors about various individuals, much of it of a personal nature, commenting on Laura Kellogg's alleged financial improprieties and Thomas Sloan's misuse of his position as an attorney. Hewitt also claimed that an SAI vice president who was trying to oust Kellogg was guilty of violating the Mann White Slave Act by "debauching" Indian girls and supplying them with liquor. He added that the Society needed to get rid of those subject to such accusations. In terms of criticisms of the Society, he claimed the inaction was the result of the disharmony and disinterestedness of the Executive Council and the Advisory Board, as the latter was not doing its job as the oversight committee. He also said the *Quarterly* was excellent, but he complained that it was of little value to the "unlettered Indian." He thought that what they needed was a functioning and effective legal aid department.[11]

Parker responded somewhat defensively but acknowledged the accusations. He admitted that he was depressed at times about the state of affairs. He supported the accusations about Coolidge lacking initiative and affirmed that Sloan had charges filed against him. The same was true for the charges against Kellogg for misappropriating funds, to which he responded, "From Boston to Los Angeles she is known for swindling business men out of funds." Parker and Kellogg had been close friends as founders of the SAI. In their early letters, they addressed each other as "Dear Princess," "Dear Seneca," "My Dear Oneida." By the end of 1912, they addressed each other very formally. Parker also told Hewitt that there were also charges of immoral behavior against two Executive Councilmen, but he believed many of the rumors were only gossip since they were unsubstantiated and may have been initiated by enemies. No one was ever found guilty of these accusations, but they made working together very difficult, if not impossible. Parker also explained to Hewitt that on the question of legal aid, hundreds of complaints against Indian Office superintendents and agents arrived in his office from reservations and that many dealings with wills, allotments, patents in fee, and withholding of funds were settled.[12] Parker's letters have an air of pessimism and a sense of him carrying too much of the burden of the Society; however, in his public statements, he was the voice of optimism about the future of the Society.

With the conference a month away, Parker sent out another invitation to the membership, pleading for attendance and attempting to squelch two rumors: that the government controlled the SAI and that a contract had been signed with the city of Denver to participate in the 1915 pageant. Parker was direct and firm: both rumors were false. In a letter to Montezuma, he assessed the Society's finances and membership. Clearly, finances were a problem, with a $600 deficit predicted for the year. The major expense incurred was printing, especially the new journal, and mailing costs. Membership had increased: 357 Active members and 414 Associate members, but he pointed out that the larger problem was a lack of cooperation, as "our work is largely paralyzed by a mutual distrust of each others [*sic*] motives, and by a spirit created by widely circulated rumors."[13] On the eve of the Denver conference, Parker's editorial in the *Quarterly* was an optimistic, self-help, "racial uplift" message, reflecting the theme of the conference: "What the Indian can do for himself, for his race and for his country, the United States of America." Parker outlined the SAI's goals: new laws, better living conditions, raising public awareness, and a clearly defined citizenship status. To achieve the latter, he proposed that a "definite series of grades should be established by which the Indian could progressively step upward into complete citizenship." This gradualist approach was contrary to birthright citizenship and was opposed by Montezuma. Parker also hoped the conference would help diminish the "vanishing" imagery, especially the "grotesquely carved" cigar-store Indian advertising the "nicotine-bearing weeds." On policy issues, Parker recommended paid officers, lobbing for better legislation, and providing a strong legal aid service. He engaged in extensive lobbying, writing letters to Cato Sells, commissioner of Indian affairs, calling his attention to particular legislation, providing supportive arguments, sending relevant literature, and asking for his support. In early 1914, he asked the commissioner to support legislation opening the U.S. Court of Claims to Indian claimants. As part of his advice to members, he warned them not to become partisan in party politics, as it would alienate others. As a solution to the financial problems of the Society, he called for 100 individuals to donate $100 and 100 individuals to donate $5–$50; he also wanted 1,000 new members and 1,000 new subscribers to the *Quarterly*.[14]

The conference proceeded as the first two, with a strong lineup of well-known, high-energy speakers, including Montezuma, Coolidge, Parker, Oskison, and Associate members McKenzie and Matthew K. Sniffen, secretary of the Indian Rights Association (IRA), one of the most active "friends of the Indian" groups. Founded in 1882 by Herbert Welsh, the IRA's mission was to "civilize" Indians, leading to citizenship and full assimilation. They hoped to accomplish this by supporting the assimilationist policies of the federal government, such as the Dawes Act. The IRA later played an important role in the peyote controversy. Sniffen, who had just returned from a tour of the Southwest, echoed a large majority of Associate members in his support of the social Darwinist or social evolutionary theory of stages that posited a development from savagery to barbarism to civilization (a theory now under assault by anthropologist Franz Boas). Sniffen and other Associates believed the theory was an essential historical truth. He said, "We cannot expect the Indian to take a step in a generation or two that has required centuries for the Anglo-Saxon."[15] Even with all the high-powered speakers at the third SAI conference, it was Chauncey Yellow Robe (Lakota) who received most of the attention from the audience and the press. His presentation, "The Indian and the Wild West Show," received considerable notoriety because of the controversy over the city of Denver's plan to spend several million dollars on the proposed pageant.

Yellow Robe grew up near Rapid City, South Dakota. At age fifteen, he was sent east to the Carlisle Indian School. He did not speak a word of English but became a prize pupil of General Pratt. He graduated in 1895 and returned to Rapid City to teach in a federal Indian school. His talk was blistering. He began with a question: "Is there anyone here that will tell me that the Wild West Show is a good thing for the Indian?" He went on to answer his own question, calling the shows terrible, degrading, demoralizing, and degenerating. He added that "tribal habits and customs are liable to be degraded for show purposes," asserting that "[American Indians are] exhibited as savage[s]" in the Wild West shows and similar movies and forms of entertainment. His paper, as published in the *Quarterly*, mostly includes his remarks on the Wild West shows, in addition to his criticism of the Buffalo Bill film *The Indian Wars*. The film, produced by Cody Historical Picture Company, was intended as a documentary, featuring General Miles and the Twelfth Cavalry reenacting the massacre at Wounded Knee (1890) as well as other so-called battles. The film portrayed Wounded Knee as a battle and the cavalrymen as heroes, concluding that it was justifiable. The federal government's support for the film added to the controversy. Franklin Lane, secretary of the interior, and Commissioner Sells approved the production and requested the War Department to supply troops and equipment. The War Department agreed, sending a thousand troops from the Twelfth Cavalry. The film was shot in 1913 and released in 1914. As the movie was filmed on the Pine Ridge Reservation, Yellow Robe was made aware of its content. He asserted that, in reality, Wounded Knee was a massacre. He also pointed out that Buffalo Bill and Miles were not there; they produced the film "for their own profit and cheap glory." He called it a "cowardly and criminal act." Historian Jacqueline Kilpatrick bluntly points out that *The Indian Wars* was a propaganda film meant to make the military action seem justifiable. McNenly describes its purpose as an illustration of progress as in "winning the West." It ends with a government message portraying Indian youth at work and in school, learning the white man's ways. The film was shown to President Wilson's cabinet and many congressmen as "official" history. Not all of Yellow Robe's remarks were published in the *Quarterly*, but they were reported in Denver newspapers. While referring to him as the "Redskin at Indian Convention," the *Denver Republican* described his remarks as "terse and cutting" and as "flaying Cody and Miles." He was quoted as saying: "Women and children and old men, my relatives, were massacred with machine guns by soldiers in a Christian nation." His talk in Denver was reported in the *New York Times*. They said it was "one of the few protests yet uttered against depicting scenes of vanishing wild Indian life in Wild West shows." They also quoted his comment about the portrayal of the Indian as a savage in every theater. Additional support for Yellow Robe's attack came from Alanson Skinner, an assistant curator in the Department of Anthropology at the American Museum of Natural History and an SAI Associate member. In a letter to the *New York Times*, he attacked the on-screen portrayals of Indians. He said they were ridiculous, with Delawares dressed as Sioux and Manhattan Island Indians living in tipis. The sad part, he wrote, was that the films served to produce prejudice in the popular mind. Yellow Robe went on to attack the proposed Wanamaker memorial in New York City: "The Indian wants no such memorial monument, for he is not dead. . . . We have not vanished." Yellow Robe gave a powerful and insightful critique, challenging the representation of American Indians and initiating a century of similar critiques by Native activists and intellectuals.[16]

The conference continued with presentations on education, law, and legislative proposals; however, one common criticism of the SAI was its failure to provide significant help for those individuals or tribes with claims against the government. The Legal Aid Committee produced a pamphlet, "Appeal to the Nation," that was introduced at the conference, published in the *Quarterly Journal*, and distributed free of charge. It was directed at Congress and

CHAUNCEY YELLOW ROBE
(Sioux)
Mr. Robe made a stirring address at the Denver Conference, scoring wild west shows and moving picture reproductions of soldiers massacring Indians. Mr. Robe is a clean-cut gentleman of high ideals.

**Figure 9** Chauncey Yellow Robe, outspoken critic of Buffalo Bill's "Wild West" shows and stereotyping of American Indians. Photo from the *Quarterly Journal of the Society of American Indians* 1, no. 4 (1913).

the public, seeking support for two pieces of legislation, known as the Carter Code and Stephens bills. The Carter Code bill proposed the codification of Indian laws and regulations. The problem, as stated in the pamphlet, was that Indians had no legal recourse to settle claims against the government in the Court of Claims, without special congressional legislation. The Stephens bill, introduced into the House of Representatives in 1912, was the remedy. It would authorize American Indians to submit claims to an Indian Court of Claims and to be able to appeal to the Supreme Court. The bill was reprinted and distributed to all interested parties. This was a major lobbying effort, but to no avail, as an Indian Court of Claims and an Indian Claims Commission was not established until 1946.[17]

According to Parker, the Denver conference went smoothly, probably because Montezuma was not there, nor was the usually bombastic General Pratt. Montezuma was protesting the possibility that the SAI would sponsor the 1915 Denver pageant. Nevertheless, Montezuma's quest to abolish the Indian Office and the reservation system was still an underlying issue. However, seeing the future from a different perspective was Oliver Lamere (Winnebago/Nebraska), who foresaw Indian cultures surviving in the long run. Lamere was a former Carlisle student and a member of SAI's Advisory Board. He served as an interpreter and informant to anthropologist Paul Radin, author of a history of the Winnebagoes. Lamere was a Peyotist and a well-known proselytizer. He did not mention the Peyote faith in his talk, but he outlined a plan for the future based on pluralism.[18] This implied room for his faith, as the government, many sectarian organizations, and almost all the Associate members, were campaigning to criminalize the use and possession of peyote. Chief Henry Roman Nose (Southern Cheyenne), a well-traveled Peyotist from the Cheyenne-Arapaho Agency, was also on the agenda. He had been a prisoner of war in Fort Marion in St. Augustine, Florida, attending Hampton Institute and Carlisle before returning home. In addition to being an adherent of the Peyote faith, he considered himself a Christian, a follower of the Ghost Dance movement, and a sun dancer. He was also a successful businessman. He gave a brief talk on how to solve problems. His answer—follow the teachings of the "Sermon on the Mount" and all will be settled. One can assume that he meant to convey a message of respecting other religions as you would expect others to respect yours. Several years later, Parker unsuccessfully tried to convince Roman Nose to give up the Peyote faith.[19] The SAI had not yet taken a position on peyote, but Parker knew it could become a serious problem, as there were Peyotists among the SAI members (five attended the Denver conference) and the new faith was spreading rapidly throughout the Plains states. In 1914, the SAI began publicizing attacks on the supposed dangers of the use of peyote in the *Quarterly*; however, they did not take an official position on peyote until 1916.

For the most part, the conference proceeded with a minimum of dissent. In his post-conference comments prepared for the press, Parker said it was a distinct success with "remarkable unanimity." He spoke more forcefully on reservations. They must go, he said, but only after all claims have been paid, the legal status is fixed, and tribal funds are broken up and distributed. In order for all this to be accomplished, Congress had to pass the Carter Code bill and the Stephens bill, as called for in the 1913 platform. He also claimed that the SAI helped settle "thousands of dollars of claims for Indians." He reported that there were a thousand members, with eighty-five attending the Denver conference—sixty-nine Active and sixteen Associates, including about 25 percent women. The platform was not significantly different from the 1912 platform, except that it had a stronger statement on education. Previous platforms called for improvements and expansion to underserved areas, but the new platform called for a complete reorganization of the federal Indian school system. This upset some of the Associate members who worked at the schools. Also, in keeping with the theme of the conference, the last item in the platform focused on rights with responsibilities and called for hard work, service to the race, and service to all mankind.[20]

The election of officers did not have the drama of previous elections. Several changes were expected, as Kellogg and Sloan were replaced (they were not in attendance). Reverend Coolidge was reelected president, and Parker remained secretary-treasurer. Sloan and Kellogg had opposition as a result of reports of their questionable behavior. Even before Kellogg went on trial (she and her husband were indicted by a federal grand jury), everyone on the Executive Council wanted her removed from office and expelled from the Society. Emma D. Goulette was elected to replace her as vice president for education. Goulette was not in Denver, as she had just given birth to a boy, who she proudly announced would be given an "Indian name." In a letter to Parker, she said that she had always been opposed to Kellogg's role in the Society and that her indictment was a "Godsend" that would save the SAI from negative publicity. Kellogg, given her strong personality, had aggravated almost everyone at one time or another. It was a foregone conclusion that she would not remain an officer, even though she had been one of the founders. Sloan was replaced by William J. Kershaw (Menominee), a prominent attorney from Milwaukee, who served as first vice president, vice president on legislation, chair of the Finance Committee, and chair of the Advisory Board. He attended Catholic school, but ran away and worked as a cowboy and lumberjack, eventually studying law and passing the Wisconsin bar at age twenty-one. He was a well-known speaker who expressed the theme of looking to the future while not forgetting the past. He later became the assistant attorney general of Wisconsin. He was a very important member of the SAI, as he added a degree of stability to the leadership amid swirling tensions. Sloan had supporters, but he also had enemies, especially among the Associate members. The opposition to him was mostly because of his support for the Peyote faith and the fear that his questionable reputation would harm the Society. The remainder of the offices were filled by Congressman Carter, vice president for legislation, and Rosa La Flesche, as assistant secretary, to run the Society's Washington office. Henry Roe Cloud remained chair of the Advisory Board, and McKenzie remained chair of the Associate members.[21]

Following the conference, Parker sent a letter and a copy of the new platform to members and friends. He said the conference was a crucial test, which "we survived," thus making the Society stronger. He encouraged all to write their congressmen and encouraged them to support the legislation described in the platform. This began a year-long campaign to lobby Congress and the executive branch for the Society's agenda. Parker also had help from William "Pussyfoot" Johnson, an Associate member and the editor of a popular prohibitionist publication, the *New Republic.* He wrote editorials in support of the Carter and Stephens bills. To follow up this initiative, the Executive Council, which held its mid-winter meeting in Washington, drew up a "memorial" or letter to President Wilson, seeking his support for the pending legislation. Parker, along with General Pratt, visited congressmen and attended sessions of the U.S. Senate.[22]

In February 1914, the Executive Council scheduled another midwinter meeting in Philadelphia. It was not just an Executive Council meeting, but a gathering that included Associate members and friends who could not travel to Denver. Despite a blizzard blanketing the city, the event went over well, with more than one hundred attendees. It was hosted by the Philadelphia Academy of Science and featured a morning business meeting and an afternoon of academic-type presentations, followed by a banquet at the Hotel Walton. The Executive Council established two new subcommittees to focus on finances and membership. Henry Roe Cloud chaired the Finance Committee. The plan was to appeal to a group of American Indians who were able to donate $10–$100 or more. The other was a committee of Indian school graduates seeking SAI membership applications from other graduates. They were supplied with of list with 2,500 names and addresses.[23] The afternoon presentations were divided between Active and Associate members. Commissioner Sells of the Indian Office was invited as an honored guest, as were representatives from various organizations such as the Indian Rights Association, the YWCA, and the YMCA. The papers focused on the relationship between education and citizenship. Before the Philadelphia meeting, Parker had a difficult situation with Father William H. Ketchum of the Bureau of Catholic Indian Missions, who was also a member of the Board of Indian Commissioners. Parker had made it known that he was not happy with how the Board was constituted. Ketchum, an Associate member, took offense and refused to attend the SAI gatherings. Parker said he had nothing against any individual member, but the Board was not constituted for the greater good of the American Indian. This incident helps explain why Parker took extra care not to alienate the Associate members, as he believed they were essential to the success of the Society.[24]

The banquet was an exquisite event. The banquet hall was carefully decorated, the women wore evening gowns, and the men wore tuxedos. Parker said he wanted it to be "equal to any in polite society." There was a long head table that included Commissioner Sells, General Pratt, and most of the Executive Council. Those seated at the table made remarks, but "the address of the evening," as Parker billed it, was Carlos Montezuma. In his usual dynamic style, he compared American Indians to immigrants. He argued Indians did not need special schools or special teachers. Like immigrants, they must enter public schools and universities, as Indian schools are weak and inefficient. He added that "we compelled the Negro, invited Huns and Italians and Irish and everyone else to come and live with us. Why not invite the Indians and give them the same chance," since the only way to learn English was to be dispersed among all Americans? He described teaching Indian art, Indian pottery, Indian basketry, and Indian music as foolish. "Where does this help the Indian children into the ways of civilization?" he added. Frank Speck, an anthropologist from the University of Pennsylvania, prepared a paper for the banquet as a rebuttal to Montezuma. When he was called to read his paper, he did not come forth to read it. He told Parker that he was greatly disappointed in the event. He said he came to hear from Indians but instead heard from "white politicians in a vein of narrow professional or religious enthusiasm." Speck's concerns were voiced by others. He apologized to Parker for not responding when called. Parker said he was sorry he did not read his paper, since it contained much that the audience should have heard. Parker asked him for a copy and went ahead and published it in the *Quarterly* right next to Montezuma's paper. Speck argued that Native cultures should not be obliterated as Montezuma seemed to suggest, but instead languages, traditions, and customs should be preserved. He wanted to know by what authority "we [are] called upon to deculturate them, to transform them completely to the likeness of ourselves." He concluded that trying to eliminate "tribes" is tantamount to "race murder."[25]

After Philadelphia, planning was underway for the fourth conference at the University of Wisconsin. A major concern for Parker and the Executive Council was the tremendous workload and the minimal resources available. Parker received hundreds of letters asking for help; voicing complaints; and requesting rulings, information, and laws. He said the Society was "in deep financial water." Parker told Kershaw and Montezuma that he had never been paid his $2,000 stipend and was rarely reimbursed for out-of-pocket expenses. The *Quarterly* had only 300 subscribers, and he was not sure if he could continue to publish it. It cost more than double to publish than receipts it brought in. The September 30 treasurer's report recorded a $1,200 deficit. Parker estimated he needed $5,000 for 1915 but was unsure how he could raise such funds.[26]

During the summer of 1914, personality issues emerged again. Henry Roe Cloud was distrustful of Dagenett. He wrote to his wife that Dagenett was trying to take control of the Society and that everything has become political with self-interest the driving force. He claimed it would be better to not attend the conference "than haggling over matters with the ungodly and unchristian set." These types of accusations against Dagenett, one of the original founders, were not new—plus his employment at the Indian Office never sat well with some members. In September, Roe Cloud resigned as vice president for membership and refused to attend the upcoming conference but retained his membership.[27] The situation was more difficult with Laura Kellogg. She was furious—in fact, seething. She had been acquitted in federal court of all charges and turned her anger against the SAI. She wondered why all the accusations and innuendoes arose even before she went to trial. She lost all faith in the Society, going so far as to initiate plans for a new competing but short-lived organization called the Grand Council of American Indians. She sent two long hastily written letters (partially illegible) to Montezuma. She described the details of her acquittal and blamed Dagenett, as a federal employee, for her arrest in Oklahoma. She was also angry at Montezuma. He had written her and asked her to come to the conference in

Madison anyway, suggesting that she should not hold on to "petty things." She blasted him and said, "To insinuate that I am quarrelling on petty things is nothing short of gross insolence." She added, "I am going to quarrel until hell freezes. . . . You are such a gullible lot of fools." In her next letter, she encouraged Montezuma not to have anything to do with the SAI and that he should join her new organization: "I say again as I said before the Society's length of life is not long—you are pouring your energy and money into a leaking bucket." She also took the opportunity to attack Reverend Coolidge: "Believe me," she wrote, "nothing is so deadly to independence of thought as a clerical collar."[28] This was not promising for the SAI's future.

Meanwhile, as part of his outreach efforts, as well as to keep in touch with his relatives, Montezuma traveled to Arizona as an SAI representative to assess the conditions among the Pima and Maricopa at Camp McDowell on the Salt River Reservation. The reservation wanted to celebrate Montezuma's visit with a dance, but in an exchange with the Indian Office, Commissioner Sells told Montezuma that he heard they were "planning to hold some old-time dances in your honor," adding, "they are not allowed to dance." He requested that Montezuma use his influence to stop them. One can understand Montezuma's insistence that the Indian Office be abolished.[29]

As the Madison conference approached, Parker was quite concerned, if not panicking, about the attendance. Only nine individuals (six Active members, Henry Roe Cloud, Sherman Coolidge, Charles Dagenett, Oliver Lamere, John Oskison, and Arthur Parker, and three Associates) attended all three previous conferences. He rushed a letter "To Every Member," telling them they had an immense responsibility, which if not fulfilled would lead to not only failure of the Society, but to the "failure of the proud blood you own." He told McKenzie that the Society was badly in debt, that Dagenett and Rosa La Flesche had resigned, and that he was worried that the upcoming conference "may degenerate into a purposeless program of merely talk." Parker did not plan to attend but urged McKenzie to attend to give the conference some stability. Parker said, "The Society looks to you as the Father." Despite private pessimism, Parker was optimistic in his public statements. Several months before the conference, Parker described the theme: "To the American Indian let there be given equal opportunities, equal responsibilities, equal equipment," especially "better education." He declared again that the root of the problem was the undefined legal status of the American Indian and that everyone must know how they can proceed from wardship to citizenship. Parker also took the opportunity to comment on the Carlisle School, which had been under investigation by Congress for lax academics, overemphasis on sports, abuse of students, and questions about the handling of athletic funds. Parker supported the investigation of Carlisle, particularly the emphasis on sports over academics. He asked why the coach should make double the salary of the school's superintendent. He also asked, "Why is walloping a pigskin more honorable and necessary than earning a worth-while sheepskin?" He supported the continuation of Carlisle, but with a renewed focus on academics. However, this was the beginning of the end for Carlisle. Their famous coach "Pop" Warner left for the University of Pittsburg. The sports program was never the same. In 1917, they played their last football game, losing to the University of Georgia, 98–0. The school closed the very next year.[30]

Despite Parker's concerns, the conference proceeded smoothly, with the usual presentations, debates, business meeting, and elections. Sixty-two people registered for the conference. On the other hand, some individuals who were lightning rods for controversy, such as Kellogg and Sloan, were not there. Also hanging over the SAI was the distant cloud of the Great War in Europe. What brought it closer to home was the concern expressed for the Canadian Indians, who had just deployed to Europe as part of the Canadian military. Aside from an addition to the platform and the elections, there were two noteworthy items: Chauncey Yellow Robe continued his assault on the Wild West shows, and Parker made the first published response to the growing Peyote faith, labeling it in an editorial as a "drug-induced religion" (as discussed in more detail later). As in Denver the previous year, Yellow Robe called the Wild West shows an evil and degrading influence. He attacked the Indian Office for supporting them and for granting special privileges, such as allowing the participation of reservation Indians and supporting the production of motion pictures. All these exhibitions and films, he argued, were "teaching young children that Indians are savages," depicting hatred and lawlessness. As the film *The Indian Wars* was just released, Yellow Robe attacked it again, explaining that Wounded Knee was a massacre, not a battle, adding that the film was a disgrace and an injustice, especially as the government had cooperated in the production of the film. He closed his talk referencing the theme of the conference: "equal opportunities, equal responsibilities, equal education."[31] Parker and other members of the SAI shared Yellow Robe's views. Parker continued the attack in an editorial describing the Wild West shows as fraudulent and deceiving the public as to the reality of the American Indian. He wrote, "The show Indian is not the real Indian any more than the circus white man is the real white man." Particularly galling was the poster advertising *The Indian Wars*, claiming it was historically correct and was approved by the U.S. government under the direction of the War Department.[32]

At the business meeting, the present leadership was reelected, indicating some stability, although the constitution had to be changed eliminating term limits so President Coolidge could be reelected. The Denver platform was reaffirmed with few changes. Two additional items were discussed: establishing local SAI centers on various reservations and submitting a petition or memorial to the president, Congress, and the commissioner of Indian affairs, to define the legal status of the American Indian and to settle Indian claims against the government. Both McKenzie and Parker declared the conference a success, especially since they raised $1,800 in cash and subscriptions. The platform did not call for the abolition of the reservation system, nor a demand for immediate birthright citizenship, as Montezuma proposed. Official SAI policy called for a path to citizenship, but it remained a vexing issue. When the conference ended, Marie Baldwin, Henry Roe Cloud, Charles Dagenett, and John Oskison, along with several of the Associate members, including McKenzie, left Madison for the long train trip to New York to attend the Lake Mohonk conference, where the issue of the Peyote faith was on the agenda. Parker did not attend the Madison conference. He wrote to Montezuma that in his absence the members could feel free to discuss his role as secretary-treasurer and assess the policies he had instituted. Parker was feeling stress from the criticism of the SAI and wanted to know what the members felt about his work. He was reelected.[33]

After the platform was approved, a committee was appointed to draft a petition to President Wilson. Dennison Wheelock was selected as chair, along with Roe Cloud, Chase, Kershaw, and McKenzie, with input from the Executive Council. They met in Washington at the office of Gabe E. Parker (Choctaw), an SAI member and the register for the U.S. Treasury. After several days of debating the contents of the petition, they decided on a moderate tone and to stress only two issues. The president agreed to meet with them. On December 10, a delegation of more than forty Active and Associate members went to the White House. It was a who's who of American Indian intellectuals, prominent missionary officials, two members of the Indian

Rights Association, and three representatives of the Indian Office, including Commissioner Sells. McKenzie and General Pratt also attended. Gabe Parker introduced the delegation to the president, who circled the room and shook hands with everyone. After a brief explanation, Dennison Wheelock proceeded to read the petition:

> *His Excellency, the President of the United States . . .*
>
> Congress has conferred special authority upon the President of the United States respecting the welfare of the Indians, regarded as wards of the Federal Government. We believe that this obligation lies close to your heart and we, therefore, feel free to suggest to you a few things which seem to us necessary to our welfare and progress . . .
>
> *Definition of Legal Status*: As a race, the Indian, under the jurisdiction of the United States, has no standing in court or nation. No man can tell what its status is, civic or legal. Confusion and chaos are the only words descriptive of the situation. This condition is a barrier to the progress of our people, who aspire to higher things and greater success. . . . *We request . . . this matter be placed in the hands of a commission of three men . . . and that they be authorized to study this question, and recommend to you and the Congress the passage of a code of Indian law. . . .*
>
> *Admission to the Court of Claims*: We plead, sir, that you give us the cheer of your word, that you consider our request and call upon Congress to grant the American Indians those fundamental rights and privileges, which are essential to release them from enforced wardship, dependence and consequent degeneracy; and that you advocate measures that will, according to the recognized principles of legal and economic development, speedily secure their admission to the field of even chance for individual efficiency and competency.
>
> For the weak and helpless, for the discouraged and hopeless of our race scattered over this broad land we make this plea and petition.[34]

Following the presentation, Wheelock handed the document to the president. Charles Kershaw read a second petition on behalf of the young men and women who were returning to their reservations after boarding school, only to find that they were under the arbitrary authority of superintendents.

They had little opportunity and no way of seeking redress for their concerns over land, leases, or inheritances. Kershaw concluded by reiterating the two points from the previous petition: the need for the Carter bill and the need to open the Court of Claims to American Indians. The president expressed his pleasure in receiving the delegation but admitted he "had not given special thought to the Indian." He promised to give the petitions his earnest consideration. They returned to the Hotel Powhatan for an informal meeting and to prepare for a large banquet that evening and two days of Executive Council deliberations. They voted to hold the next conference in Oklahoma City, but that was soon to change. They also voted to establish a Board of Trustees to oversee the Society's property. Parker was quite gratified and enthused. They had met President Wilson, presented petitions, and hoped this would lead to a positive outcome. Parker summed it up: "There were no blankets, no feathers, no relics of the past, for these men and women were the *Indians of today*" (italics in the original). Parker sent a letter and an SAI article on the legal battles of the American Indian to Indian Office officials and a number of U.S. senators, making a case for the recommendations in the two petitions to the president. Parker made it clear: "We hold it incontrovertible that our status in this nation should be defined by federal authority." Then, in an optimistic letter to the membership asking for more support, he implied that the SAI had the support of President Wilson, claiming that "the best forces for good are with us, from President Wilson down."[35] Parker was mistaken, Wilson had no intention of reforming federal Indian policies. Influencing federal policy at this point was fruitless, but there was still hope for public support. Within the next year, Parker's optimism would be dampened. He also had another concern to deal with: He had called the Peyote faith a "drug-induced religion." The peyote issue became a public debate within the SAI and a source of great dissension.

## The Origins of the Peyote Controversy

At the SAI's inaugural conference in Columbus, Ohio, the peyote issue was not mentioned, but there was concern about it. The controversy over peyote had become a national issue. For several years, the Office of Indian Affairs had been looking for ways to stop the expansion of the Peyote faith. Parker was aware early on that it was a potential problem. After the conference in 1911, Parker wrote to Dagenett, telling him that he had received two types of criticisms of the Society. One was the suspicion of government control; the other was concern about the Society being too "pagan" and sympathetic to the "mescal-peyote element." He explained that Sloan was feared by some, especially the missionaries, for his sympathy for the "mescal [peyote] eaters." Parker feared that this antagonism toward Sloan might have a negative effect on the SAI. One such letter came from Reverend Thomas C. Moffett, of the Board of Home Missions of the Presbyterian Church and an Associate member. Moffett expressed concern over Sloan and Chase and said that Reverend Alfred Riggs, a prominent Presbyterian missionary and editor of the *Word Carrier*, a missionary journal, felt the same way. They claimed that Sloan and Chase were not to be trusted and would have a harmful effect on the Society's reputation. Moffett included a quote from the *Word Carrier* criticizing Chase as a procurer of Indians for the Wild West shows and Sloan as a "lawyer who defends the mescal drunkards, and is promoting that vice." Parker wrote to Sherman Coolidge, the SAI president, pointing out that the Society was accused of harboring proponents of the "Mescal religion." A concern became a controversy.[36]

Peyote (*Lophophoro williamsii*), a small, pale blue-green cactus one to two inches in diameter, has been used as a religious sacrament for hundreds of years in pre-Columbian Mesoamerica. The name is from *peyotl*, a Nahuatl (Aztec) word. Its natural growth area is on both sides of the Rio Grande River in what is now northeast Mexico and south-central and southeast Texas. It is harvested by cutting off the top, which is sometimes referred to as a *peyote button*, and is dried in the sun. It may be chewed, made into a tea, or ground into a granular form, and with the addition of water, it is ingested during peyote services. Aided by the development of the railroad system, which facilitated the shipment of dried peyote, the use of peyote as a sacrament spread north into what is now Texas and Oklahoma, where it developed into a religious complex in the 1870s and 1880s on the Kiowa-Comanche Reservation in Oklahoma. As the Peyote faith expanded throughout the southern and northern Plains, partially through personal contacts and friendships formed by individuals attending government boarding schools, working in Wild West shows, and sharing the experience of the Ghost Dance movement, it came under assault by federal and state governments and by many nongovernmental organizations, as they believed it threatened assimilation, "civilizing," and Christianizing agendas. (The Spanish had also tried to eradicate peyote usage in Mexico.) As Peyotism emerged, it developed a moral and ethical system to guide its members along what was referred to as the "Peyote Road." This included a prohibition against alcohol, as it was believed that peyote was a gift from God that had the power to heal, especially to cure the disease of alcoholism. Peyote is commonly called "medicine," and in many Indigenous languages, the generic word for medicine is the same word for peyote. Peyote origin narratives and thousands of testimonials proclaim the power of peyote to heal both body and soul. These services were conducted by roadmen who would guide the participants along the Peyote Road. The roadmen were also proselytizers who traveled from reservation to reservation, teaching about peyote and how to run a peyote meeting. (The term "meeting" is often used to refer to the religious service.) Peyotism continued to spread throughout the early twentieth century, as it provided a degree of spiritual and cultural autonomy when political and economic autonomy was virtually impossible. It also developed variations in its dusk-to-dawn service, such as the Big Moon, Half-Moon, and Cross-Fire, the latter incorporating elements of Christianity. It was Albert Hensley, an Active member of the SAI and a well-known Peyotist, who primarily developed the Cross-Fire variation. Hensley traveled widely, extolling the virtues of the Peyote faith. As a defense against judicial and legislative assaults, Peyotists sought constitutional protection through the First Amendment. In 1918, Oklahoma Peyotists incorporated as the Native American Church, followed by similar incorporations throughout the western states. Today there are more than four hundred thousand members. Most belong to either the Native American Church of North America or the Azee' Bee Nahaghá of the Diné Nation (Peyote Ceremony of Diné Nation), which is the peyote community among the Diné (Navajo).[37]

At the second conference in Columbus, William "Pussyfoot" Johnson, an Associate member, a former employee of the Indian Office, and a virulent anti-peyote crusader, was in attendance. In his presentation, he only mentioned peyote once, but just his presence would have been very discomforting to Peyotists. President Roosevelt appointed him as a special officer in 1906 to enforce the 1897 Indian Prohibition Act, which banned the sale and use of intoxicants on reservations. In support of Johnson, Congress passed additional legislation authorizing the use of law enforcement officers to obtain evidence to prosecute offenders. However, Johnson expanded the interpretation of the law to include peyote as an intoxicant. He had spent several years in south Texas buying and destroying peyote under the guise that it was covered by the 1897 law banning "intoxicants." He was an anathema to all in the Peyote community, as his actions against peyote were widely known. In 1908, he reported that he has destroyed 174,400 peyote buttons. In 1911, he wrote, "We will be able to snuff out this peyote nuisance." This had to be upsetting to Oliver Lamere and Albert Hensley (Ho-Chunk, Wisconsin), both SAI members, especially since Johnson targeted the Ho-Chuck as the major proselytizers of the Peyote faith. Both men had been active in trying to convince the Indian Office that peyote was harmless and to leave their faith alone. In 1910, one of Johnson's agents arrested Lamere in Iowa and confiscated 2,000 peyote buttons. Johnson claimed that peyote was an intoxicant and, like alcohol, should be regulated. At the time, the possession of peyote was not illegal, but a campaign to make it so had begun. In 1911, Johnson resigned. He felt that the government was not giving him enough support for his campaign to eradicate peyote. The following year, he joined the Anti-Saloon League of America; moved to Westerville, Ohio, a hotbed of prohibitionist activity; and published the *New Republic*, a Prohibition newspaper. He continued his crusade against alcohol and peyote. His presence at conferences as an Associate member exacerbated internal tensions. Like other so-called reformers, he assumed alcohol and peyote were the same problem; however, others disagreed. In 1910, James Mooney, from the Smithsonian's Bureau of Ethnology, wrote an article on peyote for the *Handbook of North American Indians*, which indicated that peyote had medicinal value and was used in a ceremony of prayer and contemplation. The problem for the SAI leadership was that many SAI members, especially the Associate members such as "Pussyfoot" Johnson, and various secular and sectarian organizations supported the criminalization of the possession and use of peyote. The SAI needed their support to accomplish its goals—hence the dilemma and the controversy. Whatever position the SAI took on the peyote issue, it alienated one group or another.[38]

Peyotists were part of the SAI from the beginning. Thomas Sloan and Hiram Chase, both attorneys, made formal presentations at the first conference, and Hensley participated in debates from the floor. Sloan, who had been chair of the temporary Executive Council, was elected first vice president at the second convention but stepped down, partially as a result of rumors about questionable activities in his past and his defense of the Peyote faith. The Executive Council, however, appointed him as the SAI's first attorney, and he remained an important part of the SAI, even serving as the president. Chase did not play as big a role but had an excellent reputation as county judge in Thurston, Nebraska. What riled some members is that both men were witnesses or attorneys in court cases defending the Peyote faith. At the Denver conference, as mentioned previously, Oliver Lamere presented a paper on the "Indian Culture of the Future." He argued the American Indian "could union with the civic life of America." It is inevitable and we can learn much, he added, "but we should not lose the worthy features of our ancestors such as the love of and acquaintance with nature, and keeping what is good in Indian culture such as ethical and moral teachings that are as good as Christianity." He claimed that Indians should not teach this as borrowed Christianity but as "old Indian ideals." He also believed Indigenous arts should survive, such as decoration, sculpture, wood carving, and music. These are views that the Peyote community supported with its ethical system, unique music, and art forms that were becoming specialized genres of American Indian music and art. Although he did not say so, one can assume he meant a perpetual land base would be necessary to preserve "Indian ideals." His hope for the future paralleled that of his cousin Angel De Cora, who expressed similar views at the first conference in 1911.[39]

In hindsight, it seemed inevitable that this would become a divisive issue, especially as Parker was involved with various organizations that were part of the assault on Peyotism. For example, he corresponded with Samuel Brosius, attorney for the Indian Rights Association (IRA), who was lobbying Congress to criminalize the possession of peyote. They discussed strategies to persuade the government to list peyote as an intoxicant. Parker went out of his way to convince missionaries, such as Riggs and Moffett, that Christian concerns were part of the SAI conferences, pointing out the active participation of Christian members. Henry Roe Cloud also supported a similar strategy. He wanted the Indian Office to simply declare peyote as an intoxicant and hoped an objection would become a test case in court.[40] Parker's views are essential to understand the development of the controversy. As longtime secretary-treasurer and as editor of the SAI *Quarterly*, he was in contact with many people. His opinion was significant, as it affected the opinions of others. It seemed at first that he was concerned about the image of the SAI among Associate members and potential new members. He was aware of the view that peyote was a dangerous drug, but he was also aware that others saw it as beneficial. His longtime friend and SAI member Reverend Joseph K. Griffis (Osage), also known as Tahan, related his recent experiences on the Omaha Reservation, where he spoke with many people and attended a nightlong peyote service. He said that some of the worst men on the reservation have been changed for the better by "peyote worship." He added that the Christian ministers on the reservation have an extreme prejudice against "peyote people," but they could not explain the changed lives of the "pagans."[41]

Parker had cordial relations with SAI members who were Peyotists. He exchanged letters with Lamere and Hensley, never mentioning peyote but discussing ways they could work together to achieve SAI goals. Just before the Denver conference, Parker sent a letter to Lamere, addressing him as "My Dear Friend." He made several suggestions about his upcoming paper. This is significant, as it gives some insight into Parker's thinking on the future of the American Indian. Parker stressed the importance of the "old ways," especially the love of nature, reverence for God, kindness, and hospitality. He also mentioned the arts, particularly songs, stories, weaving, quillwork, and beadwork. He noted that these were good things to share with the nation. On the other hand, he stressed, in order to get along and compete with the "white man," the American Indian "must learn the same ways that the white man learns."[42]

Parker was well aware that various organizations, such as the Indian Rights Association, Board of Catholic Indian Missions, the YMCA, and the Lake Mohonk Conference on the Indian, supported the assault on peyote. The Board of Indian Commissioners condemned the use of peyote in 1912, as did the IRA two years later. Several SAI members, including Parker, belonged to these organizations, attended their conferences, and made several presentations to the Lake Mohonk group. In 1914, they officially called for federal legislation for the suppression of peyote, referring to it as the "peyote menace." They put pressure on Parker to support such legislation.[43] SAI members, such as Parker, Henry Roe Cloud, and John Oskison, regularly attended their conferences, listening to a steady diet of anti-peyote rhetoric. They heard talks such as "Liquor and Peyote: A Menace to the Indian" and heard a litany of "scientific evidence" on the harmful effect of peyote. SAI Associate members also belonged to these organizations. For example, Fayette McKenzie, General Pratt, and archeologist Warren K. Moorehead were members of the Lake Mohonk Conference. The strategy of these organizations was to have the federal government declare peyote an intoxicant. Parker encouraged Franklin Lane, secretary of the interior, to prohibit the interstate distribution of peyote. Secretary Lane convinced the postmaster general that peyote contained poison and should not be allowed to go through the U.S. Postal Service. Nevertheless, Parker admitted to George Masquequa, a friend, that he really did "not know anything about this peculiar habit of eating mescal [peyote] buttons and having visions." Parker also told Senator Harry Lane of Oregon that he believed alcohol was more damaging than peyote and pointed out that attorneys Sloan and Chase, SAI members, defended the sacramental use of peyote.[44]

The SAI had yet to take an official position on peyote, although Parker had earlier supported the Indian Appropriation Bill of 1913, which included funds for the suppression of both liquor and peyote. To the dismay of many, Congress deleted peyote from the final bill. The next year, the Indian Office campaigned to have peyote included in the 1914 Harrison Narcotic Act. Again, this effort failed, as Congress refused to add peyote to the list of illicit drugs. After the Madison Conference, Parker published his first editorial on peyote under the byline "Drug-Induced Religion." He explained how the "peyote religion has spread like wild fire" despite government and missionary efforts to stop it. He described Albert Hensley's role in its development and propagation, and that it was well organized into congregations and had missionaries. He denied the claim that peyote is a divine gift and cures alcoholism, calling it a narcotic that induced hallucinations. He did not use the harsh language of his later writings, nor did he call for its criminalization in this editorial.[45] Several clergy praised Parker for his stance, and the controversy continued to grow. The Indian Office and the "friends of the Indian" groups were determined to stifle Peyotism, as they believed it threatened assimilation policies and programs. SAI members such as Parker feared that the failure to condemn Peyotism would threaten non-Indian support for the SAI.

The mid-years of the SAI, even with the personality conflicts, slow increase in membership, and financial constraints, were fairly good years compared to future times of dissension and turmoil. In assessing the first four years, Parker pointed out that the Society had grown from a small uncertain beginning to a nationally known organization, publishing a respectable journal that gave public airing of American Indian issues. He added that the Society's journal presented the needs, aspirations, and achievements of the "race," encouraging young men and women.[46] In terms of public exposure, Parker was right. Members of Congress, the U.S. president, the Office of Indian Affairs, and segments of the media were aware of the SAI's existence and its agenda. Sectarian and secular organizations were also aware of the SAI, although this had a different twist. The SAI believed it needed these organizations and their members to help it achieve its goals; on the other hand, these organizations, especially church-related entities, wanted to use the SAI for their agendas of Christianizing and assimilating the American Indian. Turning this public exposure into concrete results was another story. Little progress was made on the SAI's legislative agenda concerning citizenship, the codification of Indian law, or access to the U.S. Court of Claims. For example, the Society had met with President Wilson, but nothing resulted from that meeting. There was no indication that the Indian Office would change any of its policies or that it was even listening to the Society's concerns, such as reforming Indian education or improving the daily lives of those living on reservations. Nevertheless, Parker maintained a public optimism that these goals could be achieved.

# CHAPTER 4

# "Let My People Go"

*1915–1916*

The mid-years were dramatic for the Society of Americans Indians, made more so by Carlos Montezuma's famous speech "Let My People Go." He called for the abolition of the Office of Indian Affairs and the reservation system, which were ongoing divisive topics. The same level of divisiveness was associated with the peyote controversy. In 1916, the Society formally endorsed the government's campaign to criminalize the use and possession of peyote. Also, in 1916, Montezuma initiated his own monthly magazine, *Wassaja: Freedom's Signal for the Indians*. He used the publication to attack the Indian Office and to rebuke several SAI policies. The Society faced additional lingering problems: insufficient membership, lack of financial resources, and intense debate on what direction the SAI should take on the citizenship issue. There were disagreements about how to support reservation communities, how to improve education, and what type of education was best for Indian students. Should the government work on improving the boarding schools or close them down and send the youth to public schools? They still had to deal with the perception, mostly on the reservations, that the Society was an arm of the Indian Office or at least influenced by it. Also, keeping the Associate members involved and supportive was a problem, as some from the missionary community were pressuring the Society to focus on "Christianizing" work. In short, this was a period of growing factionalism.

In prioritizing goals, Parker and the leadership decided the most pressing issue was clarifying the legal status of American Indians in conjunction with the demand for citizenship. It also was decided to include the *Quarterly Journal* with the membership fee, which remained at two dollars per annum, not as a separate subscription. This would save billing paperwork but also would keep the members current on Society activities. There were a number of members who did not subscribe to the *Quarterly*. Nonmembers could subscribe for $1.50. This required 1,500 copies to be printed each quarter. Parker outlined these priorities in numerous letters, editorials, and articles. He explained to the secretary of the interior the peculiar position of having an undefined standing and being the only group of people in the United States without a definite legal status. He recommended that Congress should appoint a commission to determine the status of Indian people and also codify existing law. He stressed the importance of establishing the status of American Indians as citizens, potential citizens, or under permanent guardianship.[1] Parker was blunt; he wrote to General Pratt that the Indian Office has "no conception of the fundamental needs of the race" and that the Indian Office had never asked Congress to define Indians' legal status. Parker listed several other issues he wanted the Indian Office to resolve: settle Indian claims against the government, distribute tribal funds on a per capita basis, and clarify land titles. Until this happened, the Indian Office would retain its grip on power.[2] In a powerful essay in the *Quarterly*, he wrote that both the government and the church perceived the needs of the Indian through their own lenses or eyes, based on their own standards, both expressing "the idea of the white man's burden." He described the Indian Office as a "vast bulky machine with many ill-fitting, or inferior parts, it grinds on, consuming huge sums of money for fuel and lubrication" that could be more profitably spent on Indian communities. He listed seven charges of robbery against the Indian Office:

1. Robbed a race of men—the American Indian—of their intellectual life.
2. Robbed the American Indian of his social life.
3. Robbed the American Indian of his native freedom.
4. Robbed the American Indian of his economic independence.
5. Robbed the American Indian of his moral standards and of his racial ideals.
6. Robbed the American Indian of his good name among the peoples of the earth.
7. Robbed the American Indian of a definite civic status.

In addition, Parker listed seven more denials of civic, economic, and self-determination rights. He added sarcastically that he would not mention "the awful wars against Indian women and children, the treacherous onslaughts on sleeping villages, the murder of the old and helpless, broken promises, the stolen lands, the robbed orphans and widows, done by men professing civilization and religion." These were very strong words, which were usually written in private correspondence but now expressed publicly.[3]

There was frustration within the Society. Some of the members were unclear about its policies and purposes. Parker complained to Sloan and Montezuma about his workload. He said there were not enough hours in the day for his full-time job with the state of New York, his family, the work of the Society, and his reoccurring health problems. He lamented the lack of an officer who could devote full-time hours to the Society. Many appeals for help came into the office, but there were no available attorneys, no funds to hire any, and a legal aid department that never functioned. All Parker could do was to send the appeals to the Indian Office or the Department of the Interior. Parker had secretarial help in the Washington office, but nevertheless, the workload was overwhelming—especially the correspondence. For example, the treasurer's January 1915 report listed "regular correspondence—559"; the December 1915 report listed "regular correspondence—441"; and then there was a massive effort to mail out the *Quarterly* and other publications, such as copies of the SAI Constitution and Bylaws (Parker ordered 200 pamphlets).[4]

Parker kept up a steady correspondence on legal status and citizenship. He constantly reminded the Indian Office to deal with these issues, but he knew that in order for real change to take place, it had to come from Congress. The Indian Office did not make policy, but they recommended and lobbied for policies and procedures that advanced their agendas and also administered federal Indian policies. Parker was concerned since Congress had not made it clear to American Indians what its ultimate intentions were. He asked Commissioner Sells: If not immediate citizenship, what is the legal status of American Indians? Parker encouraged the Indian Office to address these issues with Congress. Sells replied that he would take these issues into consideration. Parker invited Franklin Lane, secretary of the interior, to address the upcoming Lawrence conference on the suggested topic: "The Indian and the Plan of the Interior Department."[5] Lane did not accept the invitation, nor would any future secretary of the interior address an SAI conference, given the Society's growing hostility toward the Indian Office.

The SAI struggled with not only external forces, such as the Indian Office, but also continuing internal turmoil. Both McKenzie and John Hewitt expressed serious concern about the reputation of the Society as an arm of the Indian Office. Despite Parker's denial and no real evidence of Indian Office control, the perception persisted. McKenzie, for example, pointed out that the 1914 Philadelphia banquet gave the impression that Indian Office officials were the chief figures in the eyes of the Society. He added that the Society should make more of an effort to express its independence when "surrounded by a mass of federal employees, both Indian and white." This concern was heightened when federal officials were invited to make presentations at annual SAI conferences. In addition, many Indian Office employees were Associate members. Hewitt also made the same points, adding that to those on the reservations, the Society seemed like an adjunct to the Indian Office. With a broader analysis of the SAI, Hewitt was highly critical of the decision to hold the conferences on university campuses, far away from the reservation population. He believed this contributed to the perception problem. He felt that all conferences should be held on reservations to foster contact with the people who most needed the Society's help and who could personally identify with the SAI. Hewitt also pointed out what he thought was another failure of the Society: the inability to develop a functioning legal aid department. He added that the reservation Indians living on a restricted allotment, harassed by greed and graft, were the ones who most needed legal services. Hewitt was also critical of the Society's leadership. His choice for president was Thomas Sloan, who he believed had the intelligence and the drive to lead the SAI.[6]

While Parker was grappling with these difficult issues and planning for the conference, he was quite pleased when Yankton Sioux Gertrude Simmons Bonnin (Zitkala-Ša) and her husband Raymond, also a Yankton, became SAI members. Both were born and raised on the Yankton Sioux Reservation in South Dakota and were fluent in Dakota. Mrs. Bonnin became a very important addition to the Society, holding a number of leadership positions. She had a long career as an author, orator, musician, and activist. She was in demand as a public speaker, traveling widely and speaking to numerous groups, especially women's organizations. She held very strong opinions and sometimes clashed with other SAI members. At age eight, she was sent to White's Manual Institute, a Quaker school in Indiana, for three years; she returned back home from 1887 to 1891, then went back to White's Institute, and received her diploma in 1895. She spent the next three years at Earlham College, where she excelled in oratory. She taught music for two years (1897–99) at the Carlisle Indian School, then moved to Boston to attend the New England Conservatory of Music to study voice, violin, and piano. It was during this latter period that she combined her traditional Dakota upbringing and her negative boarding school experiences to begin her career as an author, publishing a number of short stories under the name Zitkala-Ša.

Her return home in the late 1880s seemed to stir her creative energies, as she felt she was between two worlds, belonging to neither. She wrote short stories and autobiographical essays, and assembled a collection of Sioux oral narratives, published as *Old Indian Legends,* with illustrations by Angel De Cora. Her essays and short stories were published in *Harper's Monthly Magazine* and the *Atlantic Monthly* at the turn of the century, and collected and published in 1921 as *American Indian Stories.* Her writing brought her notoriety as one of the first Native women in the publishing world. After a brief relationship with Carlos Montezuma, she married Raymond Bonnin, a federal employee, in 1902. The following year, they moved to the Uintah-Ouray Reservation in northern Utah. While her husband worked as a clerk for the Indian Office, she taught school for two years but spent most of her time doing community service work among the Northern Utes. The couple remained in Utah until 1916, then moved to Washington, D.C. Once joining the Society, Zitkala-Ša emerged as an influential leader. She was appointed to the editorial board of the Society's journal; added to the Advisory Board in 1916; and elected secretary in 1916 and 1917, secretary-treasurer in 1917, and editor of the journal in 1919. She had strong, passionate views, which she expressed very forcefully, as she was an engaging speaker. She attacked the Indian Office for its paternalism and its assimilation policies, especially when it came to protecting the reservation land base. She supported those who wanted to abolish the OIA but did not support those who wanted to abolish the reservations.

She was a strong advocate for all Native people, and as the years passed, she became more vocal about protecting social and cultural institutions. Her biographer, Tadeusz Lewandowski, argued that her ideas were comparable to those of the activists of the 1960s and 1970s—hence the title of his book, *Red Bird, Red Power,* which depicts her as a forerunner of the Red Power movement. Speroff describes Zitkala-Ša as a pioneer in the quest for self-determination. Her strong views led to clashes with SAI members on several issues. The one Indian Office policy she supported was the criminalization of peyote usage and the suppression of the Peyote faith. While in Utah, she joined several missionary groups in lobbying the Utah legislature to outlaw peyote, as she believed it had the same negative effects as alcohol. She was very adamant and did not change her opinion on peyote for the rest of her life. At the time of her death in 1938, thirteen states had criminalized peyote. Omer Stewart wrote, "I am ready to give Mrs. Bonnin the major credit." She lobbied intensely, traveling widely, speaking to politicians, and trying to convince various groups, especially women's groups, to support state and federal attempts to pass anti-peyote legislation. In 1917, her husband Raymond attended Officers Training School, became a captain in the U.S. Army, and served in Europe. (Both are buried in Arlington National Cemetery.) In a letter to Parker, she recommended that in addition to lobbying governmental agencies, politicians, and organizations, the Society also needed to focus on reservation life. Based on her experience with "local centers" in Utah, she laid out a plan to combine some adults and returned boarding school students into reservation-based community centers to spread the ideas of the Society and help prepare the local population for when they receive "a definite legal status." Parker was totally supportive. "The Indians need awakening from within by some member of their race," he added.[7]

Parker received additional advice from Dennison Wheelock, a member since 1912, elected to several leadership positions. He was one of the most prominent and accomplished SAI members, as an attorney, composer, and conductor. He was a strong supporter of citizenship and public schools for Indian children, but like his mentor General Pratt, he advocated for integrating Anglo values and opposed teaching Indian arts and music. He wrote most of the memorial for President Wilson and drafted potential legislation, but by 1917, as the SAI took more forceful policy positions, he left the organization. Meanwhile, he suggested that the conference format be changed. Instead of focusing on "abstract questions," the entire time should be devoted to developing legislation. He suggested an invitation be extended to all tribes, requesting they send delegates to the conference, bringing a list of grievances and a list of legislative or policy needs. The resulting legislation would then be drafted and sent to Congress. Parker responded affirmatively and agreed to notify various tribal officials of the plan. Wheelock took a pragmatic approach in attempting to fashion policies that would lead to the improvement for reservation life, but ultimately, he wanted to close the reservations. He consistently pushed other Society members to establish and maintain correspondence with those living on the reservations.[8]

## The Fifth Annual Conference: University of Kansas and Haskell Institute, 1915

The first four SAI conferences were held at major universities in large cities. The location of the fifth conference, in Lawrence, Kansas, was selected not only because it was home to the University of Kansas but because of the presence of Haskell Institute, a federal Indian boarding school founded in 1884. Today it is Haskell Indian Nations University, a four-year institution. In choosing the theme "Responsibility for the Red Man," Parker explained that the goal of the conference was for individuals to have the right to freedom of action without guardian oversight. To achieve this, American Indians needed to become competent as individuals and as a race and gain competency by being responsible. The suggested conference topics revolved around how to teach responsibility. Again, this was to be prefaced by the government settling all claims and accounts; then American Indians would become competent and thus responsible members of society. Parker argued for a path-to-citizenship model, claiming that this strategy would garner support from non-Indians for eventual citizenship. In addition to blaming government control, Parker also blamed reservation conditions on intemperance, improvidence, renting of land, ill health, neglect and laziness, and "tribal customs." The latter was very controversial, as it implied that Native spiritual, cultural, and social traditions were a hindrance to future success and possible citizenship. On this point, the Indian Office, "friends of the Indian" organizations, and Parker were in agreement, at least publicly.[9] This was Parker's go-slow strategy to gain support from government officials and the public, yet he continued to support the Iroquois (Six Nations) Confederacy's right to self-determination.

As Parker saw it, there were two reasons for this unhappy state. The first reason stemmed from the conditions created by the government, such as inadequate education, lack of business skills, legal restrictions, and hordes of grafters. The second was the Indians' own neglect—as they were disheartened; crushed; facing adverse social conditions; and coping with land sharks and money sharks who were after Indian land, timber, oil, and mining rights. Parker added that one thing was certain—the Indian was not to blame, yet the Indian needed to work hard and press forward in the face of adversity. The solution was for the Society to awaken Indian individuals, providing knowledge about their rights. If the government wanted to create good citizens, it was going about it the wrong way. In another preconference editorial, Parker wrote that Indians needed "efficient manhood and womanhood" and must plant hope, ambition, and inspiration that leads to action, self-help, and achievement. He asked, "Who knows better about being an Indian than an Indian?" He listed all the accomplished members of the SAI, who were highly educated, highly competent people. He asked that their ideas be given serious consideration, and he hoped that the upcoming conference would contribute to this outcome.[10] Prior to the conference, Parker received a letter from Franklin Lane, secretary of the interior, placing the burden of survival on the shoulders of the Indians. Lane wrote, "Civilization is based on the gospel of work, and if the Indian is to survive, he must adopt this gospel as his own and prove his right to live under it." He did not mention federal tutelage over the reservations, the lack of gainful employment opportunities, or obstacles to sufficient food and health care, much less the outright thievery of Indian resources. Parker published Lane's letter in the *Quarterly Journal* and followed with his own call to abolish the Office of Indian Affairs and replace it with a nonpartisan commission.[11]

The conference opened with warm welcomes from the mayor of Lawrence, the president of the University of Kansas, and J. R. Wise, the superintendent of Haskell Institute. A letter from President Woodrow Wilson was read,

**FIGURE 10** The Fifth Annual SAI Conference. Engineering Hall, University of Kansas, Lawrence, Kansas, October 1, 1915. Courtesy of the Kansas Historical Society.

sending best wishes for a successful conference. Attendance was reasonably good, with about ninety Active and Associate members. Also, many local people, including students from the university and Haskell, attended many of the events. The *Kansas City Star* reported that 1,200 "wildly cheering Indians" attended an evening event. In addition, there were a number of Peyotists there from nearby Oklahoma, along with strong anti-Peyotists such as Associate members "Pussyfoot" Johnson and Matthew Sniffen of the Indian Rights Association. The fourth day of the conference was held at Haskell. The members toured the school; saw the classrooms, dormitories, shops, barns, and kitchens; and reviewed a full military uniform dress parade. That evening in Haskell's auditorium, many of the SAI leaders, including Henry Roe Cloud, Arthur Parker, Sherman Coolidge, and Marie Goulette, gave uplifting speeches to the students, encouraging them to work hard. The theme throughout the conference was "What can the Indian do to help himself?" One answer was Gertrude Bonnin's recommendation to develop reservation-based community centers. She volunteered to manage the first center among the Utes at Fort Duchesne, Utah. She asked the members to donate books, sewing materials, surgical bandages, and anything that would promote "industry, sanitation and clean and pleasant homes." In the fall of 1915, she arrived in Fort Duchesne and established sewing classes for women, who produced clothes for the elderly and infants. She assisted with the distribution of food and generally tried to alleviate impoverished conditions. She also set up a local branch of the SAI, but little came of this effort. She prepared a report on her year's work at the Community Center, hoping it would be a model for other centers. However, given the lack of funds, this did not materialize.[12]

During the conference, several presenters adopted a new approach. Instead of presenting broad-based papers on general concerns, there were several papers on specific problems on various reservations, with the presenters asking attendees for their help. For example, James McAdams (Shoshoni) described the problems on the Wind River Reservation. He feared the loss of good farmland and water rights to local white ranchers. He wanted help so the Shoshones could have a voice in their own affairs. There were also pleas for help from the Utes and the Lac Court d'Oreilles, and from the Seminoles for land in Florida. Debates ensued about how to handle the complaints, but unfortunately, the SAI did not have the resources to handle such issues, aside from forwarding them to the Indian Office.[13]

**Figure 11** Dr. Carlos Montezuma, an SAI founder and major voice for abolishing the Indian Office and advocating for full citizenship. Courtesy of the University of Illinois Archives.

The conference followed the usual structure of presentations, entertainment, elections, voting on the conference platform, and resolutions. The highlight, however, was an hour-long dramatic speech, "Let My People Go," by Carlos Montezuma, the "fiery Apache." The speech, in part, was in response to Montezuma's ongoing battle with the Indian Office over tribal land and water rights on Arizona reservations and a lengthy all-out assault on the Indian office, the reservation system, federal education policies, and lack of citizenship status for all American Indians. Montezuma issued a call for Indians to join the fight for their own freedom. He also attacked the Society as a do-nothing organization:

> The Society of American Indians has met and met. This coming together every year has been the mere routine of shaking hands, appointing committees, listening to papers, hearing discussions, passing a few resolutions,

> electing officers, then reorganizing–and that has been the extent of our outlook and usefulness for our race. . . . The Society of American Indians is not free. We are wards, we are not free!

With praise for General Pratt, Montezuma used Pratt's argument that nothing could be better than the complete destruction of the Indian Office. In addition, he stated that "Indian Reservations, Indian Schools, Indian College, Indian Art, Indian Novels, Indian Music, Indian Shows, Indian Movies and Indian Everything create prejudice and do not help our race." Montezuma claimed there should only be one object for the Society: "Freedom for our People." With stirring words and great intensity, he added, "My Apache blood rushed into my head." He declared the reservation schools were training grounds for wardship. He attacked the "friends of the Indian" groups, along with the hundreds of Native federal employees, criticizing them for supporting the system for fear of losing their jobs. He added that "Indian employees in the Indian Service are working against the freedom of their race." He asked: "What has happened to our land? The Indian Office thinks we have too much; sometimes they flood it with dams without consulting us. Their only interest is to perpetuate themselves." He recommended the SAI send a bill to Congress to abolish the Indian Office. He concluded with quite a rhetorical flourish: "We must act as one. Our hearts must throb with love—our souls must reach to God to guide us—and our bodies and souls must be used to gain our peoples' freedom. In behalf of our people, with the spirit of Moses, I ask this—THE UNITED STATES OF AMERICA—'LET MY PEOPLE GO.'" Parker, using his editorial prerogative, chose to reprint only about one-fourth of the speech in the SAI's *Quarterly*. He included Montezuma's critical analysis of the Indian Office but did not include Montezuma's negative commentary on the SAI. Montezuma, however, had five thousand copies of his speech printed in pamphlet form. He distributed it to members of Congress, newspaper editors, libraries, college presidents, and school superintendents. After the supply of pamphlets was exhausted, he ordered another five thousand copies. Despite his negative remarks about all things "Indian," Montezuma always kept in contact with his Pima relatives and waged a continual war with the Indian Office to protect Indian natural resources in Arizona. He wanted the SAI to concentrate only on one issue: abolishing the Indian Office. He believed the only way to help American Indians was by ending federal paternalism. But why did Montezuma call himself the "fiery Apache" or refer to his "Apache blood?" While he was not Apache (although the Pima are related), he was aware of the Apache public image and thus used this notoriety to draw attention to himself and his message to abolish the Indian Office. His message was amplified by the "Red Man's Burden" drawing printed in the "Let My People Go" pamphlet (see figure 12).[14]

The response to Montezuma's speech was mixed. Some supported his attack on the Indian Office, but others wondered what would happen to the legal claims, the trust funds, the treaties, and the tribal lands. Also, there was no mention of how personal and property rights would be protected. Montezuma offered no follow-up plan. Peter Iverson, his biographer, describes him as an egotist—uncompromising, quick to be insulted, and convinced of his righteousness. People paid attention to him, but it strained his relationship with certain Society members, such as Arthur Parker, adding to the growing factionalism of the SAI. Julianne Newmark emphasizes the ideological

**FIGURE 12** Montezuma's "Red Man's Burden" drawing, depicting Indian people burdened by the federal government. Pamphlet by Carlos Montezuma, "Let My People Go," 1915. Carlos Montezuma Papers, microfilm edition, Reel 6, 1915.

differences between Parker and Montezuma, but it seems their differences were not ideological but pragmatic. Both supported the closing of the Indian Office but had differing approaches, which reflected the division within the SAI. Montezuma called for immediate closure; Parker called for gradual closure. The same with citizenship. Montezuma wanted immediate citizenship; Parker espoused a go-slow approach. Overall, Montezuma was disappointed with the response to his speech. After the conference, Parker wrote to him, supporting the idea of abolishing the Indian Office, but not without a plan for the future. He emphasized that legal matters and property rights needed to be settled first, and that using the word "abolish" without a subsequent plan contributed to a lack of support. Some members wondered if abolishing the Indian Office would leave American Indians landless beggars and peons, like the Indians of Mexico and South America.[15]

The conference papers were divided by topic. Montezuma's presentation was part of the panel on "The Responsibility of the Government to the Indian." Other papers focused on claims and legislation; establishing an American Indian Day; education; and discussions about progress, drawbacks, and problems on the reservations. Many of the ideas presented in the papers were reflected in the platform and resolutions. The platform included some past items, such as support for the Carter Code bill and the Stephens bill, to open the Court of Claims to American Indians. There was a call to reorganize the boarding schools by improving academic standards, making them equal to public schools, and making tribal funds and trust funds available to boarding school graduates so they could pursue higher education. A resolution to support the immediate closing of the Indian Office failed, but a substitute resolution passed that was part of a long-range plan to abolish the Indian Office, divide tribal trust funds into severalty, and pay out the monies in individual trust accounts instead of "annuities and doles [that] foster pauperism." A set of arguments were presented on ending federal control and setting a path toward citizenship. (This still was not a call for outright citizenship, although Parker called for full citizenship for Puerto Ricans.) One resolution received unanimous support: implore Congress and the executive branch to uphold the suppression of liquor traffic, as cited in many treaties, and to support federal and state legislation to prohibit all traffic in alcohol, as the national Prohibition movement was gaining momentum.[16]

Aside from the declaration of an American Indian Day on the second Saturday in May, the resolutions responded to specific petitions the SAI received from various tribal groups. They were mostly land issues sent in from the Seminoles of Florida, the Cheyenne-Arapahos of Oklahoma, and the Crows of Montana. The latter resolution also called for the Crows to be allowed to send their children to locally built schools and not sent away to boarding schools. It was hoped that a more assertive approach by the SAI would pressure the Indian Office to modify their policies, especially with all the talk of abolishing them.[17] The election of officers went smoothly, although there was some support for Thomas Sloan as president. Nevertheless, Coolidge was reelected president; W. A. Durant, an attorney from Oklahoma City, was elected first vice president; Henry Roe Cloud was elected vice president for education; Thomas Sloan was elected vice president for legislation; and a new officer, Estaiene De Peltquestangue (Ojibwe) from Massillon, Ohio, was elected vice president for membership. William Kershaw replaced Roe Cloud as chair of the Advisory Board. One significant change was to separate the position of secretary-treasurer. Parker was elected as secretary and Marie Baldwin as treasurer. This reduced Parker's workload and gave him more time to run the Society's daily activities. Baldwin lived in Washington, D.C., where she had access to Congress and the Indian Office. Gertrude Bonnin, attending her first conference, was appointed to the *Quarterly Journal's* editorial board. The only comment she made, aside from the discussion of community centers, was to mention that the Utes were "falling victim" to the "terrible stuff"—peyote.[18]

After the conference, Parker attended the annual meeting of the Lake Mohonk group. They passed resolutions supporting federal legislation for the suppression of alcohol and peyote. Parker applauded both. They also supported replacing the Indian Office with a commission to administer Indian affairs, as was proposed by the SAI. The Mohonk group tried to influence the SAI and vice versa. It was an informal reciprocal arrangement that included discussions of policies and exchanging speakers. Parker wrote to H. C. Philips, secretary of the Mohonk group, that it is was the Society's desire to cooperate in a friendly manner. They also shared platforms. Parker presented the Lawrence conference platform to them and he published the Mohonk platform in the *Quarterly Journal*. Parker did not always see eye to eye with the Mohonk group, but he did believe they could help each other when they were supporting similar policies, especially if they led to a reduction of federal control over American Indians and the possibility of citizenship.[19] It is important to note that while the SAI was advocating reduced federal tutelage, they were advocating more federal authority to suppress alcohol and peyote distribution.

In late 1915, Parker considered changing the name of the *Quarterly Journal.* He sought advice from General Pratt, suggesting the name *American Indian Advance,* but eventually choose *American Indian Magazine* (*AIM*). He also consulted the editorial board and some of the members. He wanted a publication with a wider appeal, not just the product of an organization; he said he felt the old name implied too much "clannishness." He hoped for increased subscriptions and newsstand sales by covering other topics, in addition to SAI material. The change was agreed upon and the new name appeared on the January–March 1916 issue.[20]

## 1916: A Difficult Year

After the Kansas conference, Parker and other members of the Executive Council lobbied for and against various bills in Congress. They lobbied for the establishment of an official Indian Day. They opposed Senator Johnson's Right of Nomination bill, which called for reservation residents to choose their own superintendents, claiming it would lead to manipulation of voters by self-interested parties. They also opposed the Hastings bill (HR 108), which called for the transfer of jurisdiction of the Five Civilized Tribes in Oklahoma from the Department of the Interior to the local superintendent. The SAI and the Indian Rights Association worked together to stop both bills. Parker and Coolidge wrote to various congressmen, opposing both.[21] But not everyone agreed. For example, Thomas Sloan, vice president for legislation, supported the Johnson bill. The question arose as to who spoke for the Society in its lobbying efforts. This created a problem among Sloan, Parker, and Coolidge, with each believing he was the spokesperson for the Society. Sloan felt excluded and upset. He was in Washington with access to Congress but now felt hamstrung by the lack of cooperation from Parker and Coolidge. Sloan wrote McKenzie, complaining that "I am wrought up" and that "we have the worst administration that we have ever had." This factionalism was difficult to overcome and hindered cooperation among the Society's officers.[22]

In May 1916, the first American Indian Day was celebrated in various places around the country. As early as June 1912, McKenzie and Parker had been discussing such a day. McKenzie recommended a date when children were in school but pointed out the growing concern over too many holidays.

He suggested combining it with Columbus Day. At the 1912 conference in Columbus, it was presented to the delegates, who voted in favor of an American Indian Day. The resolution stated that "this day should be devoted to the study of the true history of the Indian . . . and to his present social and economic condition to-day . . . consolidated with Discovery Day." Yet in some ways, the idea of combining the new holiday with Columbus Day did not seem like a good idea. Some feared Indian Day would be subordinate to Columbus Day, and thus the second Saturday in May was eventually agreed upon. Parker explained that this would enable schools to celebrate it on Friday, followed by public events on Saturday and church events on Sunday. In order to gain national exposure, Parker wrote to the *New York Times*, announcing the proposal. Between 1912 and 1915, when the SAI officially endorsed an annual Indian Day, Parker wrote to many public officials and educators, seeking support. He mailed out information about the Society and copies of the 1912 platform endorsing an Indian Day. He convinced the Boy Scouts of America to have a First Americans Day, which they celebrated for three years (1913–15). In 1914, an SAI member from Montana, Red Fox St. James (who had a number of aliases), took up the Indian Day banner. He claimed to have ridden horseback for four thousand miles, seeking signatures from the nation's governors for such a day. He acquired the signatures of twenty-four governors, brought them to Washington, and presented them to President Wilson. The SAI supported his effort and sent a letter to the president signed by the SAI leadership (although Parker did not sign it). On December 17, Red Fox, accompanied by a group of Boy Scouts, was granted a ten-minute audience at the White House. He handed the twenty-four signatures to the president and asked for his support for an American Indian Day. He picked October 12, he said, because it was when the "Red-Man first met the White-Man—when Columbus landed." He also said it commemorated the founding of the SAI on October 12, 1911.[23]

Parker was concerned about Red Fox hijacking Indian Day for himself. Parker believed he was a fraud, a showman, and an opportunist, questioning his heritage, as only his great-grandmother had some "Indian blood." Parker advised people not to affiliate themselves with him or his new youth organization, the Tepee Order of America, founded in 1915 in New York City. Parker wrote to the commissioner of education for New York, warning him that Red Fox was not an Indian—he just posed as one and also posed as a scoutmaster for the Boy Scouts of America. Parker distributed a memorandum to the membership warning them about Red Fox, who sometimes signed his name "Rev. Red Fox J. Shiuhuska." Parker also pointed out that Red Fox belonged to a spurious Freemason group that had no official recognition by the Freemasons. This was significant to Parker, as he was a committed Freemason. Reverend Moffett, an Associate member, dissociated himself from Red Fox, as did Montezuma.[24]

At the fifth annual conference in Lawrence, the SAI officially proclaimed the second Saturday in May as American Indian Day. It was one issue that was supported by almost everyone. Parker mailed copies of the proclamation to officials around the nation, including reservation superintendents. He published recommendations for its celebration in a nine-page pamphlet, which he included in the mailing. He suggested celebrating events such as Pocahontas saving John Smith, reviewing famous speeches by Chief Logan, Black Hawk, Tecumseh, and Osceola. He recommended songs, including the "Star-Spangled Banner," and included a reading list with five books written by Indian authors. Indian Day was for everyone—a day of fellowship, friendship, resolution, and patriotism—and the day also had the aim of encouraging American Indians of all backgrounds to see themselves as part of one race. Parker wrote that the Sioux is no longer a mere Sioux, the Iroquois a mere Iroquois, but a member of "a red race of aboriginal ancestry." He wrote that the American Indian should say, "I am not a red man only, I am an American in the truest sense and a brother to all human kind," and to think of themselves as belonging to a "race" first and a tribe second. The fact that a *New York Times* editorial did not approve of another holiday did not dampen Parker's enthusiasm. The most positive response came from Governor Charles Whitman of New York, who proclaimed May 13, 1916, as American Indian Day.[25] Parker claimed the first Indian Day a success. Three states, New York, Wisconsin, and Connecticut, put aside May 13 for special events. In New York, thousands of schoolchildren participated in various activities. Special events took place on several reservations and in select boarding schools. Parker was very clear on what he wanted—"that the wild west Indian was not imitated"; instead, the theme was "the American Indian as Our Friend and Fellow Citizen." The SAI was still battling the negative public image of Indians in the Wild West shows, recent films, and novels. This was all part of the SAI's overall goal—to change the public image of American Indians. Parker and Charles Dagenett tried to get Indian Office employees to stop using the terms "squaw," "buck," and "redskin." Thus the establishment of an Indian Day had sporadic success. It did not catch on nationally, although there were local activities in various places. But the idea of a special day did not die, with the SAI being one of the first (if not the very first) organizations to promote the need for official recognition of American Indian contributions to American society, thus laying the groundwork for today's National Native American Heritage Month in November and National Native American Heritage Day the Friday after Thanksgiving.[26]

As previously noted, in 1916, Montezuma began publishing his own journal, *Wassaja: Freedom's Signal for the Indians*. He chose the title *Wassaja*, as it was his Yavapai name meaning "signaling" or "beckoning," intending for his publication to signal freedom. It was a brief four-page monthly newsletter published from April 1916 until 1922, the year before his death. The publication attempted to counter those who opposed abolishing the Indian Office. The masthead of the first issue depicted a large log, representing the Indian Bureau, crushing an American Indian. He included three other mastheads in his publications, all depicting an oppressive Indian Office. Montezuma used his publication to continue his assault on the Indian Office, or as he wrote, *Wassaja's* "sole purpose is Freedom for the Indian through the abolishment of the Indian Bureau." In addition to editorializing, Montezuma's publication was also a forum for debate. The correspondence section offered individuals the opportunity to express their views and open a dialogue with other readers. Sometimes he reprinted parts of speeches. He also used *Wassaja* as an attack vehicle against the SAI, criticizing it as a do-nothing organization. Montezuma was angered that the SAI would not support his call for the immediate abolition of the Indian Office. With the appearance of *Wassaja*, working together for the unity of the Society became more difficult; however, Montezuma did not want to abolish the SAI, only change it. With *Wassaja* as a platform, Montezuma took the opportunity to attack the vanishing Indian imagery and make a personal statement via a poem about the meaning of his life, who he was, and what he stood for. In all his writings, this is the clearest statement of his essential beliefs about the future of American Indians:

CHANGING IS NOT VANISHING
Who says the Indian race is vanishing?
The Indians will not vanish.
The feathers, paint and moccasin will
vanish, but the Indians,—never!

Just as long as there is a drop of human
blood in America, the Indians will not vanish.
His spirit is everywhere; the American Indian will not vanish.
He has changed externally but he has not vanished.
He is an industrial and commercial man, competing with the world; he
has not vanished.
Wherever you see an Indian upholding the standard of his race, there
you see the Indian man—he has not vanished.
The man part of the Indian is here, there and everywhere.
The Indian race vanishing? No, never!
The race will live on and prosper forever.

Montezuma also attacked Indian Day, something that Parker had worked on for years. Montezuma opposed the holiday and said it was a farce, a fad, and would not help Indians, as it detracted from the real issue of Indian freedom. Parker's editorial response was to compliment Montezuma's sincerity as having Indian welfare at heart, but in slighting Montezuma, he wrote, "Dr. Montezuma has a splendid sense of humor and luckily for the rest of us we have also." Parker added that his "statements are worthy of psychological examination." Here, Parker was attempting to convince SAI members not to take Montezuma seriously. The relationship between the two men would henceforth be strained, with reconciliation almost impossible.[27]

## 1916: The Beginning of the End

The sixth annual SAI conference was hosted by Coe College in Cedar Rapids, Iowa. The choice of locations for the conferences had always been a source of contention. Some of the members wanted the conferences to be near reservations. Sloan was particularly upset over the selection of Cedar Rapids. His first choice was Omaha or, if not, Oklahoma City or Sioux City. He wanted local Indians to have access to the conferences. Parker defended the locations, including Cedar Rapids, claiming that Indians should see themselves as part of the larger world and have contacts beyond the reservation. Indians should "come out" from the reservations and gain wider experiences. He felt it was important to educate the public in the host cities. Parker arrived early to make the final arrangements for the conference and told a local reporter that "the Indians came to civilize the white race." The

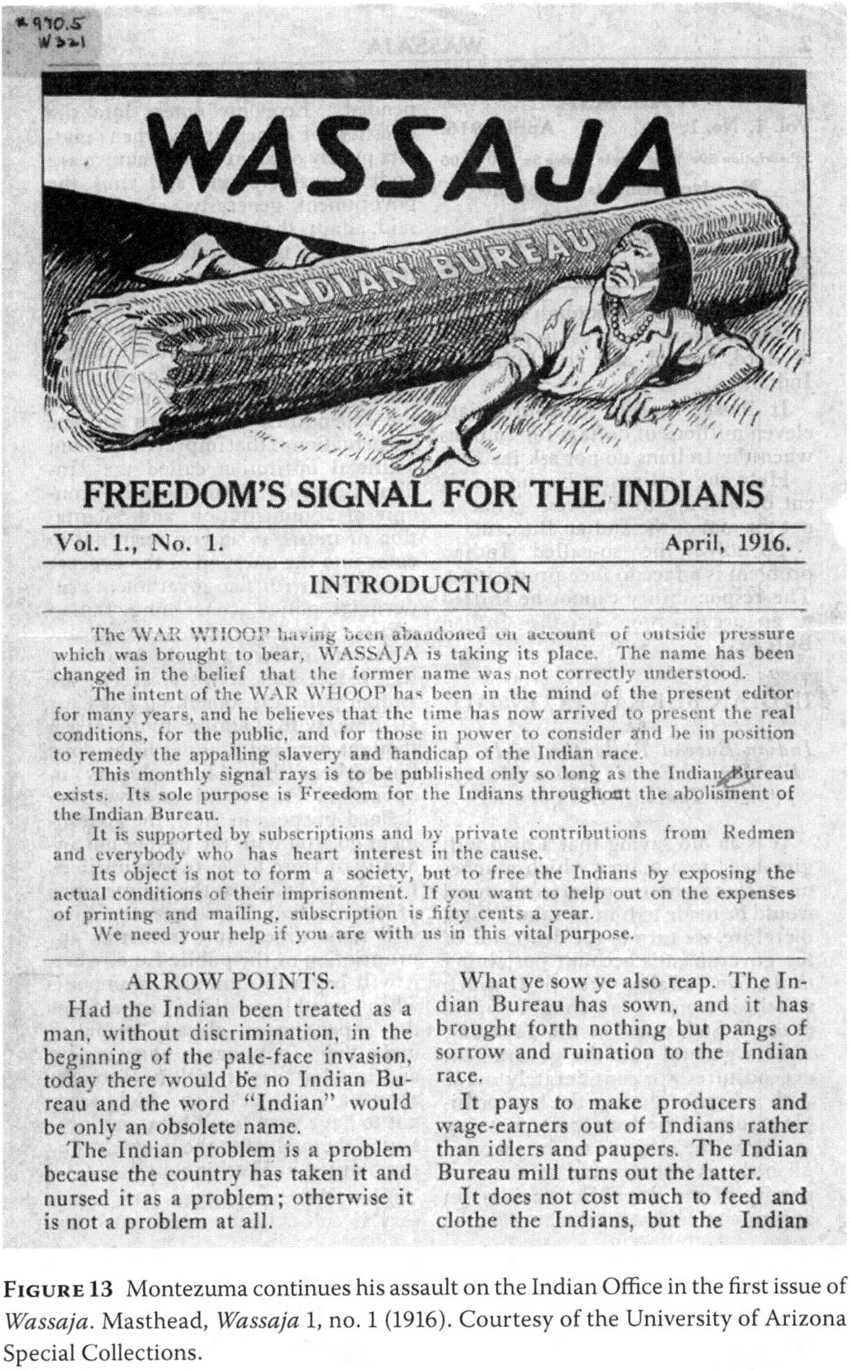



# WASSAJA



## FREEDOM'S SIGNAL FOR THE INDIANS

Vol. 1., No. 1. April, 1916.

### INTRODUCTION

The WAR WHOOP having been abandoned on account of outside pressure which was brought to bear, WASSAJA is taking its place. The name has been changed in the belief that the former name was not correctly understood.

The intent of the WAR WHOOP has been in the mind of the present editor for many years, and he believes that the time has now arrived to present the real conditions, for the public, and for those in power to consider and be in position to remedy the appalling slavery and handicap of the Indian race.

This monthly signal rays is to be published only so long as the Indian Bureau exists. Its sole purpose is Freedom for the Indians throughout the abolisment of the Indian Bureau.

It is supported by subscriptions and by private contributions from Redmen and everybody who has heart interest in the cause.

Its object is not to form a society, but to free the Indians by exposing the actual conditions of their imprisonment. If you want to help out on the expenses of printing and mailing, subscription is fifty cents a year.

We need your help if you are with us in this vital purpose.

### ARROW POINTS.

Had the Indian been treated as a man, without discrimination, in the beginning of the pale-face invasion, today there would be no Indian Bureau and the word "Indian" would be only an obsolete name.

The Indian problem is a problem because the country has taken it and nursed it as a problem; otherwise it is not a problem at all.

What ye sow ye also reap. The Indian Bureau has sown, and it has brought forth nothing but pangs of sorrow and ruination to the Indian race.

It pays to make producers and wage-earners out of Indians rather than idlers and paupers. The Indian Bureau mill turns out the latter.

It does not cost much to feed and clothe the Indians, but the Indian

**FIGURE 13** Montezuma continues his assault on the Indian Office in the first issue of *Wassaja*. Masthead, *Wassaja* 1, no. 1 (1916). Courtesy of the University of Arizona Special Collections.

theme was "A Conference on Race Progress," based on five goals: education, high moral standards, efficient administration, citizenship, and full responsibility and freedom with citizenship. The conference was not well attended, with between thirty and forty individuals. Parker admitted that he did not send out the same number of invitations as in the past, claiming he was under financial and time restraints. To make a point about his workload, he published a list of the material he had mailed out since 1911. It included 30,000 letters and 69,000 copies of printed material. He did not publish a list of attendees, but some of the Society's big names were there, including Gertrude Bonnin; Montezuma; Coolidge; Dennison Wheelock; Henry Roe Cloud; Thomas Sloan; Marie Baldwin; Delos Lone Wolf (Kiowa), a prominent Peyotist; and Father Phillip Gordon (Ojibwe), the only American Indian Catholic priest in the United States. He would play an increasingly important role in the Society as an ally of Montezuma and chairperson of the Advisory Board. He also edited the *War-Whoop* (with only three issues appearing in 1916), which was billed as a nonpolitical publication; however, in a not-so-subtle critique of the SAI, Gordon boasted that his publication would break away from the conservatism that hampered *other* organizations. Associate members in attendance included General Pratt; Matthew Sniffen of the Indian Rights Association; Robert Hall of the YMCA; Henry A. Larson, chief special officer for the Indian Office; and Reverend Thomas C. Moffett, superintendent of Presbyterian missions, soon to be elected president of the Associate members. Professor McKenzie did not attend; as president of Fisk University, he was now less involved with the SAI.[28]

The conference was split on several key issues that stirred debate, emotion, and on occasion, anger. What position should the SAI take on the Indian Office: immediate abolition, as spearheaded by Montezuma and Gordon, or settling legal and economic issues first and then, after citizenship was granted and rights were protected, closing it down? Equally as heated was the debate over SAI members working for the Indian Office. Could one serve both—could one be loyal to the "race" and work for the government at the same time? Montezuma claimed that this was not possible, but others defended the Indian Office employees, arguing that one could serve both. The peyote controversy was now out in open, as Parker and General Pratt made stinging speeches against what they saw as an evil drug. Even though there was little agreement on these major issues, Parker declared there were some basic agreements on civic freedom, citizenship, education, temperance, and speedy settlement of the government's affairs with the Indians.[29] Reverend Coolidge opened the conference by describing the present legal status of Indians as "chaos." He asked for moderation and cooperation by not talking about abolition. Disregarding Coolidge's advice, Father Gordon, Montezuma, and Pratt spoke in favor of immediate abolition. Gordon wanted Indians to have all the rights of American citizens. Pratt attacked segregation of the federal Indian schools. He wanted them closed and Indian children sent to public schools. "Get them into civilization," he argued. Montezuma also attacked the missionaries for supporting the policies of the Indian Office. He wrote, "These missionaries, you understand that, have their job waiting upon Indians. They want this thing prolonged. . . . They have an object for keeping the Indian as they are; they would not have a job. I think they are the obstacles." Marie Baldwin supported Coolidge, opposing immediate abolition of the Indian Office, claiming that too many reservation Indians needed help and support and that "they are not prepared to compete with people that surround them in a business way." She also said that as a federal employee, she never felt restricted in what she said; for example, she had always been publicly in favor of the eventual closing of the Indian Office. Delos Lone Wolf used a similar argument that there were too many elderly people that needed protection, but for others, he wanted the government "to give us what is ours." Coolidge had the final word: "Eliminate the antiquated rules, regulations and laws, by which the Indian Bureau is run. . . . Get rid of these old laws and clear the atmosphere for a new start, get ourselves on our feet as soon as we can and then abolish the Indian Bureau, but take care and do not abolish the Indians." Compromise was not possible. If you did not favor immediate abolition, then you were accused of prolonging dependency.[30]

The debate over federal employees as elected SAI officers was just as intense. Montezuma set the tone, proclaiming that one could not be loyal to both, especially since the Indian Office was not working for the best interests of Indian people. He claimed that one could not work for the Indian Office and do any good for Indians, nor could one expect to make progress with reservation Indians while being employed by the government. He added that he was disappointed that the Society did not support his proposal to close the Indian Office immediately. He referred to federal employees as "hirelings" who could not think for themselves. He added, "I cannot serve the devil and my God both, and neither can you." He concluded dramatically, "Freedom first, last, and die for it." His remarks, according to a local reporter, seemed to be aimed at President Coolidge. After Montezuma left the stage, Coolidge took the floor, defending himself and claiming that one could be "loyal to the race and the Government at the same time." Montezuma stood up and shouted, "I am an Apache; you are an Arapahoe. I can lick you. My tribe has licked your tribe before." Coolidge shouted, "Well, I am from Missouri." Laughter ensued, and the tension between the two was temporarily relieved. Father Gordon supported Montezuma, who claimed that one could not be loyal to both. Both Baldwin and Bonnin supported Coolidge. Bonnin, whose husband was an Indian Office employee, argued that many Indians in the federal service do so as a commitment to help Indians, with a "sense of duty."[31]

As if the debate over the Indian Office had not stirred enough controversy, the peyote issue added to the turmoil. The peyote controversy had been brewing since the founding of the SAI. However, 1916 was a watershed year, with an open debate as the SAI took its first official position opposing peyote, even though a number of members supported the Peyote faith. By 1915, Parker was convinced that peyote was a menace and that the SAI should be committed to its suppression. This was despite his commitment to keeping the SAI as nonpolitical as possible. He told Coolidge early in 1916 that "we can therefore stand for no specific political principle or oppose any, not even the peyote habit, without rousing the ire of large divisions of Indians." The previous year, he took a personal approach. In a letter to Chief Henry Roman Nose (Southern Cheyenne), a well-known Peyotist who had attended Hampton Institute and Carlisle, Parker spelled out a series of arguments to convince him to give up peyote and use his influence as a chief to stop the use of peyote on the Cheyenne-Arapaho Agency. Parker used a strange argument to try and convince Roman Nose that peyote was a dangerous narcotic. He gave an elaborate description of the intelligence of the "white men," who had made exceptional inventions such as the telephone, trains, and modern medicine, adding that since these same wise people say that peyote is bad, we should listen to them. Parker added that peyote was not given by the Great Spirit: "It [peyote] is after all only the devil's way of getting hold of you." Parker's arguments proved ineffective, as Roman Nose remained a Peyotist.[32]

By the time of the fifth annual conference in 1915, Parker and the SAI were under continual pressure from the Associate members and "friends of the Indians" organizations concerning peyote. They received many letters, especially from clergy, asking for cooperation to suppress the use of peyote in order to stop the "peyote craze." For example, Parker received a letter from George Gibbs of the American Baptist Home Mission Society, who was stationed in Oklahoma among the Cheyenne. He said that peyote "is an insidious foe of our work here." He asked for Parker's cooperation in fighting peyote, adding that it would be greatly appreciated by missionaries.[33] The factionalism over peyote deepened at each conference. Representatives from twenty-five western tribes attended the 1915 conference, including a number of Peyotists from Oklahoma, such as Howard Whitewolf (Comanche), Paul Boynton (Cheyenne/Arapaho), James R. Murie (Pawnee), and Cleaver Warden (Southern Arapaho). The latter three had attended Carlisle and played a major role in the defense of the Peyote faith, as they later testified in defense of peyote before a 1918 congressional committee. Bonnin, attending her first SAI conference, became part of the anti-peyote faction. The platform voted on by the delegates included support for state and federal legislation to suppress "the liquor traffic in Indian country." Surprisingly, the suppression of peyote was not mentioned in the 1915 platform. It is difficult to assess the reason for the omission, but it was possibly a reaction to the presence of Peyotists at the conference or, as Parker noted, the fact that the conference was disorganized in nature, with people speaking out of turn on topics that were not part of the agenda.[34]

By 1916, however, concern over peyote and the Peyote faith (soon to be incorporated as the Native American Church) had become a national issue. As the Peyote faith was spreading, it became an intense SAI issue. In addition, the Indian Office was lobbying Congress to criminalize the use of peyote through the recently introduced Gandy bill, making it a crime to transport, sell, or use peyote, punishable with fines up to $500 and a year in jail. Representative Harvey Gandy of South Dakota led the legislative effort to suppress peyote. There was considerable publicizing of pro and con positions. For example, Francis La Flesche (Omaha), a Smithsonian ethnologist and SAI member since 1913, worked to defeat the Gandy bill. In April 1916, he led a delegation of Omaha Peyotists to Washington to testify in defense of their faith. Given all the pressure Parker faced, he moved from concern about Peyotism to full-fledged opposition. For the first time, he clearly articulated the view that peyote was harmful to American Indians and should be eliminated via federal legislation. Despite the presence of many other contentious issues, the controversy over peyote came to the forefront in the Society's *American Indian Magazine*. As the magazine's editor, Parker had previously argued that taking a particular stance on political issues would be disruptive to the organization; nevertheless, he went ahead and reprinted a controversial article by Gertrude Seymour, "Peyote Worship: An Indian Cult and a Powerful Drug." By reprinting the article, the SAI avoided any direct endorsement of anti-peyote legislation, since they were only presenting someone else's opinion. Seymour, a journalist, had contacted Parker for information for the article. She said she had read his 1914 editorial, "Drug-Induced Religion," and wanted to know how peyote was imported and what impact it had on students. Parker responded by saying the peyote traffic was now commercialized and that schoolchildren who had experienced peyote could no longer concentrate. Seymour wrote a harsh indictment of peyote and Peyotists, calling for the passage of the Gandy bill. Parker's decision to have Seymour's article reprinted in the Society's journal added to the controversy.[35]

Meanwhile, two weeks before the sixth annual conference in Cedar Rapids, Iowa, the SAI became indirectly involved in a peyote case, as attorney Thomas Sloan, an SAI officer, assisted in the legal defense of a Peyotist. Harry Black Bear (Lakota) from the Pine Ridge Reservation was arrested for the distribution of peyote under the 1897 statute prohibiting the distribution of intoxicants. That September, Black Bear went on trial in federal court in Deadwood, South Dakota. Sloan went to Deadwood to serve as an advisor and a witness for the defense. The jury found Black Bear guilty; however, his attorney asked the judge to overturn the verdict since the statute he was accused of violating did not include peyote. The judge agreed and vacated the jury's decision. The local press reported on Sloan's testimony and cited comments by Black Bear's attorney, who credited Sloan's testimony for the judge's decision. Sloan said that peyote was not a "habit-forming drug," had no serious effect on the body from long-term use, and was a cure for alcoholism. The press article also pointed out that Sloan used peyote. Parker then chose to reprint the article on Black Bear's trial. Sloan's defense of peyote, not as an attorney but as a witness, was contrary to SAI policy, so one could speculate that the decision to reprint the article was intended to harm Sloan's reputation.[36]

As described previously, the sixth annual conference was quite contentious on two particular fronts: Montezuma's call to abolish the Indian Office and the peyote issue. The strategy used by those opposed to peyote was to link peyote with alcohol and seek federal and state legislation for its suppression. There was a strong anti-peyote group that included Parker, Reverend Coolidge, Henry Roe Cloud, Montezuma, Gertrude Bonnin, Father Philip Gordon, General Pratt, and almost all Associate members. The group was driven by the fact that while the Gandy bill had failed in Congress, it soon would be reintroduced. Bonnin, now fully involved with the SAI, spoke about the evils of peyote. She cited the damage it had done to the Utes, describing how they became "crazed," with some running wild and others committing suicide. It was a powerful, emotional appeal. The local press said she spoke with much fervor. She was interviewed by a reporter who complimented her for working with the untutored individuals of a semi-savage race. She did not take kindly to the statement, retorting that people like Geronimo and Sitting Bull were heroes, not outlaws, and that the government had "no right to break up the sun dance, a religious ceremony."[37] Henry Larson of the Indian Office linked the use of peyote with alcohol. He claimed that all the evils of alcohol also applied to peyote and that "peyote, whiskey, cocaine, hashheesh [*sic*] are all the same." He added that peyote "excites unusual passions," with a deteriorating effect on the human body. He asked the SAI to take an official stance against peyote. General Pratt argued that the campaign to suppress peyote should be tied to the temperance movement. He proposed a resolution to urge Congress to pass the Gandy bill. His motion carried. The resolution was entered into the final conference platform and read: "We urge unequivocally upon Congress the passage of the Gandy bill to prohibit the commerce in and use of peyote among our people, because of its known baneful effects upon the users [*sic*] mind and morals."[38] The SAI was now officially on record supporting federal legislation to criminalize the use and possession of peyote. The vote was not unanimous. Delos Lone Wolf, a Carlisle graduate and football star from the 1890s, who was now a cattle rancher, Peyotist, and prominent Kiowa leader, spoke on behalf of the Peyote faith. He said that talk about peyote killing people, as some had alleged, was ridiculous. "I know," he affirmed. "I used peyote for fifteen years." He added that Peyotism and Christianity were not mutually exclusive, since he was also a Christian. He claimed to speak to people about Jesus through the "instrument of peyote." The local press focused on the peyote issue, reporting all the horror stories they heard. They did not mention Lone Wolf's testimony. With such a variety of perspectives and individuals with strong personalities, a reporter from the Native newspaper the *Tomahawk*, edited by SAI member and future vice president Gus Beaulieu (Ojibwe), wrote that poor attendance, only fifteen to twenty Indians, and internal dissension threatened the organization. His assessment was correct.[39]

Bonnin emerged as the leading SAI spokesperson for the criminalization of peyote. As a political activist and publicist, she used a wide range of strategies. Through one-on-one conversations, she tried to convince individuals to give up peyote as she did on the Uintah and Ouray Agency in Utah. She traveled with several SAI members through the reservation, meeting with John McCook, a Northern Ute Peyotist leader, trying to convince him to give up peyote.[40] She also wrote to Commissioner Sells, urging him to use his influence to convince Peyotist leaders to desist. She successfully lobbied state legislatures. (Nevada, Utah, and Colorado criminalized the possession of peyote in 1917.) She wrote to organizations such as the Indian Rights Association and the Lake Mohonk group to support the Gandy bill. She also wrote to Samuel Brosius of the IRA, outlining her views on the evils of peyote. Brosius included her views in his article "The Ravages of Peyote," an intense diatribe against peyote. She wrote that peyote "was undermining the uplift work of churches." She compared peyote to opium, morphine, and cocaine, claiming that it excited the baser emotions, that it was demoralizing, and that at least twenty-five Utes had died from ingesting peyote. She ended with a flourish calling for "the prohibition of peyote, twin brother of alcohol, first cousin of habit-forming drugs."[41] She shared the same views with Parker, describing the physical and psychological danger of peyote and claiming that its spread was due to "peyote agents" who were pushing it for profit. As the anti-peyote efforts were not successful, Bonnin, Parker, and others tried to explain its growth by arguing that drug dealers and drug agents were involved in a "peyote lobby" to keep it legal. As it became increasingly difficult to get Congress to suppress peyote, the anti-Peyotists used harsher language and more extreme arguments to make their case, thus creating more dissension within the SAI.[42]

On the last day of the conference, the members voted on a platform and officers. Reverend Coolidge stepped down as president, although he was proclaimed the honorary president. Arthur Parker, who had worked tirelessly for the Society, was elected president by acclamation; John Oskison was elected first vice president; Margaret Frazier became vice president on membership; Gabe E. Parker became vice president on education; William Kershaw became vice president on legislation; Gertrude Bonnin became the secretary; Marie Baldwin became the treasurer; and Father Gordon was

**Figure 14** Zitkala-Ša (Gertrude Bonnin), editor, *American Indian Magazine*, 1918–19. Found in *American Indian Magazine* 5, no. 4 (1917), reprinted in *American Indian Stories*, 1921. This photo appeared in one of her short stories published at the beginning of the twentieth century. Courtesy of The Ohio State University Libraries.

elected chair of the Advisory Board. The debate over the platform was again contentious. The battle was led by Montezuma and supported by Pratt and Reverend Moffett, calling for the immediate abolition of the Indian Office. The final platform, however, reflected Coolidge and Parker's views in taking a moderate stance toward the Indian Office. The platform called for the Indian Office to be closed only after all federal obligations to American Indians were settled. It called for the use of the federal Indian schools as stepping stones to "white schools" and as "Schools for Citizenship," with a gradual path to U.S. citizenship. It also supported the suppression of liquor and peyote traffic and reaffirmed the principles and platforms of previous conferences, referencing the legislation the Society had supported in the past.[43]

The Cedar Rapids conference and platform exhibited the internal divisions that had beset the SAI since 1911. The seeds of demise were obvious, and the Society would not recover from the divisive issues and turmoil of 1916. The factionalism had become entrenched. There were viewpoints and opinions that could not be compromised, and sometimes the debates became personal. Montezuma's *Wassaja* added to the climate of divisiveness, even though the publication was not intended to directly compete with the Society's journal but to express Montezuma's views. *Wassaja* alarmed many members, both Active and Associate, with its blunt criticism of the government, particularly the four mastheads depicting an authoritarian and evil Indian Office. The Society would never recover from this point, especially as finances and memberships continued to languish and several prominent members left the organization. They had a new president but were besieged by a series of new controversies involving World War I, the draft, and citizenship.

## CHAPTER 5

# The SAI Struggles

*The Great War, the Draft, and Citizenship, 1917–1918*

The war years presented the Society of American Indians with new challenges and controversies. The Progressive Era's spirit of reform was fading in the midst of gathering war clouds as the nation focused on the Great War in Europe. The war intensified the debate over citizenship, as the drafting of noncitizen Indians became a possibility. When Parker accepted the presidency of the Society in 1916, he could not foresee the rough terrain ahead. For all his commitment and hard work, he could not put the SAI on a firm foundation, as there were too many forces working against a unified organization. As in virtually all wartime eras, change was a dominant reality. The Prohibition movement, for instance, was in full swing. By 1917 twenty-one states had banned the sale of alcohol. The SAI officially supported Prohibition, and some of the Associate members were active in Prohibition organizations. Parker personally supported Prohibition and reprinted Prohibition articles in the *American Indian Magazine*.[1] A coalition of forces led to the Eighteenth Amendment to the U.S. Constitution (ratified in 1919), extending Prohibition nationwide. The woman's suffrage movement also gained momentum during the war years, spurred on by women's contributions to the war effort. The SAI did not take an official position on women's suffrage, but several of the women in the SAI were active suffragists, especially Treasurer Marie Baldwin, now living in Washington, D.C. She was a leading activist in the struggle for women's rights. The Nineteenth

Amendment establishing women's right to vote was ratified in 1920, and the irony of the women's suffrage movement was not lost on SAI members. Many Americans supported women's rights but not American Indian rights. There was a similar irony regarding the great influx of immigrants. There was a growing anti-immigrant sentiment, yet SAI members were perplexed. Why did immigrants have a path to citizenship while "real" Americans did not? The same sense of irony prevailed as the United States entered the Great War in the name of democracy and freedom: Where was democracy and freedom at home? The peyote controversy also deepened during the two-year span of 1917–18. Congress, with the encouragement of the Indian Office, held hearings on the criminalization of peyote. SAI members testified on both sides of the issue, creating animosity that could not be overcome.

Upon taking office, one of Parker's first official duties as president was to send a letter to Congress, asking for justice for American Indians by granting citizenship, but before that could happen, he advised, "tribes must be dissolved as social, commercial and political entities. The Indian must come into the nation as individual units." He reiterated all the points he had been making over the years—that Congress should codify Indian law, individualize trust funds, open the U.S. Court of Claims to all, and provide adequate education. He hoped that his new strategy would seem more convincing to Congress, adding that these were legislative issues in need of "haste and action." There was no plea for birthright citizenship and no mention of closing the Indian Office. Parker believed he could gain more by not antagonizing President Wilson, Congress, or the Indian Office. This go-slow strategy infuriated Montezuma. Parker's goal as president was to speed up the work of the Indian Office to hasten the granting of citizenship. He became more direct toward the Indian Office, yet not as uncompromising as Montezuma. He explained his goals to Father Gordon, the chair of the SAI Advisory Board. Parker used the metaphor of a train on the wrong type of track to describe the Indian Office: "The wheels won't budge." He continued: "They do not understand the extent of the task at hand, they are not preparing the Indian for the day they are no longer wards of the state. They suffer from blindness." Parker's goal was freedom for the strong, and freedom and protection for the weak. The government's strategy for protecting the Indian had not worked. He gave several examples—Louisiana Indians were plundered, the Mississippi Choctaw were beaten to the earth and servile, California Indians were starved and murdered, and Florida Seminoles needed to fight to keep but a few pieces of swampland. Parker's answer was to provide the tools for people to protect themselves; metaphorically speaking, "they must enter the fight with a blade in hand."[2]

The Society was not functioning as the founders had envisioned in 1911. Continuing turmoil among the members, funds in short supply, and too much work for too few people were taking a toll. Parker was always pressed for time. It was difficult to continue all the mailings and get the *American Indian Magazine* published. In fact, he considered ceasing the publication altogether. Parker's biographer, Joy Porter, citing the previously noted factors and his intermittent health issues, claimed that he became depressed during this time.[3] Making things more difficult for Parker, turmoil erupted between Secretary Gertrude Bonnin and Treasurer Marie Baldwin. The position of secretary-treasurer had been separated to make the functioning of the office in Washington more efficient. The Bonnins had left Utah and moved to Washington, and Baldwin, who worked for the Indian Office, also lived in Washington. Each complained to Parker about the other. Baldwin took the account books home without permission; Bonnin moved the SAI office to a room in her apartment without informing Baldwin, who decided to do the treasurer's work at home. Baldwin was angry that Bonnin charged the SAI rent for the office in her apartment. There was a failure to communicate and cooperate, which had an impact on finances, as the two were late in getting out notices for annual dues. Bonnin became quite perturbed. She was working without pay and needed the account books to know what finances she could count on as secretary. The situation was partially resolved by Reverend Thomas C. Moffett, who met with both women and worked out a temporary modicum of cooperation between them, but Parker admitted that separating the secretary-treasurer office was a mistake. In a letter to Coolidge, Parker called both women petty and spiteful and wished they would resign. Parker wondered about the organization's survival but insisted that it must live on "in spirit strong, if weak in body." At the 1918 conference, the offices of secretary and treasurer were again combined.[4]

Parker added to his own difficulties on the issue of race. In the last issue of *AIM* in 1916, he included an article he wrote on assimilation that contained several extremely negative remarks on African Americans. The article was an attempt to compare the possibilities for assimilation among European immigrants, African Americans, and American Indians. He saw America as a melting pot and assumed everyone's goal was assimilation. For European immigrants, he argued, assimilation was not difficult, as the immigrant "is a white man from a civilized country," citing an example of German immigrants to the United States. He indicated that American Indians, with the proper education and their traditional love of freedom, have the potential for "civilization" and assimilation, but have not been given the same opportunities as immigrants. Indians were segregated on reservations and kept away from economic and educational opportunities by a society not willing to open the door. He asserted that African Americans could "adapt" to "civilization" because of their "natural servility" and "imitativeness." He added that the "Negro admired his master and wanted to be like him"; however, he added, imitation is evidence of "feeble character and inferiority." For assimilation to be possible, the "Negro" must eliminate their "darky habits," and he believed that Anglo Americans were still determined to protect "racial purity" and maintain strict segregation. Then, in a statement that presages his later involvement with the American Eugenics Society, he described "White-Negro" marriage as "a danger to the white element." This was quite an unusual article for the president of a national organization. It alienated some SAI members, especially Associates who had ties to the African American community. Montezuma immediately attacked the article in the pages of *Wassaja*. He called it "shallow." The article was not helpful for Parker's reputation or the SAI. But some of this controversy was nothing new. In 1912, when the federal government stopped funding American Indians attending Hampton Institute, a predominately African American institution in Virginia, Parker agreed with the government's decision, since he opposed American Indians attending school with African Americans. Earlier, Marie Baldwin encouraged Parker to support segregating African Americans and Native Americans in schools. She claimed the former would have a negative effect on the latter. She also opposed the hiring of African Americans by the Indian Office, since, as she claimed, "the negro is immoral—dangerous." It is difficult to ascertain Parker's motive in publishing this article. One factor he and several other SAI members may have feared is that the American public would see American Indians and African Americans through the same prejudicial gaze, thus impeding opportunities for Indians to escape the racial confines of the American landscape. His answer was to try to separate the two groups in the public mind. His goal was the empowerment of American Indians, and any association with the "Negro problem" could be detrimental to this goal. This helps explain the SAI's hesitancy in working with African Americans. Lucy Maddox's assessment seems rather accurate. Parker wanted to make it clear that the "Negro problem" was a problem with the "Negro"; the "Indian problem" was not a problem with the "Indian." Indians were not a problem; Indians *had* a problem. Parker's views on race were complicated and changed over time, especially in the 1920s as he used eugenic theories to oppose immigration and "racial blendings." However, in his years as SAI secretary-treasurer, he used the term *assimilation* more as accommodation as he distinguished between the two. *Assimilation*, he explained, was for American Indians to support "American ideals," as he often wrote, to adjust to changing circumstances in order to function and compete in the contemporary world. Despite these factors, he continued to support the sovereignty of Native nations, particularly the nations of the Iroquois Confederacy. He expressed pride in his Seneca heritage, reinforced by his multiple books and articles on the Iroquois Confederacy.[5] As wartime issues emerged after 1916, Parker became more outspoken about the self-determination of the Iroquois Confederacy.

## The Great War

The outbreak of what became known as World War I provided the SAI with an opportunity to demonstrate patriotism, hoping participation in the war effort would convince the nation that all American Indians should be granted U.S. citizenship. The SAI saw this as a major opportunity to pursue its goals. Unfortunately, President Wilson was not interested in American Indian issues. Despite the SAI's 1914 meeting with the president, they made little headway with him, Congress, or the Department of the Interior. The war in Europe demanded the full attention of the Wilson administration. In 1914, the United States declared neutrality, but in 1915, Wilson began a "preparedness" program for possible American entry into the war. In the 1916 presidential campaign, Wilson used the slogan "He kept us out of the war." Nevertheless, the war hit home with the sinking of American merchant ships by German submarines and close cultural and economic ties to the Allies. On April 2, 1917, Wilson asked Congress to declare war "to make the world safe for democracy." His words were not lost on American Indians and other colonized people around the world. In January 1918, Wilson issued his "Fourteen Points," which included a declaration that all nations and colonized people have a right to self-determination. The irony was obvious: Wilson's words were used by the Society as the basis for continuing protests. The issue became immediate when Congress passed the Selective Service Act of 1917, requiring men eighteen to forty-five to register for a draft, which embroiled the citizenship issue with the draft. By war's end, twenty-four million men registered and about four million served in the armed forces. SAI members wanted to know: If you are not a citizen, do you have to register for the draft? Can you still be drafted? It was unclear how President Parker and the SAI leadership would respond to this situation. It was several months before the Selective Service issued guidelines on registering and inducting American Indians into the military.

Cato Sells, commissioner of Indian affairs, and Franklin K. Lane, secretary of the interior, saw the Great War as an opportunity to expand the government's "Americanization" programs. Both had been appointed by President Wilson in 1913. Sells had been an attorney active in Democratic party politics but had no experience working with American Indians. This was contrary to the SAI's demand that a commissioner be a nonpolitical appointee. Sells used the war to encourage reservation officials to develop Anglo-style agriculture and stock breeding, arguing that additional production was needed for the war effort. Both men believed that American Indians should participate in American society as individuals and not as members of Native nations, implying that patriotism and "tribalism" were incompatible. Their policies reflected this view. They continued the implementation of the allotment system, individualizing Native land and selling or leasing the so-called surplus. Sells was charged with administering the Selective Service Act for the Native American population. He declared that all Indian males, twenty-one to thirty-one (later changed to eighteen to forty-five) must register for the draft, whether a citizen or not. He required all men of age to fill out a questionnaire, which was more like an interrogation, asking if they knew anyone who was not registered for the draft or anyone who was advising against registration—providing the names and addresses of offenders so that their "grave offense" could be dealt with. The guidelines also stated that American Indians who were citizens were eligible for induction, but those who were not citizens would not be inducted. Unfortunately, the citizenship status of many Native Americans was not clear. Sells issued guidelines on who was considered a citizen, hoping to resolve the issue. One was considered a citizen if one acquired land by means of the Dawes Act of 1887 or through the Burke Act of 1906, if fee-simple deeds to land were issued and citizenship granted, if one lived apart from one's "tribe" in "white society," or if one's parents were citizens. It was still confusing. Sells avoided making individual decisions on who was a citizen by delegating the responsibility to local draft boards, who were even less informed. He added that, when in doubt, authorities should declare the individual a noncitizen. It was estimated that approximately 50 percent of Indians were citizens in 1917. This brought a sense of immediacy to the citizenship issue, as the prospect of being drafted became a reality.[6]

Parker and the SAI supported the war effort. Their strategy was to focus on the patriotism of American Indians. Parker encouraged Indian participation in all aspects of the preparedness programs, including volunteering for military service. He believed involvement in the war effort would lead to the granting of citizenship. In his editorial support for the war effort, he used Wilsonian language, calling the war a "conflict for the principles of freedom and democracy" and a "war for universal justice." He hoped the war would result in the recognition of the rights of "smaller divisions of mankind." He also used the War Office's language of fighting evil "to eliminate barbarism from its grip on men and nations." In a speech in Philadelphia to a group of "friends of the Indians," he argued that making the world safe for democracy included American Indians. Patriotism was his theme: "Our American Indians are today in France on the battle line, fighting that liberty, fraternity and equality of opportunity may prevail throughout the world." In a later editorial, he reiterated Indian loyalty to the nation and called for the doubling of agricultural production on the reservations.[7] The goal was clear: support the war and demonstrate patriotism, leading to citizenship.

For the most part, the American Indian population supported the war effort and the draft. For example, the Navajo offered ten thousand men "to take to the war path for the United States." The Oklahoma Cherokee offered to establish a regiment to "to defend the flag." Parker published these examples to show the public that Indians were patriotic. There were exceptions. Some, such as the Goshute of Utah and Nevada and several members of the Iroquois Confederacy, argued that noncitizens were not obligated to register with the Selective Service and be drafted. There was an increase in farm production and the sale of Liberty Bonds and Liberty Stamps; by the war's end, more than $25 million was raised from the nation's Indians. Thousands volunteered for the American Red Cross as nurses, clerical workers, and fund-raisers. According to the Indian Office, 17,313 registered for the draft, with 6,500 inducted and the remainder volunteering. Approximately 12,000 recruits served in the U.S. Army, 1,000 recruits served in the U.S. Navy, and a smaller number served in the U.S. Army Air Service. Scholars do not agree on the number of Indians who served in the military because of unclear local draft board records. (For instance, Iverson estimates 16,000 while Grillot estimates 12,000—probably the more accurate number.) Commissioner Sells wrote that this shows a "sure basis for the strong and trustworthy citizenship to which our efforts are directed." Although not well-known at the time, a group of Choctaw soldiers from the 142nd Infantry served as the first "code talkers," sending messages in Choctaw that the Germans could not translate. They became the model for the famous "code talkers" of World War II. Also, during the Argonne Forest offensive, the Germans were intercepting military communications between U.S. artillery units. Two Sioux soldiers were assigned to communicate in their "own tongue." One moved forward to an advanced artillery position; the other remained behind to receive the messages and direct artillery fire. Parker published this in a story titled "Played Joke on the Huns."[8]

As with President Parker, the SAI as an organization supported the mandatory registration of all male American Indians and the induction of citizen Indians into the military. The exception was Montezuma, who railed against noncitizen Indians being required to register or be inducted. Montezuma came under investigation by the Department of Justice, as it was a crime to speak or write against registration, the draft, or the war effort. Montezuma argued that wards of the state should not have to register or be subject to induction into the military. He asked if it was fair or just to do this to people with no rights. He put his objections into print in *Wassaja*. He wrote that he was not against the war or voluntary participation; he was against forcing noncitizens to comply. If Indians were made citizens, then they should be drafted and would "will march side by side under the same flag with the brave patriots to victory, then in behalf of THEIR COUNTRY."[9] Early in the war, the government established the Committee on Public Information. They developed wartime propaganda to instill support for the war by stimulating patriotism and loyalty and arousing anti-German hatred. They also encouraged Americans to report instances of disloyalty. Congress reinforced the committee's work with the Espionage Act of 1917 and Sedition Act of 1918. It was now a crime to speak against the war, the draft, or draft registration. Overall, it was a massive campaign to stifle free speech in the name of the war effort.

Montezuma's articles in *Wassaja* came to the attention of the American Protective Association, a private vigilante group with a nationwide membership of a quarter million. They saw themselves as the protectors of Protestant America. They were generally anti-immigrant and specifically anti-Catholic, as their stated goal was to prevent Catholics from holding public office. They were also watchdogs in their communities, as they believed they were protecting America from aliens and disloyalty. In October 1917, they brought Montezuma and *Wassaja* to the attention of the Department of Justice and accused him of disloyalty to America. They also pointed out that he had a German wife who had a "strong willed mother" from Germany. Montezuma defended himself, claiming he was not disloyal. His attack on the Indian Office was not an attack on the government, nor was he against the war. He was against the American Indian not having a voice and being a ward of the state. His goal was to inform the public of this unjust reality. He continued his attack on "Indian Bureauism" and "Kaiserism in America." Montezuma used the term "bureauism" to attack the Indian Office, castigating it as an imperialist and colonialist institution. For example, he defended the Yavapai, Pima, and Tohono O'odham in Arizona against the "bureauism" that was suffocating them. He questioned why America could combat injustice abroad but not at home—especially toward American Indians. He labeled this as hypocrisy: "Just think, Christian nations killing each other by the millions and sending missionaries to teach thou shall not kill." A Department of Justice investigator visited Montezuma in his home in Chicago. During a long interview, Montezuma made the same assertions that he had written in *Wassaja*. Opposing the Indian Office was not being disloyal. His purpose was to free American Indians from government control by granting citizenship. At this point, the Department of Justice dropped the case and lost interest in Montezuma.[10]

The complexity of the war, the draft, and citizenship was brought home with the case of the Six Nations Iroquois Confederacy. Parker, a Seneca, was involved in the controversy. He was appointed adjunct general of the state of New York to act as special advisor to New York Indians for Selective Service. He was also a member of the New York State National Guard. He supported the government's requirement that noncitizen Indians must register for the draft. Some members of the Iroquois Confederacy claimed the Selective Service Act did not apply to them, since the Treaty of 1794 with the United States guaranteed their "nation within a nation" status, and therefore state and federal law did not apply to them. According to Indian Office policy, all Indians, including the Iroquois, had to register. It was ordered by the U.S. provost marshal general to New York Indians. The government proclaimed that "Failure to Register Violates the *Pledge of Peace and Friendship* Made in Treaties between the Six Nations and the United States and Will Bring All the Penalties as Provided by Law."[11] This was a very dubious argument. Sells chose not to challenge the Six Nations, since most Iroquois men had already registered and many had volunteered to serve in the military. Also, as an expression of their sovereignty, the Oneida and the Onondaga of the Six Nations Confederacy declared war on the Austrian and German Empires and enlisted in the U.S. military as allies. Parker wrote the declaration for the Onondaga and tried to convince the Seneca to do the same, arguing that this would be a reaffirmation of their sovereignty. Parker was a complex individual. His defense of Iroquois sovereignty may seem like an anomaly, given his earlier statements comparing American Indians to immigrants. In Parker's public persona, his views have to be considered in conjunction with his perceived audience. His arguments, which may sound as if he was advocating assimilation, were geared toward acquiring citizenship rights as Americans, not as cultural assimilation. This argues against labeling him as an assimilationist. Parker's personal letter to Walter Kennedy, a Seneca leader, is striking:

> If I were you and Mr. Hoag [Seneca], I would have a Declaration of War prepared against Germany and Austro-Hungaria, just as the Senecas did in [the War of] 1812. Once that was done you would again establish your independent right to act as a Nation and not as a ward-bound tribe that had no powers of a nation. The Senecas have lost none of their sovereignty since 1812 and a war declaration would serve to emphasize your status. The fighters could then enter the U.S. Army the same as now. I had the pleasure of writing out the declaration of war for the Onondagas recently. . . . The Senecas should not lack for ginger in this matter, and they ought to put themselves out of the neutral, bossed-around class into an assertive power.[12]

This may be Parker's clearest statement of his view on self-determination and sovereignty.

As the debate over draft registration subsided, and as large numbers of American Indians volunteered for or were inducted into the military, a new issue emerged about the placement of these troops within the armed forces.

Should they be integrated into existing predominantly white male units or separated into Indian-only units, as was the case with African Americans? The SAI, including President Parker, General Pratt, Gertrude Bonnin, and Dr. Montezuma, supported integration into preexisting military units. Parker and Montezuma were allies on this issue. Bonnin, now living in Washington, met with Commissioner Sells and other officials to argue against segregated units. Sells, in a letter to Reverend Coolidge, now the honorary president of the Executive Council, stated that he was "not in sympathy" with those calling for separate units.[13] There were voices calling for separate Indian units; however, only two SAI members supported this view: Francis La Flesche and Red Fox St. James. Red Fox gave several speeches claiming that thousands of Indians wanted to be in separate units. He suggested they be mobilized to guard the Mexican border, and in return, they should be granted citizenship. Several members of the Board of Indian Commissioners and Joseph K. Dixon of Wannamaker expedition fame also supported establishing separate units. He lobbied both houses of Congress to establish separate units and began his own campaign to build public support for his idea. He supported separate units using a racist argument that Indians had special "racial abilities" as warriors. Bills for separate all-Indian units were introduced in Congress, which included granting citizenship with enlistment. Both bills failed, as the War Department was opposed to the idea, partially because it was impractical to establish new units during a war when units were already available. Parker appealed to Newton Baker, the secretary of war, to allow Indian men to join established divisions. He said that Dixon's claim that thousands of Indians wanted to enlist in Indian-only units was untrue, as there was no indication of such petitions. In an editorial, he attacked Red Fox and did all he could to discredit him. He argued that fighting in integrated units was part of a larger process aiming to grant American Indians complete citizenship, adding that if Indians wanted to "volunteer" for a separate unit, he would not be opposed but he knew the War Department would not be supportive. Parker was correct. Secretary Baker, supported by the Indian Office, ordered Indians into established units. While Baker's policy was pragmatic, Commissioner Sells supported integrated units for another reason. He believed they would have a "large influence in moving him [American Indian] away from tribal relations and toward civilization." He later said that Indian troops should be "mixed indiscriminately among the whites, elbow to elbow, so they may absorb the English language, habits, and civilization of their white brothers."[14]

Gertrude Bonnin had an interesting take on the issue. In a very friendly letter to Parker that she addressed to the "Dear Seneca President" and signed "Truly, Sioux Secretary," she adopted a cynical view in her argument for Indian-only units: "Indian Battalion! Why those would hide the greatest scheme to utterly annihilate the Red man, by a whole-sale slaughter!" She had been equally cynical on the establishment of segregated African American units. She wrote to Parker that "secretly I wonder if it is not a cute idea to reduce the Negro population. This sounds like treason, so you better not quote me." In November 1919, Congress granted citizenship to American Indians who served during the war and received an honorable discharge; however, it was not automatic. Individuals had to petition and go through a court hearing regarding their competency, and only then would they receive a certificate of citizenship. Some veterans did not even realize they needed to petition to be granted citizenship. Regardless, not much changed for the veterans on the home front, as they returned after the war to poor living conditions, few job opportunities, no real voice, and no guarantee of voting rights. The only exception came when they returned home to their reservations, where they were celebrated and honored. Meanwhile, the service of American Indians abroad and on the home front helped dispel the myth of the "vanishing Indian."[15]

## Citizenship

The Great War did not settle the citizenship issue, but it did move the debate in the direction that the SAI had advocated since its inception in Columbus in 1911. Citizenship for American Indians was complicated, as birthright citizenship and the sovereignty of Indigenous nations came into conflict. Also complicating the issue was the position of the Indian Office and some in the SAI, especially the Associates, of earned citizenship, or a path to citizenship by the process of becoming "civilized" or "competent," as the Indian Office called it. The SAI members were in agreement on the granting of citizenship, but there were major disagreements on the best process for acquiring citizenship. Montezuma led the group that advocated for birthright citizenship—the immediate granting of citizenship to all American Indians based on birth in the United States. Parker and others took a moderate view that citizenship should follow the government settling its legal responsibilities to tribes and individuals while Indians acquired the education and skills to cope with modern America and thus became able to protect their economic resources and compete with other members of society. For those advocating birthright citizenship, the assumption was that citizenship would end federal guardianship and control over Indian resources, but this was not to be the case.

The issue was also complicated by the history of American citizenship. The basis for citizenship was contested, in the words of historian Eric Foner, between the ideals of citizenship based on liberty, equality, and democracy, yet tied to racial and ethnic criteria, such as enslaved persons born in America who were not considered citizens. The latter became ingrained in the Naturalization Act of 1790. Congress restricted the naturalization process to "free white persons." Upon the writing of the Constitution, Indians were considered part of sovereign nations and thus outside the jurisdiction of the United States. However, as Native nations were brought under the jurisdiction of the federal government, citizenship was not extended. The Civil Rights Act of 1866 declared that anyone born in the United States was considered a citizen (making former slaves citizens), overturning the Supreme Court *Dred Scott* decision of 1857 ruling that African Americans, free or enslaved, could not be citizens. The 1866 law was the basis for the Fourteenth Amendment (1868) to the Constitution, which established birthright citizenship. Section 1 states that "all persons born or naturalized in the United States, and subject to the jurisdiction thereof, are citizens of the United States and the State wherein they reside"—the key word being "jurisdiction." The language of the Fourteenth Amendment was specifically meant to exclude American Indians, as they were members of quasi-sovereign nations. As the reservation system was established and American Indians came under direct federal authority, they were under the guardianship of the United States, without citizenship rights.[16]

Once the reservation system was established, the government developed its programs to "Americanize" the Native population. The explicit view, informed by social Darwinian theory, as described earlier, was that American Indians, as primitive and uncivilized people, were not eligible for citizenship until they were shorn of their tribal ties and cultural practices. Then, and only then, as "competent" individuals, could they be granted citizenship. There were precedents that were ignored for incorporating people from new territories into the United States as citizens. In 1803, when the United States acquired the Louisiana Territory, European residents of that territory, mostly living in New Orleans, were granted all the rights of American citizenship. It was the same with the Mexican-American War. The Treaty of Guadalupe Hidalgo (1848) declared Mexican residents of the new territories American citizens. This did not apply to Indians in the land conquered from Mexico. The treaty referred to Indians in these territories as "savage tribes," with no mention of rights.

The government developed its plans for Americanization in the 1870s, leading to the General Allotment Act (Dawes Act) of 1887, which sought to destroy Indian communal life and tribal structures by dividing reservation land into 160-acre parcels to a head of a family and 80-acre parcels to an individual, with the remaining land sold to non-Indians. With the allotment, citizenship was granted; however, other conditions had to be met. The law read, "Every Indian born within the territorial limits of the United States who has voluntarily taken up, within said limits, his residence separate and apart from any tribe of Indians therein, and has adopted the habits of civilized life, is hereby declared to be a citizen of the United States." The parcels of land were then held in trust for twenty-five years, after which the allottees were given a fee patent, declaring unrestricted ownership. Within the next four decades, approximately 150 million acres of reservation land was reduced to less than 50 million acres. The goal was to replace a communal lifestyle with an individualistic, Anglo American lifestyle. The Dawes Act, one of the most devastating government policies, remained the law until 1934. Some Department of Interior officials believed that the allotment process was too slow. In response, Congress passed the Burke Act of 1906, which amended the Dawes Act. Charles Burke, a congressman from South Dakota and future commissioner of Indian affairs, proposed that allottees who were declared "competent" by the secretary of the interior be awarded a fee patent and citizenship immediately. This still was not birthright citizenship—it was earned citizenship, even though Indians were born on American soil.

Between the Dawes Act and the Burke Act, there was a significant Supreme Court decision that impacted birthright citizenship. In 1898, the court ruled (*U.S. v. Wong Kim Ark*, 169 U.S. 649) that based on the Fourteenth Amendment, the children of Chinese immigrants born in America were citizens. However, the court excluded American Indians from their ruling, who were thus excluded from birthright citizenship. This was partially based on an earlier Supreme Court case (*Elk v. Wilkins*, 112 U.S. 94). The court concluded that the Fourteenth Amendment excluded American Indians from citizenship. Following the Burke Act, the process of declaring Indians "competent" progressed slowly. In 1913, Franklin Lane, the new secretary of the interior, was under pressure from settlers who wanted access to more land. Once an individual received a fee patent, they could sell or lease the land. Many Native Americans living in poverty sold all or part of their land only to find themselves in a short time penniless and landless. For example, in 1913 the superintendent of the Yankton Agency in South Dakota reported that 75 percent of those who received a fee patent had already sold their land. The indiscriminate issuance of fee patents and subsequent loss of land led Secretary Lane and Commissioner Sells to establish three competency commissions. In 1915–16, they traveled from reservation to reservation to examine the competency of individuals. This process speeded up the granting of fee patents. Historian Francis Prucha put it aptly when he said they "pursued the termination principle with a vengeance." Individuals applied for a fee patent by filling out a questionnaire asking about education, business experience, use of intoxicants, and why a fee patent is being requested. The expected answer to this last question was to say that you wished to sever all ties with your tribe. The superintendent then made a written recommendation to the commission that declared "competency." If an individual was declared "competent," he or she was expected to participate in a public citizenship ceremony, symbolizing one's rejection of the past and entrance into a new status as an American citizen. The citizenship ceremony was part of the government's long-range goal of assimilating American Indians into an Anglo American lifestyle.[17]

The first of such ceremonies by the Competency Commission was on the Yankton Sioux Reservation in 1916. The Indian Office believed, incorrectly, that the Yankton were well on their way to full acculturation. The ceremony was a public ritual as well as a public relations event to showcase the success of federal policy. In May, Franklin Lane, the secretary of the interior, traveled to the Yankton Reservation in Greenwood, South Dakota, with reporters and a camera crew, to conduct the citizenship ceremony himself. The applicant stood with the secretary, who said, "I hand you a bow and arrow. Take this bow and shoot the arrow." Lane continued, "You have shot your last arrow, that means you are no longer to live the life of an Indian. You are from this day forward to live the life of the white man." Lane continued on, giving the applicant a purse, symbolizing the need to save money, and an American flag, for recite an oath of allegiance to the United States. The ceremony was repeated for almost 150 individuals. The Indian Office considered this a great success. In reality, it was a dismal failure. By the time Lane arrived in Greenwood, most of those receiving fee patents had made arrangements to sell their land to non-Indians.[18]

It is unclear if President Parker supported the Competency Commissions, but he did support declaring individuals competent. He offered an alternative path to citizenship in which Indian students in public schools or Indian schools were educated to become citizens and, after graduation at age twenty-one, were granted citizenship. Parker still did not advocate birthright citizenship. In the name of the SAI, he asked Congress to clarify the issue, reminding them that they had never stated in any legislation that the ultimate goal for the American Indian was citizenship. He recommended that Congress do so—declaring all Indians who held allotted land, were slated to be given allotted land, or had received a fee patent as citizens, with said land subject to taxation. As part of his explanation, he wrote, "The tribe should not be considered; the individual should. . . . Citizenship should come as a matter of course as tribal organization disintegrates. The tribal break up should come when the Government pays its bills to the tribe and settles its legal obligations."[19]

Congress was not ready to pass a citizenship bill; however, the stellar war record of American Indians in Europe and the strong support for the war effort at home helped build pressure toward citizenship. The SAI focused on this patriotism to bolster their case for citizenship. In addition, President Wilson's language on self-determination for all colonized peoples and the similar Paris Peace Conference declaration on self-determination added pressure on Congress to declare citizenship for American Indians. Congress had already established citizenship for members of the so-called Five Civilized Tribes and the Osage in Oklahoma. In November 1919, Congress passed the Indian Veteran's Citizenship bill, offering citizenship to every American Indian who served in the military during the war and received an honorable discharge. Several citizenship bills were introduced in Congress, including one by Representative Carter of Oklahoma, still an SAI vice president. His bill stated that "every Indian born in the United States is declared a full citizen." The SAI supported this bill, but with concern over a contradiction in the bill, pointed out by Dr. Eastman, that some Indians who were supposedly not competent would still have their property administered by the Indian Office. One could be a citizen and still be under the guardianship of the government. Historian Tom Holm (Cherokee, Muskogee Creek) labels these contradictory and inconsistent citizenship policies as part of a larger source of confusion in Indian affairs. None of the proposed bills called for outright citizenship for all Native Americans. By 1923, an estimated two-thirds of American Indians were already citizens by one means or another. Without significant controversy (except those who saw it as a violation of their sovereignty), on June 2, 1924, the Indian Citizenship Act was passed, asserting that all Indians born in the United States be issued certificates of citizenship. The bill also resolved a major concern—that the granting of citizenship would not impair "the right of any Indian to tribal or other property." Unfortunately, citizenship did not guarantee one's civil rights, such as voting or being free from federal guardianship. In 1916, the Supreme Court had ruled in *U.S. v. Nice* (242 U.S. 591) that Native individuals who acquired citizenship through receiving an allotment could simultaneously be under the guardianship of the federal government. The majority decision stated that "citizenship is not incompatible with tribal existence or continued guardianship, and so may be conferred without completely emancipating the Indians or placing them beyond the reach of congressional regulations adopted for their protection." The Indian Citizenship Act of 1924 did not alter this, giving citizenship a hollow ring, especially since virtually every state with a significant Indian population placed restrictions on voting. In addition, the new law changed little on the reservations. Poverty and poor health remained endemic, and land loss continued. Nevertheless, the new law provided a platform to continue the fight against the government in a never-ending struggle for self-determination. Given these severe limitations on citizenship, why did the SAI choose this issue as a primary focus when there were many other pressing issues? Citizenship issues were part of the Progressive Era. There was a broad movement or struggle as immigrants were on a path to citizenship, African Americans were struggling for citizenship rights, and the women's suffrage movement was fighting for political equality. The pervasive belief was that citizenship and voting provided a better life through reducing or eliminating guardianship. The SAI pursued citizenship based on this belief. Hoxie describes it as "The Good Citizenship Gun," as the SAI believed that citizenship status would provide access to legal equality and political power.[20] But however one views the granting of U.S. citizenship, it did not end government guardianship over American Indians.

## Annual Conferences, 1917–1918

During the spring of 1917, Parker was overwhelmed with planning for the fall conference in Oklahoma City. He was appointed an adjunct marshal during the draft in New York State, serving in the 100th Regiment of the New York National Guard, in addition to his everyday job at the New York State Museum. Many SAI members also had war-related responsibilities. Parker wondered if an effective conference could be held with the nation at war. Yet there were other reasons than the war for postponing the conference. Parker feared for the future of the Society, as a disastrous conference or an underattended conference would hurt its reputation. As far as he could ascertain, only three members of the executive committee planned to attend. He also believed that there were forces, which he did not specify, attempting to undermine the SAI. He told Bonnin that "there are influences at work that spell harm not only to the Society but to the future of the race." He wondered why other organizations he belonged to flourished while the SAI floundered. He added that he was "between the millstones of those who hear [listen to] the Bureau and those that hate the Bureau." Under these difficult circumstances, the conference was canceled. In his next editorial, Parker wrote that the "weaknesses of our own Society have existed because there was too much a belligerent spirit and even personal animosity."[21]

Amid the internal dissension, Gertrude Bonnin took a more active role in SAI leadership and helped plan the 1918 conference. She was appointed to *AIM*'s editorial board and used her influence to publish a "Special Sioux Issue," with a photograph of Chauncey Yellow Robe on the cover. In this same issue, Parker, still editor, made his sharpest attack yet on the Indian Office, which may have been influenced by Bonnin and the continual attacks by Montezuma in *Wassaja*. Parker referred to the "evils of the reservation system, the failure of a paternal policy and the incompetence of the Bureau itself." He also made reference to incompetent and crooked superintendents. He titled his editorial "Break the Shackles Now—Make Us Free." It must have pleased Montezuma, as he often used prison metaphors to describe reservations. In advocating for closing the Indian Office, Parker pointed out, "We are not advocating the abandonment of the legal and moral obligations of the Government."[22] The remainder of the issue covered Sioux schools, treaties, soldiers who served in the war, and a listing of successful Sioux men and women to counter the nineteenth-century public image of the Sioux warrior. There were also extended essays on Bonnin and Eastman. Bonnin was referred to as the most remarkable living Indian woman, and Eastman was proclaimed the "greatest Sioux of the century." In praising Eastman, the article pointed out how he linked the past and the present. Eastman believed that one could adjust to the modern world without giving up one's moral base. He had written previously: "I have never lost my Indian sense of right and justice. I am for development and progress along social and spiritual lines rather than those of commerce, nationalism or material efficiency. Nevertheless, so long as I live, I am an American." There was a concerted effort to get Eastman back into the Society. Eastman was expressing a view held by many SAI members that one could adjust to the new world without giving up the old.[23]

With the 1917 conference canceled, Bonnin and Parker planned for a special February meeting to discuss legislative issues and to ensure the continuity of the Society. Bonnin sent invitations to the Executive Council and Advisory Board to meet in Washington for a two-day conference. However, prior to the Washington meeting, there was a "friends of the Indian" meeting in Philadelphia sponsored by the Indian Rights Association, who believed Indian issues were being ignored amid wartime concerns. It was attended by members of various "friends" groups, such as the YMCA, the Lake Mohonk group, and missionary organizations. Many SAI members attended. It was a who's who of Associate members, such as General Pratt, Fayette McKenzie, R. D. Hall, Samuel Brosius, Mathew Sniffen, and Herbert Welsh. Arthur Parker, now SAI president, presided over the meeting. The Philadelphia gathering demonstrated the symbiotic relationship between the SAI and these "friends" groups. There was not total agreement on policy issues, yet they saw the need to coordinate their work. Parker gave the major address outlining his more recent stand against the Indian Office. He argued that the Indian Office must release its grip on the Indian people. He did not call for abolishing the Indian Office but said it should limit its activities to fulfilling treaty and contract obligations. He insisted that Congress either declare all Indians citizens or consider them as candidates to become citizens. He emphasized the "war for democracy," pointing out that the Indian Office's actions were not consistent with democratic ideals. He reiterated complaints against the Indian Office but wondered if American society was also to blame for the nation's focus on material acquisition at the expense of spiritual values. He asked why society had allowed the American Indian to be plundered and why such autocratic policies existed in an alleged democratic nation. He concluded that while the United States was in a war to make the world safe for democracy, democracy must be also made safe for American Indians. Other speakers, such as R. D. Hall and General Pratt, offered their thoughts on the "peyote menace." Hall said that peyote was destroying the "sacredness of the family tie," as Indians were being drugged into oblivion. The final recommendations called for the passage of the Carter Code bill, the passage of the Hayden bill (to criminalize the use of peyote), the punishment of federal employees who abused their positions on reservations, the hiring of thousands of Indians as workers to fill the wartime labor shortage, and finally, in order to increase the responsibility of the individual Indian, the severance of "tribal relations" by closing the tribal rolls and distributing communal funds to individuals, granting citizenship to all allotted Indians. This last point was stressed very strongly by the Associate members. The resolutions indicated the policy differences between Active and Associate members.[24]

Bonnin and Eastman drew up a program of reports and speeches for the February business meeting in Washington. President Parker gave the opening address, followed by the vice president's reports and an open discussion of the SAI's work on the behalf of Indian welfare. The remainder of the conference was filled with talks by General Pratt and Parker's talk on "The Attitude of the American Indian in the World's War." The highlight of the conference was the appearance of Dr. Eastman, who had been estranged from the Society. His return to the SAI was mostly thanks to longtime friend Gertrude Bonnin, now the Society's main lobbyist.[25] The large number of attendees in Washington was related to the upcoming congressional hearings on the use of peyote. Many SAI members were scheduled to testify. It was also recommended that the next conference be held in Pierre, South Dakota, in the center of Sioux country, again thanks to Bonnin. There was some debate about trying Oklahoma City again, but Delos Lone Wolf, now a member of the Advisory Board, warned Parker against it because the Peyote community in Oklahoma was upset with the SAI over its stand against peyote. Bonnin agreed that the Society should not hold a conference in peyote country. Parker agreed with Pierre as a conference site and wrote to Bonnin, encouraging her to get in touch with people in South Dakota and invite them to the conference. The choice of Pierre was also supported by Montezuma, who despite his criticisms wanted a strong organization to do effective lobbying on behalf of Native people. He encouraged all to attend.[26]

By the spring of 1918, Parker decided not to seek reelection to the presidency. He was overworked, frustrated, and suffering from lingering health problems. Bonnin wrote to Parker, suggesting he try to talk Eastman into accepting the presidency. Parker wrote a melancholy letter to Reverend Moffett, chair of the Associates, lamenting that he should never have accepted the nomination for the presidency. He did so at the request of friends, he said. He claimed he did not have enough time or funds to do the job and that he spent too much of his own money on the Society, and as a result, he did not have the funds to attend the next conference. He said he would resign immediately if one of the vice presidents would accept the office. He suggested Roe Cloud or William Kershaw, but said Bonnin wanted Dr. Eastman.[27] With Parker reducing his work for the Society, including stepping down as the editor of *AIM*, others had to plan for the upcoming conference. Bonnin, Eastman, Pratt, and McKenzie collaborated to develop a program. Parker continued editing *AIM* (6: 1918) through the summer. He edited issues 1 and 2, and then passed the editorship to Bonnin. Most of the material in the 1918 issues was devoted to the war effort, with photographs of American Indian soldiers on the cover of three issues. Parker continued to encourage full cooperation with the war effort at home by being thrifty with food, money, and clothing, and working hard to produce. He wrote, "Your laziness is the Kaiser's best encouragement." He also made special mention of those in the Society who were in the military. For example, John Oskison, a longtime SAI member, was a lieutenant in the U.S. Army in command of a machine gun company. Both Bonnin and Parker emphasized American Indian involvement at home and abroad in the war effort, hoping it would influence Congress and public opinion on the citizenship issue.[28]

During the summer, Bonnin sent out a conference announcement, choosing "Indian Patriotism, Production, Progress" as the theme. In order to finalize the arrangements, Bonnin arrived in Pierre several days before the opening. She told the press that President Parker could not attend because he "is in military service." This was not exactly the truth, but she would not publicly discuss the Society's internal problems. This seventh annual conference was the most poorly attended yet, with only twenty-five to thirty Active members and several Associates; however, Pierre residents attended many of the programs. The focus of the conference was citizenship, as most speakers discussed strategies for achieving this goal. City officials gave the SAI a warm welcome and invited them to use the capitol building and the

**Figure 15** SAI spent time and energy trying to convince America of American Indian patriotism in World War I. The Great War issue of *American Indian Magazine* 6, no. 1 (1918).

Pierre Opera House as conference sites. The conference received front-page coverage in the local press, and a number of local officials spoke, including Governor Norbeck of South Dakota, welcoming the delegates to the *former* home of the great Sioux tribe. Montezuma gave several speeches. He focused on the politics and patronage of the Indian Office, pointing out that many of its employees had large salaries that would be eliminated if it was abolished. He praised the loyalty of Indians for their voluntary response to the war effort and argued that the American Indian ought to be granted full citizenship immediately. A line of speakers, both SAI members and local officials, followed. Gertrude Bonnin spoke briefly, calling for the rights of citizenship and the same educational advantages that were offered to white youth. Henry Standing Bear, one of SAI's founders, told the story of how difficult it was for him to acquire a decent education.[29] The following evening at the St. Charles Hotel, Chauncey Yellow Robe, always an entertaining presenter, spoke on Indian patriotism. The explicit goal of the conference was to link patriotism and loyalty to the granting of citizenship. Yellow Robe told stories of the valor and bravery of the Indian soldiers fighting in France, giving examples of several who died in the service of America. He was followed by Matthew Sniffen of the Indian Rights Association, who also called for citizenship. He had just returned from travels through Oklahoma, New Mexico, and Arizona, visiting reservations, and described the miserable conditions, especially the lack of health care and the tuberculosis epidemic. Reverend Coolidge also described the founding of the SAI. He told the audience how he came to Columbus, Ohio, as a child only to return later, invited by Dr. Mc Kenzie's to help establish the Society.[30]

The next night, at a very crowded Pierre Opera House, Montezuma began his speech with "I am an Apache," but he assured the audience that he was perfectly tame. Now that he had their attention, he told his life story, detailing his mother's death; his capture and sale to a white man for thirty dollars; his education, from public school to medical school; and becoming a practicing physician in Chicago. He ended with a strong plea for citizenship. A local reporter wrote that his talk was so real that you could picture a "helpless little Indian boy." He was followed by Bonnin, who appeared on stage in full regalia and read a poem, "Song of the Ogallalas [*sic*]," which she had written in 1898. Reverend Sherman Coolidge spoke again and, not to be outdone by Montezuma, told the story of his youth, his adoption at age four, and how he was named after General William Tecumseh Sherman. He focused on the war effort and the thousands of Indian men in the military, along with the thousands of men and women who supported the war effort at home. He said the Society was proud of its work in the defense of the flag. He concluded by asking the audience if after the war you are going "to make democracy safe for the Indian."[31]

One of the highlights of the conference was another powerful speech by Montezuma with the dramatic title "Abolish the Indian Bureau." It was a long speech, beginning with a history of the quest for "the rights of man," which the United States was presently fighting for in Europe. He said the barrier to civil rights for Indians was the Indian Office, with its seven thousand employees, with "fat salaries" and patronage. He asked, How could the American people tolerate the tyranny of the Indian Office? While Indians supported the war at home and abroad, they were "caged on small tracks of land called Indian Reservations." He took a strong stand on every issue, claiming that the trouble with the Society was that they all too often "stood on neutral ground." He detailed a litany of government abuses and in his conclusion demanded, "Give us citizenship, O America people! Give us freedom. Oh you boys in blue! The Indian Bureau defies law, divine as well as human. It defies the Constitution of the United States. It defies justice, and most of all it defies the righteous object of this world-war, namely freedom, equal rights, for all. Humanity. Democracy." He ended dramatically with "My country tis of thee. Sweet land of liberty."[32]

The conference speeches and platform indicated a significant turn to more strident language against the Indian Office and demands for citizenship. The platform called for the immediate abolition of the Indian Office, something Montezuma and Pratt had advocated since the founding of SAI, which was now supported by a large majority of the leadership. Parker's absence from the conference was significant, as he represented a less strident voice in calling for a moderate approach to the Indian Office. He believed it did not help to alienate federal officials. He never agreed with Montezuma's approach or style.[33] The platform also included strong support for the war and extolled American Indian loyalty. Other parts of the platform again included a demand for a definite legal status and a call for quality education. The election of officers marked a changing of the guard. Parker was gone; Eastman was back in. Even though Eastman was not present, he was elected president. He was supported by Bonnin and Montezuma. Reverend Philip Gordon was elected vice president, Bonnin was secretary-treasurer, Reverend Coolidge was chair of the Advisory Board, Henry Roe Cloud was vice president of education, and Congressman Carter was vice president of legislation. Montezuma was quite satisfied with the platform and the election. After a history of criticizing the Society in *Wassaja,* he now supported it in his editorials. He praised the new officers and encouraged people to join the Society.[34]

Several days after the conference, Bonnin wrote to Parker describing the election, informing him that he was elected the general editor of *AIM*; however, if he declined the position, Bonnin would become the editor, according to a vote by the members. Bonnin also told him that Dr. Eastman, the new president, appointed a board to approve all articles for the Society's magazine. Parker responded by complimenting Bonnin's work for the Society, but he would not accept the editorship due to the new "committee of censors," which would make it difficult to get a publication to press, with all the back-and-forth of mailing drafts of articles for approval. He added that while he could continue, he felt it was best if Bonnin "grip the editorial reins." Parker continued backing away from the Society, as he had been doing for the past year.[35] As the general editor, Bonnin appointed Montezuma and Gordon to the editorial board. In her first editorial, she emphasized the themes of patriotism and loyalty as a basis for Indian citizenship. Writing with a flair for words, she said "American Indians are watching democracy, baptized in fire and blood overseas." She argued that the battle for democracy abroad should be brought home—a theme she expanded on in 1919 as the Paris Peace Conference was under way. Much of her rhetoric was similar to W. E. B. Du Bois in his analysis of African Americans in the war, such as the Harlem Hellfighters, who fought in the trenches in France yet suffered segregation, violence, and racism at home.

Sniffen and Moffett also wrote to Parker, describing their assessment of the conference. They reported an overall harmonious conference. They mentioned that Father Gordon arrived on the third day and that he and Montezuma did most of the talking and took control of the voting. In terms of voting, Eastman received nine votes and Coolidge received five. They wrote, "You [Parker] were not even nominated." For vice president, Gordon received twelve votes and Coolidge received two. Sniffen and Moffett were unhappy with the election but decided to accept it, hoping that the Society would get back on its feet (although Moffett resigned as chair of the Associate members). They also expressed a growing concern among the Associate members who were expected to attend the conferences at their own expense and support and fund the Society, but without a voice in its policies. This chasm with the Associate members hurt the Society. Parker had worked very hard developing a cadre of influential non-Indians to help impact federal policies, influence public opinion, and change the public image of American Indians.[36] The growing split between Active and Associate members had always been a concern. Both groups supported citizenship but for different reasons. Associate members believed citizenship would lead to full assimilation; Active members believed they could better control their own lives and have more power as they moved away from federal tutelage toward self-determination.

## The Peyote Controversy

One could make the case that up until 1916, the SAI was on an upward swing and that 1917–18 was a turning point, leading to a downward spiral and the SAI's ultimate demise in 1923. Parker gave the Society a degree of continuity as secretary-treasurer and editor. The journal was published regularly, dues notices were sent out, correspondence was answered, and conferences were planned. With the exception of his one-year presidency, he maintained stability with set principles and goals, although few of the goals were actually realized. In 1918, and again in 1919, there were major leadership changes, resulting in previous officers pulling back or even withdrawing from the Society. The Peyote controversy added to this downward spiral.

The Indian Office was thwarted in its campaign to criminalize the use and possession of peyote. In 1918, it renewed its efforts to convince Congress to pass such legislation. The OIA lobbied Congress to hold public hearings on the issue and made a concerted effort to get as many prominent individuals to testify against peyote as possible. This culminated in two years of intense activity by the Indian Office and secular and sectarian organizations to build public opinion and pressure Congress. During these two years, Congress made its first attempt to criminalize peyote. The Indian Office also hoped to gain support from the courts; however, it was not forthcoming. In cases where arrests were made, charges were dropped or guilty verdicts were dismissed. Even when reservation officials arrested Peyotists, the Indian Office had to order them released since they did not have the authority for such arrests, as no laws were broken. Nevertheless, pressure was building to do something about the "mescal craze," and thus a legislative solution was sought. Various Christian churches and humanitarian organizations were alarmed. These groups exerted pressure on Congress to pass a law prohibiting peyote. "Friends of the Indian" groups such as the Women's National Indian Association, the Indian Rights Association, and the Lake Mohonk Conference supported such a law. They believed their attempts to "save the Indian" by "civilizing" and Christianizing them were threatened by the Peyote faith. These and other groups published a steady stream of anti-peyote literature. Herbert Welsh, president of the Indian Rights Association, issued a pamphlet with an alarming title, "Peyote—An Insidious Evil." He claimed that connecting peyote to religion was just a pretense for drug use. The most active organization in the anti-peyote campaign was the Lake Mohonk Conference. They worked closely with the SAI in their anti-peyote efforts. In their 1914, 1915, and 1916 conference reports, they used inflammatory language such as "peyote menace" and "mescal fiends." They added that "thousands of our Indians are now peyote drug fiends." They called on the U.S. Congress to outlaw peyote. Yet they realized the dilemma of this position when one member pointed out that as a religious practice, the Peyote faith fell under the protection of the Constitution of the United States.[37]

Up to this point, there were many attempts to stop the use of peyote, but they all failed. In 1914, the Indian Office began its campaign for a legislative prohibition. Two years later, Representative Harvey Gandy, as described in chapter 4, introduced the first such bill in the House of Representatives. It was also introduced in the Senate. Support for the Gandy bill came from the Department of the Interior, Christian denominations, reform groups, and some American Indian converts to Christianity. These groups issued significant anti-peyote literature, some of which made its way into the media, such as Gertrude Seymour's article "Peyote Worship: An Indian Cult and a Powerful Drug." Despite the nationwide campaign, the Gandy bill failed in 1916 and again in 1917, but in 1918, as the nation focused on the World War, the anti-peyote forces coordinated their activities in a final push to convince Congress to criminalize the use or possession of peyote.[38]

Throughout 1917, Bonnin and several other SAI members increased their lobbying and were part of a full-scale assault on Peyotism. There was much dismay that the Gandy bill failed in 1916, but proponents knew it would be reintroduced in 1917. Bonnin and Parker corresponded frequently, discussing strategies. Bonnin made copies of her writings on peyote, including her "data," and mailed them to several individuals. She told Parker, "Peyote! We dread peyote," adding that she felt they had gone too long doing nothing. She sent Parker the names of Ute Peyotist leaders and accused the superintendent of the Uintah-Ouray Agency of tolerating peyote usage because he may have accepted a bribe. She also described her campaign to enlist Mormons and Episcopalians in the struggle against peyote, lobbying the Utah and Colorado legislatures. She was able to enlist the support of the Women's Christian Temperance Union and the Anti-Saloon League to lobby the Colorado legislature. Both states passed laws to prohibit peyote, as did Nevada.[39]

Parker wrote an inflammatory piece for the Society's magazine, "The Perils of Peyote Poison." He described peyote as poison, citing several extreme accusations that it was a dangerous drug and an extreme narcotic, that it had caused the death of several adults and poisoned several babies, and that peyote users were impoverished and had lower moral standards. Parker was now fully committed to the anti-peyote campaign. Why did Parker now advocate such an extreme view? Did he really believe in the so-called evils of peyote, especially since there were Peyotists around him in the SAI, or was this an opportunity to gain support from the Associates, sectarian organizations, and the Indian Office? It would seem the latter is the case, as Parker believed such support would benefit the SAI. At the same time, Bonnin moved to Washington and actively lobbied Congress to support the Gandy bill. She met with Representative Gandy to coordinate their efforts. Despite their lobbying, the Gandy bill failed again; however, the anti-peyote groups persisted and redoubled their efforts for 1918.[40]

## Congressional Hearings: Criminalizing Peyote

The Indian Office requested Carl Hayden, a highly respected representative from Arizona, to reintroduce the anti-peyote bill in the House of Representatives. The Hayden bill (HR 2614) was slightly different from the previous Gandy bill. It did not directly outlaw peyote but sought to revise the liquor traffic laws to include peyote as an intoxicant. Supporters of the bill called for extensive hearings in order to build a case against peyote. A three-person subcommittee, chaired by Representative Robert Tillman of Arkansas, of the Committee on Indian Affairs, conducted the hearings in February and March 1918. It was in this atmosphere of prohibition and suppression that Oklahoma Peyotists considered incorporation as a strategy they hoped would give them First Amendment protection. The intensity of the assault on peyote was heightened by the growing fear that the Peyote faith was spreading throughout the West. A wide array of spokespersons gave testimony on both sides of the Hayden bill. The Indian Office submitted a lengthy document to the committee, providing a long legal history of federal responsibility for controlling intoxicants on reservations, hoping to add peyote to the list. The plan to use the courts to control the dissemination of peyote was not working. Testifying in favor of the bill were government scientists, missionary and church groups, humanitarian organizations, and medical doctors. Opposing the Hayden bill were several ethnologists from the Bureau of American Ethnology, scientists and doctors, and American Indians who were Peyotists and several who were not but supported the Peyote faith.[41]

Many groups and individuals submitted supporting documentation at the hearings, including the Board of Indian Commissioners, the Anti-Saloon League, the National Women's Christian Temperance Union, the YMCA, the National Congress of Mothers and Parent Teachers Associations, and the Bureau of Catholic Indian Missions. Representatives from the Indian Rights Association who had been working closely with Parker also testified. This was by far the most determined attempt to pass a federal law prohibiting the use of Peyote. During the hearings, a long list of prominent individuals was arrayed on both sides of the issue. Representative Hayden began the testimony by stating that he had reintroduced the bill at the request of the Indian Office. He submitted two encyclopedia articles on peyote and hashish for the record. Interestingly, the article on peyote did not describe it as a dangerous, habit-forming drug and claimed that "it effectively checks tendencies toward alcoholism." This was not what the Indian Office wanted to hear. Brosius, from the IRA, followed with his testimony. He pointed out that he had no firsthand knowledge of peyote but would submit letters from reservation doctors testifying on its harmful effects. He claimed that calling it a "religious ceremony" was a pretext for drug use. He also requested the article "Ravages of Peyote" be added to the *Congressional Record*. Brosius was asked by Representative Snyder of New York about Delos Lone Wolf, a longtime SAI member and Peyotist, who (along with his wife) had just visited Snyder. He asked Brosius to account for Peyotist Lone Wolf as "an intelligent man, and his wife [who seems] to be a hardy, healthy, and intelligent woman." Brosius said that peyote did not adversely affect Lone Wolf because he was such a strong man—that Lone Wolf was an exception or anomaly. The next witness, Fred H. Daiker, from the Law and Order Division of the Indian Office, challenged the idea that peyote reduced alcoholism. He brought an envelope full of peyote buttons to show the committee what they looked like. He also submitted a list of affidavits on the deleterious effects of peyote. Many of the documents were written by SAI Associate members, such as R. D. Hall of the YMCA; Father Ketcham, director of Catholic Indian Missions; and William (Pussyfoot) Johnson. What was significant for the opponents of the Hayden bill was that none of the Associate members who testified for the bill had ever attended a peyote service.[42]

As the anti-peyote forces amassed their arsenal of evidence and testimonials, the peyote community, led by James Mooney, an ethnologist from Smithsonian's Bureau of American Ethnology, began the defense. As a government employee, Mooney angered the Indian Office and the anti-peyote groups, as they viewed him as a threat and a traitor. He was a major factor in the conflict between the Indian Office and the Bureau of American Ethnology over federal Indian policy. He was already well-known for his study of the Ghost Dance movement and had been studying and participating in peyote meetings since 1891. Mooney had argued for almost three decades that peyote was not harmful and that Peyotism was a genuine American Indian religion that deserved First Amendment protection. Because of his experience and knowledge, some of his colleagues nicknamed him "Indian Man." He gave the lengthiest testimony of the hearings, followed by vigorous questioning. He was not associated with the SAI, but he knew many of the individuals and several years earlier had written to Marie Baldwin, who had invited him to participate in an SAI conference. He declined the invitation, citing poor health, but added that the "organization seems to hold the promise of good for the Indians, if it can secure the cooperation of the intelligent full blood leadership."[43] Mooney presented a history of the Peyote faith, a description of the peyote cactus (he also showed the committee his own sample of peyote buttons), explained how peyote was harvested and sold, and gave a detailed account of a peyote ceremony. He attacked Bonnin before she even testified, hoping to weaken her credibility and raise doubts about her authenticity. His comments about her were based on a long interview she gave to the *Washington Times*, which included a photograph of her wearing traditional regalia. His testimony against her was high drama. He pointed out that although she claimed to be Sioux, her regalia was not Sioux. Her dress was from a southern tribe, she wore a Navajo man's belt, and ironically, she was holding a peyote feather fan. He said that she had never attended a peyote meeting, nor had she ever tried peyote. Mooney's comments about her clothing during the hearings and her later admission that she never attended a peyote service were embarrassing—but not as embarrassing as the misleading newspaper article that Mooney presented. Mooney brought in a copy of the article and asked that it be entered into the *Congressional Record*. He pointed out that, contrary to the article, Bonnin had never been a student at Carlisle and Sitting Bull was certainly not a relative of hers, as she had claimed. Mooney denied her accusations of orgies, or any other type of immoral activity, and defended peyote as a curative for alcohol addiction and its use for medicinal purposes. He stated that peyote could have medicinal value like quinine, reminding the committee that quinine, originally used by Indians, was condemned by the Spanish. He said it was untrue that peyote renders one physically impaired or mentally incapable. He claimed that peyote was not something one took habitually: "Men who drink liquor drink generally whenever they can get it. . . . The Indians use this [peyote] in connection with their religious ceremonies." He asked the committee to look at the Indians in the hearing room waiting to testify and see if they are physically or mentally degenerate. In the end, Mooney's dynamic testimony, peppered with sarcasm and insult, did not impress the committee. They questioned his assumptions and ultimately did not accept his arguments.[44]

Gertrude Bonnin was the key witness for the anti-peyote group. It was hoped that as a prominent American Indian, she would carry extra weight in testifying for peyote prohibition. She already was the center of attention as a result of the *Washington Times* article. Four days before the congressional hearings began, Bonnin, aware of the impact of public opinion on the hearings, agreed to an interview with the *Washington Times* (February 17, 1918, Sunday edition). The headline read, "Indian Woman in Capital to Fight Growing Use of Peyote Drug—Mrs. Gertrude Bonnin, Carlisle Graduate, Relative of Sitting Bull, Describes Effects of Mind Poison." In the article, Bonnin claimed extensive knowledge of peyote as she saw it spread among the Utes. She claimed that peyote was the same as alcohol and that a belief in its powers was superstition. She appeared before the House subcommittee wearing the same regalia as in the newspaper photo. This was not unusual for her, as she explained to Parker that she used "Indian dress" to attract attention as a "drawing card." During the hearing, she continued her vigorous attack on the use of peyote and proceeded to describe the supposed horrors of using it. She said when outsiders such as Mooney or La Flesche attend peyote services, they are prearranged to seem benign. She denied that Peyotism was an Indian religion and claimed her personal knowledge of peyote use led her to raise charges to combat the peyote culture of intoxication and wild orgies that involved men, women, and children. She claimed that peyote use had caused thirty deaths among the Utes, and she linked peyote to increased alcohol abuse, warning that if it was not stopped immediately, peyote would spread like "wildfire" and be introduced into the white population. Then, in an angry tone, she expressed her disbelief at the idea that peyote should be given constitutional protection. She submitted an article she had written for the *Congressional Record*: "Peyote Causes Race Suicide." In her final statement, she called peyote "the twin brother of alcohol and first cousin to habit-forming drugs." Bonnin then played the race card, pointing out that James Mooney was white and she was Indian; thus she was in a better position to know the truth about peyote. She was a creditable, intriguing, and dynamic witness. Her testimony helped carry the day for the Hayden bill. Mooney was accurate in his testimony about peyote usage, but he was overbearing and too combative for the committee members to accept his views. The day after her testimony, Bonnin wrote to Parker, telling him "It was some fight" and that Mooney had made lame arguments. However, one significant flaw in Bonnin's argument was that she had never attended a peyote service, whereas Mooney had attended dozens. Bonnin's biographer, Lewandowski, refers to her campaign against peyote as a "divine mission." In examining her motives, he claims she had "good intentions" and that her motives were to protect Indian interests in general and specifically to protect young women from "sexual predation." This assertion is not examined herein, as anyone with knowledge of Peyote services would know that this is a spurious argument. It also points to another anomaly in Bonnin's arguments: If the peyote prohibition became law, it could only be enforced by the federal government. This ran contrary to Bonnin's continual assertion that the government should not control Indian lives; in fact, she wanted the Indian Office abolished.[45]

**FIGURE 16** Zitkala-Ša (Gertrude Bonnin), outspoken advocate for American Indian citizenship and cultural autonomy, as indicated by her traditional attire. Courtesy of the J. Willard Marriott Library at the University of Utah.

Dr. Eastman was also a significant witness during the proceedings. He was one of the most well-known Native Americans of his era, as a noted author and a well-traveled lecturer. His testimony contrasted with Bonnin's high energy level; he was calm and moderate in his tone but not his words. He was one of the SAI founders and soon to be its president and fully supported the Hayden bill. He believed the Peyote faith was a step backward for American Indians and that defending Peyotism on religious grounds was a falsehood. He claimed that calling it a religion was a subterfuge for drug use and that it was not an Indian faith, comparing it to the "ghost-dance craze," which he claimed "was gotten up by irresponsible, reckless and unprincipled people." He claimed that due to peyote use, some of the brightest young people from Indian schools were ruined, with no moral stamina. He also disagreed with the previous commentary on Lone Wolf—that despite what was said, peyote had made him "an old man in body and mind." Eastment warned that peyote was a dangerous substance and should be prohibited by law. Given his medical background and creditability, it was difficult to ignore his testimony.[46]

General Pratt, the most important non-Indian spokesperson for the Hayden bill, followed Eastman. He was well-known to the committee as an enemy of the Indian Office and the Peyote faith. He stated that he opposed the work of the Smithsonian's Bureau of American Ethnology, as they, and especially Mooney, encouraged traditional ceremonies. He denied any direct knowledge of the harmful effects of peyote, offering only hearsay, but he wanted to challenge the testimony of Mooney. He claimed that Mooney and the Bureau did nothing but print vast volumes of useless books, adding that "it was well established at the time of the ghost-dance craze among the Indians that white men were its promoters if not its originators. That this peyote craze is under the same impulse." He added that Mooney's testimony, as well as that of Francis La Flesche, could not be trusted since they were guilty of leading Indians back to the past. When asked directly about peyote, Pratt replied, "I am absolutely against peyote." Mooney responded immediately and rebutted Pratt's attack on ethnologists as staging ceremonies, particularly on Pratt's accusation that he had staged a sun dance. It was a testy exchange of views.[47]

Several other federal government employees testified against the Hayden bill. William E. Safford, an economic botanist from the Department of Agriculture who had previously written about the "Peyote Gardens" and the harvesting, drying, and sale of peyote, had claimed that there was no problem with ingesting peyote, except in excessive amounts. He added that even excessive amounts of coffee were bad for you. He reaffirmed what Mooney had said—that peyote was not habit forming and that nothing immoral occurred during peyote services. He said he foresaw much harm to American Indians if peyote was taken away. Dr. Truman Michelson, an ethnologist from the Bureau of American Ethnology, had attended a peyote service among the Northern Arapahoe. He testified that he saw nothing unusual. He did not support the Hayden bill but recommended further study.[48]

All of the Peyotists who spoke at the hearing confirmed Mooney's testimony. Most of them were Peyotist leaders (usually referred to as *roadmen*) in their communities and prominent in their own right. Attorney Thomas Sloan was a longtime SAI member, who had served on the first executive committee in 1911, with a brief stint as president and first vice president, and would soon be elected president again. He said he was familiar with peyote among the Winnebago (Ho-Chunk), Yankton and Rosebud Sioux, Ponca, and among his people, the Omaha. He added that it had turned drunkards into sober people and that some of the immorality stories come from "old time medicine men" who were opposed to the new faith. Two of the most impressive Native speakers were Fred Lookout (Osage) and Francis La Flesche, an ethnologist in the Bureau of American Ethnology and coauthor of *The Omaha Tribe* (1911). Lookout, a Carlisle graduate, was a prominent religious and political leader of the Osage nation and a lifelong defender of the Peyote faith. He was principal chief of the Osage for twenty-six years and a roadman in the Peyote faith. He claimed that peyote was not harmful and was only used in church services to pray to God. He said it stopped the use of alcohol, and he referred to peyote as "medicine," a term all Peyotists used. When asked how many Osage were members of the Peyote faith, Lookout replied, "Most all full-blood members." La Flesche, who had been attacked by Pratt, gave a lengthy and moving testimony. In addition to being a noted author and a government employee, he was the only Native speaker who was not a Peyotist. He had never tried peyote but had attended peyote services. He said he watched as peyote spread among his people. He gave a very dramatic testimony on how peyote reduced alcoholism on his reservation. He said, "I have a respect for the peyote religion, because it has saved my people from the degradation which was produced by the use of the fiery drinks white people manufacture." He also said he had heard all the horror stories before but saw none. He inserted a letter into the testimony he had written to the Lake Mohonk Conference group, telling them that if peyote was harmful, "many of my best friends and relatives would be dead—or in an insane asylum." Speaking as an attorney, he said that the right to worship as one pleases is protected by the Constitution.[49]

After all the hearing ended, the subcommittee voted to support the Hayden bill. Their last action was to release a twenty-four-page report, "Prohibition of the Use of Peyote." It reaffirmed Bonnin's assertion that peyote was dangerous and that the Peyote faith was a cover for narcotic use. The report also included her paper "Peyote Causes Race Suicide." The chair of the subcommittee, John H. Tillman of Arkansas, concluded that Peyotism should not be defended on religious grounds. The bill was sent to the Committee on Indian Affairs, which voted in support and passed it on to the full House, which also voted in the affirmative.[50] Bonnin continued to lobby for the Hayden bill, as it had yet to be voted on in the Senate. She sent a long letter to President Wilson, encouraging him to support the Hayden bill. She added a litany of the charges against peyote usage and included a copy of the bill and a list of organizations that supported it, such as the National Women's Christian Temperance Union and the General Federation of Women's Clubs. She sent a similar letter to Commissioner Sells. Before the Senate voted, Bonnin continued to lobby for the Hayden bill. She produced and distributed a brief pamphlet titled "The Menace of Peyote." She used the same alarmist language—that with peyote "in their midnight debaucheries there is total abandonment of virtue." Her lobbying did not affect the outcome in Congress, but it did impact several state legislatures. Thirteen western states criminalized the possession and use of peyote. The congressional hearings on peyote, specifically the verbal clash between Bonnin and Mooney, have received a questionable interpretation by Bonnin's biographer. Lewandowski clearly sides with Bonnin, calling Mooney ethnocentric, racist, and having "assimilative imperatives," accusing him of calling Peyotism a crude imitation of Christianity. Mooney did not say that in his testimony. He gave a very accurate description of Peyotism and the spiritual services associated with it, referring to it as a "regular religion" that deserved constitutional protection. Bonnin's alarmist declarations that Peyotism is immoral and leads to orgies and degradation are indicative of an individual who never even attended a peyote service. She soon left the SAI but continued the anti-peyote campaign for the remainder of her life. Her biographer asks why she was so adamant about this cause: his answer is that she truly believed that it was socially and physically damaging to the Indian people. The historical record does not bear this out.[51]

Several months after the hearings, Mooney wrote an unfriendly letter to Parker, pointing out that of the twenty-odd people who testified for the

Hayden bill, not one had ever attended a peyote service. He added that "it is well-known among the tribes that a large portion of the S. A. I. is Indian only by remote ancestry or otherwise out of touch and knowledge of the Indian people as represented by their Chiefs and tribal delegations to Washington." He also said the linking of alcohol and peyote is either ignorant or a deliberate misrepresentation.[52] In July 1918, before the Senate voted on the Hayden bill, Mooney returned to Oklahoma, fearing the worst. He visited many of his old friends among the Comanche, Kiowa, Wichita, and Caddo. Knowing of his testimony, they gave him a warm welcome. However, he received hostile treatment from reservation officials. They saw him as a threat and wanted him removed from Oklahoma. Fearing an outright prohibition of peyote, Mooney concluded that the incorporation of the Peyote religion as a duly constituted church was the only way to secure constitutional protection. In August 1918, Peyotists from Oklahoma met in El Reno to draw up a charter. Mooney was at the meeting and recommended they organize, choose officers, and pick a new name. It was Mooney who supposedly recommended the name "the Native American Church." The articles of incorporation included the new name, an organizational structure, a governing body, and a clear articulation of peyote as a holy sacrament. The delegates agreed to the name "the Native American Church," as it was intentionally all-encompassing. Also "Native American" implied that it was an Indigenous faith. The term "Church" was chosen specifically with the belief that this would give them the protection of the free exercise of religion clause in the First Amendment. This was significant since the Senate had not yet voted on the Hayden bill. The document was signed by ten prominent Peyotists, including several who had attended SAI conferences. Delos Lone Wolf, an SAI member, was elected to the Board of Trustees. The document was submitted to the state of Oklahoma for incorporation, which was granted on October 10, 1918. This made it more difficult for the supporters of the Hayden bill.[53]

Mooney's role in the incorporation of the Native American Church was not well received in Washington. The superintendent at Anadarko, Oklahoma, wired the commissioner of Indian affairs, requesting that Mooney be removed. The commissioner ordered the Smithsonian to remove him, charging him with obstructing administrative policies and being detrimental to the peace and welfare of the Indians. On November 12, 1918, Mooney left Oklahoma. The anger against Mooney was intense. Gertrude Bonnin wrote to General Pratt, asking him to use his influence to have Mooney removed from government service. In 1919 and 1920, Mooney asked the Indian Office to grant him permission to return to Oklahoma; he was denied.[54]

The testimonies at the House subcommittee hearings were often fiery and acrimonious, especially the exchanges between Mooney and Bonnin. Aside from their intensity, the hearings were also interesting in another way. American Indians spoke on both sides of the issue, non-Indians spoke on both sides of the issue, and SAI members spoke on both sides of the issue. Government employees and expert witnesses were also divided. The only groups that consistently supported the Hayden bill were the SAI Associates, the non-Indian humanitarians, and the missionaries, who believed they were acting in the best interests of American Indians. After the House of Representatives passed the Hayden bill, it was met with difficulty in the Senate. The two senators from Oklahoma, under pressure from their own constituents, persuaded their colleagues not to support the prohibition of Peyote. They argued it was a First Amendment, religious freedom issue and were able to convince a majority of senators not to vote for the bill. The bill failed, and a federal prohibition of peyote was not enacted into law. Many individuals and groups inside and outside the government were unhappy with this turn of events. The Indian Office did not accept this defeat. Throughout the 1920s, they continued to promote additional legislation and also sought other means to suppress the use of peyote, such as encouraging state legislatures to criminalize the possession of peyote.

The peyote controversy deepened the fissures within the SAI. It also weakened the SAI's image in several western reservation communities, especially where the Peyote faith was expanding. It was one of the leading factors in the demise of the Society. Other consequences of the SAI's policy positions, such as confusion over citizenship and abolishing the Indian Office, alienated almost all Associate members and had a negative effect on the Society's reputation. All this hindered the SAI's plans to increase its membership, funding, and influence. By 1919, the SAI was a much-weakened organization.

# CHAPTER 6

# The Final Years

*1919–1923*

The Society of American Indians did not suddenly collapse or vote itself out of existence. Its demise was slow and punctuated by several attempts to revive it. There was a significant change in leadership in 1918 with the election of Dr. Eastman as president, succeeded by Thomas Sloan the following year. Attendance at conferences became sporadic, funds were in short supply, membership declined, and the Society had little contact with reservation communities. Members who were not happy with the turn of events began to leave the organization, opening the way for more controversial leadership, some with partisan political agendas.

Most telling, in regard to the Society's demise, was its decision to cease publication of the *American Indian Magazine*. Since 1913, it had been an expression of the Society's philosophy, ideals, policies, and goals. It had been a source of information and communication, a forum for debate, a tool to recruit members and raise funds, and a vehicle to put American Indian issues before the American public. Parker had hoped the success of the magazine would lead to the success of the Society. The last issue appeared in August 1920. By the early 1920s, the stalwarts of the organization were no longer involved. Parker backed away in 1918, Bonnin and Eastman withdrew after the 1919 conference, and Roe Cloud resigned from the Advisory Board. Competing organizations also emerged. Society members were recruited by the Tepee Order of America (TOA), which had been established in 1915, and the

American Indian Association, established in 1922. There was not an official SAI conference in 1923, although the remaining SAI members attended an American Indian convention in Chicago and proceeded to elect officials for 1924, but to no avail.

## Eastman's Presidency: 1919

With new leadership, a new *AIM* staff, and newfound energy and enthusiasm, the SAI could have rebuilt itself into a more effective entity. Eastman began his presidency with an optimistic letter to friends and fellow members. He called attention to the reorganization of the Society and the major change that occurred with the new leadership. He wrote, "The mass of the Indian people and many leaders would not co-operate with us while there remained any suspicion of a controlling influence on the part of the Indian Bureau," pointing out that at the 1919 Pierre conference, the vote to abolish the Indian Office settled this concern. His goal, he wrote, was to free the Indian from bondage by granting full citizenship. Eastman hoped his agenda would bring in more members and more donations.[1] The leadership continued to use *AIM* as it had in the past. Editorials, papers by members, commentary on local issues, and reprints of articles that reflected the SAI's policies were intended to gain public support for the Society. For example, Bonnin reprinted a harsh anti-peyote statement by Dr. Harvey W. Wiley of the Federal Bureau of Food Sanitation and Health. He had just appeared before a Senate committee to testify in favor of reintroducing legislation criminalizing peyote, asking why peyote was still unregulated when the U.S. Constitution had been amended to control alcohol. He concluded with a rhetorical question: If there is a peyote church, will there be an alcohol church, a cocaine church, a morphine church, a tobacco church? While some SAI members were slowly backing away from the peyote issue, Bonnin continued her attacks. Now, as the general editor, she had a platform. She had support from Eastman, who added his wife Elaine (the only non-Indian), Montezuma, and Father Gordon to the editorial staff. Elaine Eastman, fluent in Dakota, had considerable experience with several Sioux groups in South Dakota. She was a significant source of support for Bonnin, whose editorials were direct and blunt, calling for access to the U.S. Court of Claims, full citizenship, and support for Montezuma's continuing effort to close the Indian Office. She reprinted his 1918 speech, "Abolish the Indian

Bureau," where he used President Wilson's language about the Great War—"make the world safe for democracy."[2]

In the continuing struggle for citizenship, Eastman and Bonnin used the power of the pen to foment public awareness. They used an argument similar to the one Parker used in reference to President Wilson's pronouncements on democracy. The Paris Peace Conference in 1919 was also a prime opportunity for the SAI, as colonized communities from around the world were demanding self-determination. Bonnin used the magazine to focus on events in Paris, which she said provided an unmatched opportunity to make the case for citizenship. In her editorial, she said there never was a more opportune time as when the eyes of the world were focused on the Paris conference to grant the "little peoples" of the world self-determination. She added: "Immortal justice is the vortex around which swing the whirl of human events! . . . The Red man asks for a very simple thing—citizenship in the land that was once his own." Bonnin included Eastman's essay "The Indian's Plea For Freedom" in the same issue. He proclaimed that it was time for "little peoples" to plead for their rights, as this opportunity might never come again. As part of his critique of Western civilization, he commented on the hypocrisy of Christians, a common theme for him: "Christ has been preached in vain. His unequivocal teachings have been overwhelmed by excess of material development and social injustice." Eastman's request was direct: "All we ask for is full citizenship." He followed with an assessment of Native contributions to American civilization, such as friendship, toleration, dignity, and sincerity; moreover, he stated that the basic principles of America's Articles of Confederation either unconsciously or knowingly were from the Iroquois League of the Six Nations and the Sioux Confederacy. He believed that Indigenous values could benefit America.[3]

Eastman's presidency was beset by many personal and professional difficulties. Just after his election, his second daughter passed away during the influenza epidemic. The SAI faced financial restraints and internal dissension; however, he was determined to make a success of his presidency and make the Society more effective. He hoped to build public support for citizenship and the abolishment of the Indian Office. In January 1919, along with General Pratt, Gertrude and Raymond Bonnin, Roe Cloud, and Parker, Eastman attended another annual gathering of "Friends of the Red Men," as it was now called, in Philadelphia. These annual events, planned by the Indian Rights Association, were important to the Society leadership. They provided a venue for publicizing their views and policy goals. They were attended by many important community leaders and were usually covered by the press. The agenda was education, legislation, religion, and support for the Carter citizenship bill and the Hayden anti-peyote bill. The speakers focused on American Indian participation in the war as an argument for citizenship. However, the resolution they passed called for less than full citizenship. Citizenship was granted to all war veterans; others could acquire citizenship only after demonstrating fitness for assuming such responsibilities. Mrs. Bonnin took the opportunity to continue her assault on the Peyote faith, now incorporated as the Native American Church (NAC). She described it as hindering the progress of the "red race," comparing peyote to hashish, cocaine, and strychnine. At the end of the Philadelphia conference, the resolutions supporting the Carter and Hayden bills were forwarded to the commissioner of Indian affairs. It would be difficult to assert that attending these events advanced the agenda of the SAI. They generated some publicity but not much else.[4]

In May 1919, Eastman, along with Father Gordon, the new vice president, and Montezuma, undertook an extensive lecture tour through Wisconsin to build support for the abolition of the Indian Office and the granting of full citizenship. They believed these two issues could unite all American Indians. They were also seeking new members and new contributions, hoping that they could garner support from church groups. At the same time, Montezuma was pushing for unity through editorials in *Wassaja*, indicating that there was no excuse to miss the next conference, now that the war was over. He was concerned about the perception of the SAI's connection to the Indian Office, as some believed it was controlled by the government. He reminded his readers that this rumor was unfounded, since the Society voted to abolish the Indian Office. He asserted that the Society works for the Indians, not the Indian Office, and emphasized the Society's independence: "We are able to take care of ourselves without the crippling aid of the Indian bureau." He recommended that each tribe send at least one representative to the eighth annual conference in Minneapolis.[5]

In August, Bonnin sent out the conference announcement, which included the theme: "American Citizenship for the Indians." She requested that each person prepare a ten-minute presentation on living conditions in their locality, with suggestions on how to remedy injustices. The conference was better attended than most of the earlier ones. The local press reported about two hundred in attendance (one paper said three hundred), representing almost one hundred different Native groups (a later report indicated twenty-five groups). The total was swelled by local people, especially local Ojibwe and Sloan's supporters, wanting to defend the Peyote faith. Many of the past, present, and future officers were there: Montezuma, Gertrude and Raymond Bonnin, Reverend Coolidge, Father Gordon, and James Irving and Theodore Beaulieu (Ojibwe), who was soon to be elected vice president. The conference theme on citizenship presented a potential for unity but became very contentious, as there were varying options for implementation. The conference included an unusual event, in which Society members marched in a parade "in full war paint and feathers," something that would not have been considered appropriate at earlier conferences. The idea was that a display or performance of so-called Indianness would attract attention to the SAI's messages.[6]

President Eastman, attending his first annual conference since 1911, called the conference to order with an inspirational speech about American pride. He asserted that he was proud to be American and asserted the American identity of all Indians: "We are Americans." He pointed out that America gives aid to other countries, so why not share a little at home to help Indians get on their feet? "We want strong people, not weaklings and beggars." He reminded the audience of Indian contributions to America, pointing out that "we Indians had freedom, equality and democracy before white people came." He added that, even with full citizenship, Indians should retain their time-honored characteristics and traditions that had contributed so much to American culture. He closed with a flourish: abolish the Indian Office, respect treaties, and grant full citizenship. It should be pointed out that Eastman's statements about Indians being "proud" Americans were always paired with accompanying comments on the values of Indian cultures. Bonnin followed with an uplifting, high energy speech, calling on all to stand up, organize, and find new members. She reiterated Eastman's call for the preservation of traditional values and to be proud of one's "Indian blood."[7] Reverend Coolidge, the honorary president, followed with a speech on the founding of the SAI. He described a meeting he had held many years prior with brothers Charles and John Eastman to discuss the establishment of an Indian organization. He retold the story of how he, Eastman, and Montezuma were invited to Columbus in 1908 by Fayette McKenzie to give a series of lectures at The Ohio State University. He reflected on how out of this gathering came a plan to start a national organization composed of Indians of all tribes. The remainder of the conference focused on Eastman's theme: "We were born free, we want to be free now."[8]

The citizenship debate was divisive. Associate member Robert Hall recommended citizenship for all veterans, yet he used language that implied that nonveterans were incapable of exercising citizenship. Sloan responded angrily, asking why only veterans proved capable, since it is a "universal rule of civilization that one is a citizen in the country in which one is born." Sloan proposed endorsing the Carter citizenship bill, but that was confusing, as Eastman pointed out that it was not a clear-cut proposal for birthright citizenship; however, he still supported it. Others spoke about going slowly, particularly Henry Fielder (Sioux), a Hampton graduate; he and others asked about the elderly, who needed protection. Montezuma interrupted Fielder, who retorted that one should not interrupt when someone is speaking and promptly walked out. He returned later to finish his speech. Montezuma spoke again with his usual flair, describing the Indian Office as fat and getting fatter on Indian money. The heated exchange continued, framed by the legal question of who was a U.S. citizen. Eastman's answer was clear: if you do not have control of your money, you are not a citizen. At this point, individuals spoke at will, interrupting each other and not following any order. Montezuma spoke again, accusing the Indian Office of "criminally" ruining American Indians. He explained that "on reservations Indians sleep, eat, gamble and loaf." The debate ended with confusion and dissension. Sloan withdrew his resolution, and thus the conference with the slogan "American Citizenship for Indians" could not produce a resolution with a unified voice on citizenship.[9]

However, the conference attendees all seemingly agreed with Montezuma's plea to abolish the Indian Office. A resolution was introduced: "A calm and dispassionate study of past and present results of all government activities with reference to the American Indians, discloses a long line of gross injustices and overwhelming failures and mismanagement with attendant results of physical and moral degradation of the Indian peoples." It concluded: "Be it resolved that immediate and most urgent plan be formulated by this Society for the speedy abolition of the Indian Bureau, root and branch, thereby establishing the American Indian in normal citizenship." After the resolution was read, a reporter wrote, "Two hundred Indians sprang to their feet with hilarious shouts reminiscent of their ancient tribal war cries." The resolution passed unanimously. Five SAI attorneys were appointed to go to

Washington to deliver the resolution to Congress: three were longtime SAI officers, Thomas Sloan, William Kershaw, and Dennison Wheelock, along with Judge Robert Allen, tribal attorney for the Creek/Muskogee of Oklahoma, and Arthur Beaulieu.[10] In the next issue of *AIM*, Bonnin included all the arguments in favor of abolishing the Indian Office.

On a sad note, a resolution was passed to commemorate the passing of Angel De Cora Dietz, February 1919, age forty-eight. She had a long struggle with respiratory issues and fell victim to the influenza epidemic. She had been a member of the SAI since its founding in 1911, serving on the Advisory Board from 1912 to 1915. She was beloved by almost everyone in the SAI and was especially close to Dr. Eastman, his wife Elaine, and Gertrude Bonnin, who was at her bedside at the end. Bonnin made the funeral and burial arrangements. De Cora was a dedicated teacher, lecturer, and artist, and a strong voice for the inclusion of Native arts in Indian boarding school education. She chaired the Art Department at Carlisle, 1906–15. She also influenced the American arts and crafts movement. The last months of her life were devastating. Her husband, on trial for draft evasion, divorced her in November 1918, and her sister Mary died the following month, struck by influenza. A photograph of De Cora graced the cover of the *AIM*, and Elaine Eastman wrote a touching eulogy and a poem, "Indian Love Song." De Cora's famous painting *Fire Light* was reproduced in the magazine. She left three thousand dollars from her estate to the Society.[11]

On the next to last day of the conference, SAI members put on a pageant that was open to the public, selling tickets for twenty-five and fifty cents. It was another strategy to gain attention and to awaken the public to the plight of American Indians. President Eastman wrote the play *The Conspiracy of Pontiac*, depicting Chief Pontiac's eighteenth-century rebellion against British colonialism. The drama was an obvious metaphor for the present struggle against U.S. settler colonialism. Eastman played Pontiac, and Montezuma played a medicine man, with a cast of SAI members who wore traditional clothing, sang, and danced. The nine-scene play was done in pantomime, with a synopsis read to the audience before each scene. In closing, Bonnin thanked the audience and said the play was a plea for citizenship. She also made an important plea to "Chiefs and Headman" to do all they could to hold on to a land base. She said, "For the sake of our children's children we must hold onto a few acres," an argument that many SAI members had been making. She was very aware of the so-called citizenship ceremonies on the

Yankton Sioux Reservation and the subsequent loss of Yankton land. This event clearly illustrates Redmond's analysis of clothing and resistance—in particular, the wearing of traditional regalia as an anti-colonial statement. The performance by SAI members, with song and dance in Native regalia, was also a display of resistance. The message of the performance was clearly anti-colonial.[12]

Elections were held on the last day of the conference. There was a dramatic unexpected shift in leadership, which in hindsight doomed the SAI. The election of officers was chaotic. Sloan, with twenty-five votes, bested Eastman and Raymond Bonnin (Gertrude's husband), with eight votes each. Eastman moved that the election be made unanimous. Montezuma was nominated for vice president but declined. Father Gordon, with Sloan's support, nominated Theodore Beaulieu, the editor of the *Tomahawk*, for vice president. Sloan nominated Mrs. Bonnin to continue as secretary-treasurer, but she declined. Her husband Raymond was nominated for the same position, but he also declined. More confusion arose as Montezuma recommended that the elected officials just appoint a secretary-treasurer. Eastman opposed the idea. Bishop was then nominated for the position and declined, but he changed his mind and was elected as the new secretary-treasurer. Other elected officers included John Carl, from Minnesota, vice president on membership; James Irving (Sioux) editor of the *Woodstock News*, vice president on education; and U.S. Representative Carter, one of the original SAI members, reelected as vice president for legislation. Some longtime members were appointed to the Advisory Board, such as Parker and Roe Cloud; however, they no longer played an important role in the Society. The confusion, if not chaos, over the election was such that only one resolution was passed. The election of Sloan put the peyote issue on the sideline. It was barely mentioned throughout the conference, even though the Indian Office was still lobbying Congress for restrictive legislation. One of the most devastating blows to the future of the Society was the failure to choose a general editor for the SAI's magazine. Bonnin was no longer interested. The fall of 1919 was her last issue as editor. Eastman and Montezuma were nominated for the position, but both declined. The magazine ceased publication after one final issue. It was a great loss for the Society. Eastman and Bonnin disengaged from the SAI, with Eastman feeling that it was now too political, as Sloan was campaigning to be appointed commissioner of Indian affairs. Sloan believed the Republicans would win the presidency, so he publicly supported Warren Harding. Previous leadership had taken great care to avoid any openly political stance.[13]

## The Sloan Presidency

Sloan was a well-known attorney on Indian legal issues. He had met with and advised various Indian groups and had often appeared before congressional committees. However, he had a difficult task ahead of him in trying to rebuild the Society. There were significant problems, but none more serious than the absence of a national publication. Montezuma still published *Wassaja,* but it had less circulation and clearly was his editorial voice. From 1919 on, he became less strident toward the SAI, still hoping for a revival of the organization, but he remained extremely hostile toward the Indian Office. His editorials were direct and focused: abolish the Indian Office. His theme was strong and consistent: "A reservation Indian has no rights. He is a ward. His rights are in the hands of the Indian Bureau." The last two years of *Wassaja* featured a new masthead (figure 17) depicting an older Indian in a pillory labeled "The Work of the Indian Office" while another Indian saluted the sun as a sign of hope and freedom. How influential was *Wassaja*? It is difficult to assess. It appeared monthly, containing editorials, information about the SAI, correspondence from readers, and items about reservation conditions. It was now the only public voice of an SAI member, but Montezuma had enemies, as his stance on the Indian Office had alienated some. Despite his editorials and persistence, there was little consideration within the federal government of abolishing or even weakening the Indian Office. On the other hand, there was a widening audience for declaring American Indians citizens—something Montezuma had been advocating for decades.

The Sloan administration published one last issue of *AIM* 7, no. 4 (August 1, 1920), with a revised format, style, and content, with President Sloan as editor-in-chief. Sloan had grand ideas about a refurbished magazine. It was still referred to as the "The Official Publication of the Society of American Indians," with a new staff of associate editors, mostly non-Indians, including Frederick W. Hodge, anthropologist and editor of the *Handbook of American Indians North of Mexico.* Sloan and his staff envisioned a high-quality literary and artistic publication equal to *Harper's, Collier's,* or *National Geographic.* Their proclaimed purpose was to impress upon serious-thinking Americans the problems that affect American Indians. The revamped pub-

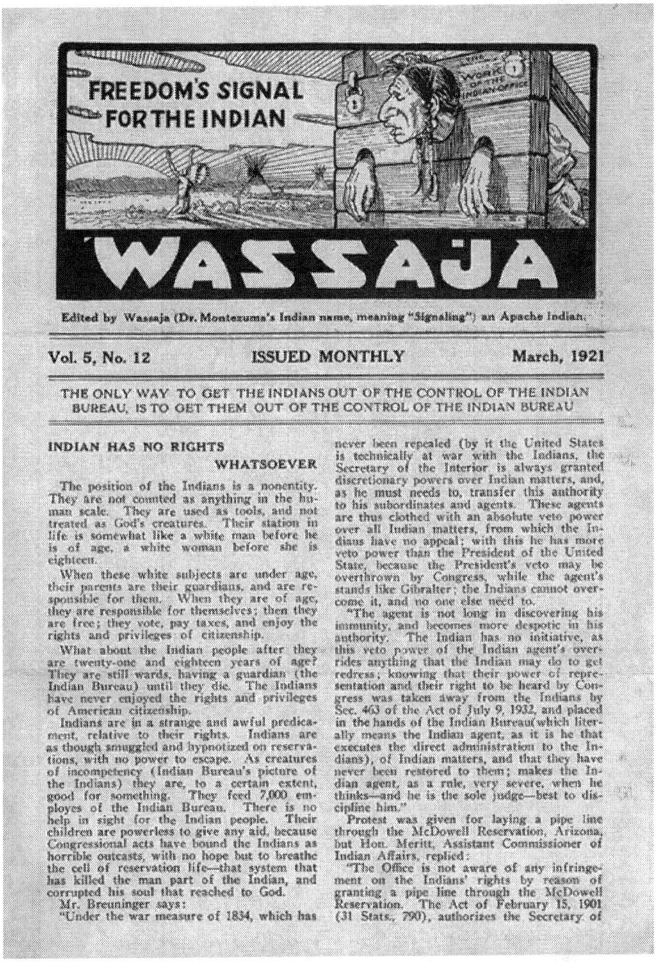


WASSAJA

Edited by Wassaja (Dr. Montezuma's Indian name, meaning "Signaling") an Apache Indian.

Vol. 5, No. 12 ISSUED MONTHLY March, 1921

THE ONLY WAY TO GET THE INDIANS OUT OF THE CONTROL OF THE INDIAN BUREAU, IS TO GET THEM OUT OF THE CONTROL OF THE INDIAN BUREAU

**INDIAN HAS NO RIGHTS WHATSOEVER**

The position of the Indians is a nonentity. They are not counted as anything in the human scale. They are used as tools, and not treated as God's creatures. Their station in life is somewhat like a white man before he is of age, a white woman before she is eighteen.

When these white subjects are under age, their parents are their guardians, and are responsible for them. When they are of age, they are responsible for themselves; then they are free; they vote, pay taxes, and enjoy the rights and privileges of citizenship.

What about the Indian people after they are twenty-one and eighteen years of age? They are still wards, having a guardian (the Indian Bureau) until they die. The Indians have never enjoyed the rights and privileges of American citizenship.

Indians are in a strange and awful predicament, relative to their rights. Indians are as though smuggled and hypnotized on reservations, with no power to escape. As creatures of incompetency (Indian Bureau's picture of the Indians) they are, to a certain extent, good for something. They feed 7,000 employes of the Indian Bureau. There is no help in sight for the Indian people. Their children are powerless to give any aid, because Congressional acts have bound the Indians as horrible outcasts, with no hope but to breathe the cell of reservation life—that system that has killed the man part of the Indian, and corrupted his soul that reached to God.

Mr. Breuninger says:

"Under the war measure of 1834, which has never been repealed (by it the United States is technically at war with the Indians, the Secretary of the Interior is always granted discretionary powers over Indian matters, and, as he must needs to, transfer this authority to his subordinates and agents. These agents are thus clothed with an absolute veto power over all Indian matters, from which the Indians have no appeal; with this he has more veto power than the President of the United State, because the President's veto may be overthrown by Congress, while the agent's stands like Gibralter; the Indians cannot overcome it, and no one else need to.

"The agent is not long in discovering his immunity, and becomes more despotic in his authority. The Indian has no initiative, as this veto power of the Indian agent's overrides anything that the Indian may do to get redress; knowing that their power of representation and their right to be heard by Congress was taken away from the Indians by Sec. 463 of the Act of July 9, 1932, and placed in the hands of the Indian Bureau(which literally means the Indian agent, as it is he that executes the direct administration to the Indians), of Indian matters, and that they have never been restored to them; makes the Indian agent, as a rule, very severe, when he thinks—and he is the sole judge—best to discipline him."

Protest was given for laying a pipe line through the McDowell Reservation, Arizona, but Hon. Meritt, Assistant Commissioner of Indian Affairs, replied:

"The Office is not aware of any infringement on the Indians' rights by reason of granting a pipe line through the McDowell Reservation. The Act of February 15, 1901 (31 Stats., 790), authorizes the Secretary of

**FIGURE 17** Montezuma's continued assault on the Indian Office. Masthead, *Wassaja* 5, no. 12 (1921). Courtesy of the Missouri History Museum.

lication was to be issued monthly, at twenty-five cents a copy, be sold on newsstands, and include advertisements, such as one from the American Indian Film Company, which produced films with negative portrayals of Indians. The publication was printed in a larger magazine-style format, with glossy paper.[14] Despite the new approach, the revised format drew criticism from nearly every quarter. The new issue contained a number of articles by non-Indians, including several anthropologists. It included photographs of Indigenous people in traditional settings, described as "primitive," with *National Geographic*–type articles such as "The Indian and His Horse," by Clark Wissler of the American Museum of Natural History, content that Parker would have never included. (Parker always wanted the focus to be on the "new" Indian.) The publication also included a lengthy biography of President Sloan—almost hagiographic in tone. It pointed out that he was elected president by a unanimous vote, and in accepting this post, he became "the official representative of every Indian in the United States of America." This statement drew much negative commentary and did not help the reputation of Sloan or the Society. In a letter to Pratt, Sloan described the new format and that he hoped to print fifteen thousand copies—ten thousand for newsstands and five thousand for subscriptions. Sloan said if he could finance three issues, there would be enough funds to sustain publication. Unfortunately, it was not to be; subscriptions and sales never materialized. Sloan's attempt at a revamped publication failed; this was the last issue.[15]

One of Sloan's major goals was having an American Indian appointed commissioner of Indian affairs—and, if not him, at least another Native person. James Irving, the new vice president for education, had written to Parker suggesting either he or John Oskison, a veteran of the Great War, as possible candidates, or perhaps one of the two Indian U.S. senators—Charles Curtis, Kansas (Kaw-Osage), or Robert L. Owen, Oklahoma (Cherokee). Irving wrote that the Jews had their Moses and African Americans had their Booker T. Washington—and that it was now time to have a real Indian leader for the next commissioner of Indian affairs. Some considered it contradictory or at least ironic to push for a Native commissioner while calling for the abolishment of the Indian Office. Another Sloan initiative was to lobby Congress to pass legislation encouraging the Indian Office to redress local problems, particularly land sales, leases, inheritances, and uncooperative superintendents.[16] Parker wrote back to Irving, criticizing the leadership for departing from the original purposes of the Society. He added that "the entire tone of the magazine is shoddy and the hysterical wailing of men who are supposed to be educated." With a touch of sarcasm, he wrote, "Since I am not in a position to be of constructive service it ill becomes me to criticize." Wheelock was also unhappy with the new leadership. He complained that he was never consulted about anything, yet they continued to use his name.[17] As former SAI officers were resigning, Sloan turned to General Pratt for support, complaining that Commissioner Sells and Assistant Commissioner Edgar Meritt had been slandering him to members of Congress. His goal was to create strong public opinion to support American Indians. He invited Pratt to the upcoming conference in St. Louis, planning a reunion of Carlisle graduates. He hoped that Pratt's presence would generate publicity, especially if he gave the keynote address. Despite the mounting criticism of his leadership, Sloan had Montezuma's support. They both agreed on the abolition of the Indian Office. However, given Montezuma's recent brush with the FBI, Sloan made it clear that he was very patriotic and not against the United States, only against the Indian Office and its bad policies, while referring to Commissioner Sells as the "Warden of the Indian Reservations."[18]

Sloan made it clear that, although he was a Democrat, he supported Republican Senator Warren G. Harding in the upcoming presidential election. He argued that President Wilson and the Democrats had done little for American Indians. The *New York Times* reported that Thomas Sloan, as president of the Society of American Indians, would visit Senator Harding on his famous front porch in Marion, Ohio. Sloan also reportedly told a Republican official that because some Indians could now vote and were largely opposed to the Wilson administration, they would campaign for Harding. Sloan, with a delegation of more than fifty Indians from twenty-three tribes, met with Harding, who by this time was the Republican nominee. The group included Montezuma, Thomas Bishop, and Father Gordon. They wanted Harding to pledge support for full citizenship for the "first Americans." Harding said his goal was to "bestow ideals, humanity and democracy on America first, rather than waste American lives in forcing these principles abroad." He added, "The American Indian is just as much entitled to a square deal as any one [*sic*] else in the Republic." Montezuma explained how his "people were oppressed and mistreated," and asked Harding to use his influence with Congress to push for citizenship legislation and to give American Indians a greater voice in national affairs. Montezuma said, "I wish to God that you would have the spirit of Lincoln." He then read a pledge he wanted Harding to repeat: "Before I leave my office here at the White House, I will see that the Indians receive their freedom, and that they become equal with all other races that have had the freedom of a liberty-loving country." It is unclear if Harding repeated the pledge. Meanwhile, Montezuma attacked President Wilson, writing in *Wassaja* that his "enthusiastic manifestation of patriotism is all a sham, false and void." After the election, Harding's promise to assist American Indians did not materialize. He appointed Albert Fall as secretary of the interior. Fall displayed harsh attitudes toward Native cultures and facilitated the process of alienating Indian land. He later became embroiled in an oil scandal for accepting bribes, and was tried and convicted of leasing government oil reserves to private businesses. Much to the chagrin of Sloan, President Harding appointed Charles Burke, a former congressman from South Dakota, as commissioner of Indian affairs. Both Burke and Fall were no friends of American Indians. Despite these appointments, Sloan continued to support President Harding. He wrote to Burke, reminding him that the president had promised Indians a "square deal." A policy of alienating Indian natural resources and land by sale or lease to non-Indians continued unabated during Harding's years in office. The Harding administration was partially responsible for the 1920s being a decade of unemployment, hunger, and disease on many reservations. His administration pursued a policy of economic retrenchment and reduced appropriations for health and education—there was no "square deal."[19]

Sloan's visit with Harding, as well as the reformatted magazine, upset many members and certainly contributed to the demise of the Society. Representative Carter, a Democrat, sent a scathing letter to Bishop. He was angry that the SAI would be so blatantly partisan, especially as they distributed political material with his name on the letterhead. Specifically, Carter cited a circular letter with an attachment from the Republican Senatorial Committee with the heading, "Importance of the Election of a Senate that will protect the United States against the Democratic Program of Internationalism." The SAI letterhead, with the name of all the officers and members of the Advisory Board, made it appear as if the SAI endorsed the Republicans. Carter said, "[The SAI] was organized and conducted strictly on nonpartisan grounds, and that its purposes would never be prostituted for political purpose." He asked that his name be removed from the SAI letterhead and that his communication be sent to all who received the "rankly partisan" material. He added angrily, "I cannot afford to be a party to any transaction that drags the Indian's rights into the vortex of politics." Carter, who had worked so long and hard for the SAI, was now quite alienated. Pratt wrote a similar letter to Sloan, describing his disappointment with the new magazine, writing that "the whole force and power of the magazine seems to have been committed into the hands of those who make their living through study and writing upon the alleged past of the race and through exploiting his alleged peculiar qualities." He indicated that if this was the direction of the SAI, he wanted nothing to do with it and would discourage his friends from supporting the Society.[20]

Before the ninth annual conference in St. Louis, there was more bad news for Sloan and Bishop. Henry Roe Cloud, one of the most respected members of the Society and the president of Roe Institute in Wichita, Kansas, was angry over the extremism of Sloan and Montezuma and their open partisanship. He asked to be removed from the Advisory Board, so not to compromise his name or his school with such propaganda. He pointed out that the Society was founded for nonpartisan purposes. Parker also resigned from the Advisory Board. He was already disengaged from the Society, as he was now involved with Iroquois affairs as president of the New York Indian Welfare Society. Bonnin also added to Sloan's problems, as she openly opposed him. Sloan's partisanship also alienated some Associate members. On the other hand, Sloan and the upcoming conference received much-needed support from Montezuma, who used *Wassaja* to encourage friends and members to attend the conference. Montezuma was highly critical of SAI members of significant talent who no longer attended conferences or helped their people. He also praised the SAI, now that it was on the right track. Again, he reassured his readers that the SAI had no connection whatsoever with the Indian Office.[21]

The new SAI leadership and some longtime members, such as Father Gordon, Emma Goulette, Delos Lone Wolf, Dr. Montezuma, and General Pratt, attended the St. Louis conference, which differed from previous meetings in several ways. There was more entertainment, more display of regalia, but fewer papers and speeches. The press went out of its way to photograph and write about the attendees wearing regalia. In its later years, SAI members wore traditional attire more frequently, as a way to attract public attention. Sometimes it attracted so much attention that it distracted from the messages being delivered. Local reporters were fascinated by the contrast between those wearing headdresses, buckskin trousers, and beaded vests versus men wearing tailored suits and women wearing "fashionable gowns." For example, Charles E. Drew (Ojibwe) attracted considerable press attention. He wore an eagle-feather headdress that the press described as a "war bonnet" and a doe-skin jacket trimmed with beadwork. Drew claimed the headdress was the one pictured on the 1899 U.S. silver certificate series of the five-dollar bill. He said the headdress belonged to Chief Hollow Horn Bear (Ojibwe) and was worn by him when he posed for the photo that was engraved for the bill. (The U.S. Treasury claims the likeness is Chief Running Antelope, Sioux.)[22] The conference supposedly opened with three hundred delegates, but the estimate was later lowered to one hundred. Sloan gave interviews to local reporters, telling them that the government was guilty of neglect and the conference would take up specific cases of government abuse. The opening reception was hosted by several professional organizations, including the St. Louis Academy of Science and the Missouri Historical Society. The mayor of St. Louis welcomed all to the city. Sloan gave the opening address, mostly of a historical nature, pointing out that many Indian mounds in the area had been destroyed and the soil used to build beds for railroad tracks. In commenting on the conference, a *St. Louis Globe-Democrat* editorial stated that it was obvious that the American Indian had not vanished.[23]

As at other conferences, General Pratt drew considerable attention from the press. Carlisle Indian School alumni sponsored a reception for the general. Now eighty years old, he still attracted an audience. As a cavalry officer in the Civil War, an "Indian fighter," and founder of a famous Indian school, people were interested in his story. This was also one reason why the SAI wanted his support: he made headlines and usually gave reporters quotable statements. For example, he was quoted as claiming, "The Indian, unlike negroes and Japanese are assimilable." At the reception for Pratt, Montezuma introduced him as the greatest living friend of the Indian. Pratt reiterated his view that the Indian Office must be closed. He maintained that it existed only to provide jobs for its seven thousand employees, and that in "all the years of its existence, I do not believe the Indian Bureau has had one sensible or constructive idea." He added that, based on the birthright clause of the Fourteenth Amendment, it was indisputable that all American Indians should be American citizens. Another troubling factor for the Society was that Red Fox St. James, who now referred to himself as Reverend Red Fox St. James Skiuhushu, began to play a more important role in the Society. In 1915, he had established the Tepee Order of America, a Boy Scout–type organization for Anglo-Protestant youth. Now, in 1920, he changed it into an adult organization for Indians and "friends" of Indians. He hoped to blend it into the SAI—or at least absorb some of its members.[24]

While in St. Louis, Sloan and several delegates were invited to speak at a Women's Exposition being held at the same time as the SAI conference. Sloan and twenty male and female delegates, many dressed in "Indian costume," were greeted by a standing-room-only crowd. Sloan told the women in the audience that since they now had the right to vote, they should help

American Indians get their right to vote as well. He claimed it was only just and fair, since America was possessed by American Indians before Columbus voyaged to the New World. He was followed by a humorous Montezuma, who said, "I have lived in Chicago for fifty years so you don't blame me for being wild." Once he had the audience's attention, he attacked the reservation system. He compared it to slavery: "Indians on the reservations today are held in slavery worse than the darkies used to be on the plantations." The SAI often used women's suffrage and slavery metaphors to argue for citizenship.[25]

Another theme used to build support for the citizenship campaign was to compare the status of American Indians with immigrants. Red Fox, who was vehemently anti-immigrant, pointed out how "foreigners of the lowest class" arrive, find jobs, remain in America for several years, and become full-fledged citizens. With this in mind, why should the original inhabitants of America not have citizenship? In order to stress his point, he focused on Indian loyalty during the recent war, asking the audience if there was even one incident of disloyalty. "The Indian is 100 percent American," he added. Red Fox spoke on several occasions, but the press focused on his Wednesday morning speech. His talk was little more than an anti-Japanese rant. He said that if the "Japs" were allowed to continue immigrating to America, they would eventually take over the Pacific coast. He accused Japanese immigrants of leasing Indian land on the West Coast and dominating various industries, such as lumber mills and fish canneries. He reflected the growing anti-Japanese sentiment in America that culminated in the 1924 Oriental Exclusion Act, prohibiting Asian immigration to the United States. This was just the beginning of Red Fox's anti-immigrant as well as his anti–African American diatribes. America was in an era of intolerance, as the anti-immigrant mood deepened and race relations were at a low point with the revival of the Ku Klux Klan and a firmly entrenched Jim Crow system; however, Red Fox's views did not help the SAI recruit more members. He also took the opportunity to criticize the Indian Office's campaign against traditional dancing. He attacked those who called Indian dancing "wild." He argued that traditional dances were mild and austere compared to the "shaking up and shimmy dances" of American women who "display more paint in ballrooms than the braves going into battle." Other speakers followed up on similar themes of government mismanagement. Especially compelling was a representative from the San Carlos Apache Reservation, who described impoverished conditions, a lack of opportunity, and the Indian Office's refusal to do anything to alleviate the situation. He said he visited the Indian Office in Washington and was told to leave the building or he would be thrown out.[26]

Speaking at the St. Louis Thomas Jefferson Memorial, President Sloan again made the case for closing the Indian Office and full citizenship rights, supporting his argument by reminding the audience of Indian service and loyalty during the Great War. He mentioned individual examples of bravery and heroism by Indian soldiers. He pointed out that he had received support from several members of the House of Representatives and from Senator Seldon P. Spencer, who also spoke at the conference in support of President-Elect Harding's promise of a fair and just settlement for the American Indian.[27] On the next to last day of the conference, SAI members debated resolutions and voted for officers. The Executive Council announced that the Society was applying for a charter in all forty-eight states. A committee of five, chaired by Sloan, was appointed to follow through. They were also instructed to develop new policies for the Society's magazine. The need to expand membership and revive the *American Indian Magazine* was essential. Unfortunately, neither of these proposals was carried out. A number of other resolutions were also proposed, apparently with little disagreement. The first resolution called for the "complete abolishment of the Indian Bureau" and full citizenship for Indians, with copies of the resolution sent to congressional committees and the press. It passed unanimously. A second resolution asked the government to stop taking away people's homes and turning Indian land into reservoirs for power projects without the approval of local residents. A third resolution requested that Indian affairs be administered in such a way as to prevent starvation on reservations, as had happened in the past when Indians died in a land of plenty. The resolution listed the Blackfeet and Crow of Montana, Fort McDowell Reservation in Arizona, Fort Belknap Reservation in Montana, and the Pimas and Maricopas of Arizona as most susceptible to starvation. Sloan was reelected president, and Thomas Bishop was elected secretary-treasurer. One new officer, Robert Hamilton (Blackfoot), was elected as vice president for legislation, replacing Representative Carter, who had resigned. All the other officers were reelected.[28] Unfortunately for the SAI, little came from these resolutions.

One of the highlights of the conference was an evening of entertainment at a local high school. Approximately 2,500 St. Louis residents attended a variety of performances and short speeches. The program included drama, dance, poetry, and song, intermixed with selections by a local high school band. The program opened with "My Country," sung by SAI delegates, some wearing traditional regalia. Montezuma was unhappy with the trend of performing "traditional entertainment" in "Indian garb." He questioned if it did any good for advancing the Society's agenda. Tsianina Redfeather Blackstone (Creek/Cherokee), the famous mezzo-soprano opera star known as "Princess Tsianina," was the evening's featured performer. "Princess" was a common stereotypic term used for female Native vocalists. She began her singing career as a teenager performing in traveling concerts. She always performed wearing traditional regalia. During the Great War, she entertained American troops in France and Germany. Prior to the SAI conference, she had performed at the Metropolitan Opera in New York City. The program described her as a "special entertainer" who had received accolades from American generals. She appeared on stage wearing beaded Native attire and sang her signature song, "From the Land of Sky Blue Water." It is unclear if she was a member of the SAI, but she had attended the Denver conference in 1913. Tsianina continued her musical career for several more decades before retiring. She died in 1985, at the age of 102.[29]

The following morning, a group of SAI delegates visited Monks Mound in Illinois, just across the Mississippi River from St. Louis. They traveled by chartered streetcar, as arranged by the St. Louis Convention Bureau and the Missouri Historical Society. It is unclear how many delegates went to the mound—probably several dozen, some wearing regalia. Monks Mound is part of the Cahokia earthworks complex (today it is Cahokia Mounds State Park, Collinsville, Illinois). The mound, which is terraced, is approximately one hundred feet high; its base is one thousand feet wide, north to south, and eight hundred feet wide, east to west, and it is surrounded by numerous other mounds. The top of the mound is flat, and at one time, a large wooden structure rested on the upper terrace. Monks Mound and Cahokia are part of the vast Mississippian culture complex that reached its apogee between 800 and 1200 CE. Monks Mound is the largest constructed mound in North America and was the center of a vast ceremonial, political, and economic complex, based on a trade network that extended throughout the Mississippi valley and southeastward toward the Atlantic coast. When the delegates reached the top of the mound, three men and three women danced and sang. Dr. Whelpley of the Missouri Historical Society followed with a talk on the history of the mounds. Before departing, a number of delegates sang a Yankton Sioux women's song. This trip was reminiscent of the SAI's 1911 excursion to Pope's Mound (renamed Toepfner Mound), just outside of Columbus, Ohio.[30]

Following the conference, Sloan told reporters that he considered the conference a success. He thanked St. Louis officials for the great hospitality and said he hoped to return the next year. In fact, he said, it was the most successful conference ever and accomplished more than any other conference by beginning a "new era" for Indians, as we worked hard for "complete and unrestricted citizenship," a position now fully agreed upon by Society members. He promised to appear before any congressional committee and meet with any government official who would listen. He was confident and hopeful, and believed the American public was on his side. As a conference, one would have to conclude, it was a success. Attendance was good, the program ran smoothly, resolutions were passed, elections held, and the public entertainment was successful, but it did not solve inherent problems. There was little follow-up to expand membership, and the magazine never appeared again. The increasing role of Red Fox in the SAI was more of an impediment to success rather than an asset. And, most importantly, there was no noticeable effect on federal policies.[31]

As the conference ended, a new problem emerged for the Society. As mentioned previously, Red Fox's organization, the Tepee Order of America (TOA), became a competitor. At their conferences, they focused on Indian lore, songs and dance, and "Indian Ceremonials," as advertised on their flyers. Dr. Eastman was the main speaker at TOA's official opening in 1915. This was not unusual for Eastman, as he had been active with the Boy Scouts and Camp Fire Girls. He became involved because he believed certain Indian values, particularly spiritual values, could modify America's materialism, or as David Martínez had written, "to get the Indian's white brothers to Indianize themselves." Now, in 1920, with a revamped organization and a branch known as the American Indian Tepee Order, Red Fox hoped to attract SAI members. Whether he wanted to blend the SAI into his organization or replace SAI is not clear. It was organized as a fraternal group with a Masonic-type structure and corresponding titles, rituals, symbols, mottos, colors, and a series of degrees. The members were divided into tribes or councils, and clans or bands. Red Fox remained active in both organizations. Membership and leadership positions were open to American Indians and non-Indians, but specifically excluded African Americans. Also, in 1920, as the SAI ceased publishing its journal, Red Fox published his own magazine, *American Indian Tepee.* He included SAI news in his publication and pursued some SAI initiatives, such as calling for a nationwide observance of an Indian Day.[32]

In the months after the St. Louis conference, Sloan faced a number of difficulties. Over the years, he had accumulated several enemies. Some of these hostilities arose from Sloan's assertion that he was the official representative of all American Indians in the United States. Sloan also drew criticism as a result of the demise of the Society's magazine, his earlier support for peyote, his partisan politics in support of Harding in the 1920 election, and unproven accusations of fraudulent activities in the past as an attorney. When it became known that Sloan sought a nomination for commissioner of Indian affairs, the opposition grew. A group of American Indians, including Gertrude and Raymond Bonnin, sent a four-page petition to the secretary of the interior opposing the appointment of Sloan, arguing that his appointment would be an "injustice to the Indians of this country and viciously detrimental to their interests." The petition also pointed out that Sloan had supported the abolition of the Indian Office but now wanted to be its leader. On the other hand, Sloan had supporters. Montezuma gave his full support to Sloan for commissioner of Indian affairs. He editorialized in *Wassaja* to argue for an Indian appointee. He encouraged all to write to their senators, their congressmen, and all the influential people they knew to encourage their support of Sloan. He wrote: "It means wardship or citizenship; it means freedom or slavery." In March, a delegation of twenty-five Indians visited President Harding in support of Sloan; however, he was not under serious consideration by the White House. Charles Burke was soon appointed as the new commissioner. It probably did not help Sloan that Montezuma had written that the Indian Office was an "army of blood-sucking grafters" and that outgoing commissioner Cato Sells was the worst commissioner in history.[33]

With all the problems the SAI faced, some believed it was dead as an organization. Montezuma tried his best to discount that assertion and defend Sloan's leadership. In one of Montezuma's last attempts to revive the Society, he wrote:

> They tell you that the Society of American Indians is dead. It makes "Wassaja" [referring to himself] laugh. Dead? No, never! You may say, "it is dead," but saying it does not kill it. Those that say it is dead are those who never did

> stick to the Society. They are dead, but not the SAI. A society that stands for freedom and citizenship and the abolishment of the Indian Bureau cannot die. You may as well get rid of God as to get rid of the Society. . . . Cease publishing the "Indian Magazine" does not mean that the Society is dead. We admit that the Society has gone through the valley of death, but it is far from giving up the ghost. Some people so hate the President [Sloan] that they would love to see the Society go under. . . . Do not let anybody try to make you believe the Society of American Indians is dead. It is the greatest Indian organization in America. We must join and stick together. It will help you, your tribe, your people, your country and the world.[34]

Another harsh reality that emerged from Sloan's pro-Republican partisanship was that Harding's promise of a "square deal" never materialized. Thomas Bishop, the SAI secretary-treasurer, addressed the issue with Charles Burke the new commissioner. Bishop outlined the reasons why some SAI members supported Harding, noting that the Democratic candidate offered no changes in federal Indian policy. Bishop pointed out that after six months, there were no changes—only unfulfilled promises. He asked why the unpopular Edgar Meritt was still the associate commissioner of Indian affairs. He also asked why so many incompetent and corrupt superintendents were still working on reservations and making life so difficult for those living there. He gave Burke their names and locations. It seemed that little change was forthcoming from either a Democratic or Republican administration. Montezuma proclaimed that President Harding had turned a deaf ear to the Indians. He was correct.[35]

Prior to the 1921 Detroit conference, Montezuma took the opportunity to assess why the SAI was not successful. He wrote that it had gone wrong but could still potentially right itself. He believed the Indian Office was interested in the SAI in the early years, since so many members worked for it. He said it was strange that many Indians would not join the Society because some members worked for the government. There were accusations that the Society was run directly by the Indian Office. He also said there were misunderstandings. Some members believed that the Society could work with the Indian Office; others wanted the Society to have nothing to do with it. He lamented the loss of important people, especially Gertrude Bonnin: "She was the backbone of the Society." He also said it was the same with the loss of the Society's magazine, which was taken over by "magazine promoters" who led the Society into fiscal difficulty. The Society could not survive without a regular publication. However, Montezuma was still optimistic. He claimed there was still a strong nucleus of committed people and that "out of the calamities of the Society of American Indians there still stands untarnished, unmoved, that greatest of principles, that greatest of life—freedom and citizenship." He added if the Society had stood firm on these principles from the beginning, then it would have been more successful. He said bluntly: "Our discord hurt us. . . . We wasted our fire on lesser issues such as archeology, ethnology, native arts, Indian missions, etc." From now on, he advised, "we must aim and fire, shoot straight right at the Indian Office." While these are characteristically strong words, it is difficult to refute his assessment.[36]

The tenth annual convention in Detroit, October 1921, was a disaster. It effectively marked the end of the Society. Only eight Active and Associate members registered. There were others in attendance, but they were from other organizations. The publicity for the conference was published by the Tepee Order's magazine, *American Indian Tepee*, and by Montezuma's *Wassaja*, but neither had the circulation or status of the defunct *American Indian Magazine*. The Tepee Order billed it as an "International Convention of American Indians under the Auspices of the National Society of American Indians," and invited members of other organizations to attend.[37] President Sloan presided over the conference, which opened with a welcoming address by the mayor of Detroit. After the mayor's welcome, Red Fox, referred to as the Assistant Great Incohanee and business manager, joined the mayor on the stage of the YMCA auditorium and, as described in *American Indian Tepee*, "performed the sacred rights [*sic*] of ceremonial Peace Pipe with the mayor." Sloan followed with the opening address, focusing on the same theme of reducing government control. This time he compared the situation to Russia under the late czar and to American slavery, where "the Negro slaves were property of individuals, the plight of the Indian is the same, for he is the slave of the Indian Bureau." His answer: declare citizenship for all American Indians and abolish the reservations. Some of the other presentations focused on the continuing public stereotypes of American Indians, especially the use of the term "wild." A campaign was announced to fight these stereotypes, particularly the "whooping, feathered, superstitious roughneck carrying a tomahawk in one hand and a scalping knife behind each ear." The plan was to send letters to members and friends, encouraging them to combat these stereotypes. There is no evidence that this plan was ever implemented. Montezuma followed with a presentation about closing the Indian Office, describing the plight of citizen Indians who were still under the control of the Indian Office. He said that these individuals were not free to conduct business as they pleased and that "these thousands [Indian citizens] are still tied to the bureau in one way or another. In Oklahoma citizen Indians still have agents. Tribal leases allow the Indian Bureau to hang onto the Indian citizen. Money deposited in the treasury compel the citizen Indian to transact his business with the bureau." He added that these controls "treat the Indian as a slave and an inferior creature." His rhetorical conclusion posited, How could one be a U.S. citizen and continue to be a ward of the state?

Except for a successful evening of entertainment, the conference ended with confusion. Sloan and Montezuma measured success by a full house in the YMCA auditorium. Red Fox gave an "Illustrated Lecture" and sang "America" in "the Indian tongue." Also, many play-Indian groups (made up of non-Indians) participated in the entertainment, such as "Indian Songs and Recitations by members of Degree of Pocahontas, Red Men Lodges of Detroit, and the Improved Order of Red Men."[38] The entertainment was quite different from the earlier conferences, where almost all of the entertainers were American Indians usually SAI members. This was clearly the influence of Red Fox. The confusion at the end of the conference resulted from a failure to muster a quorum at the business meeting—hence there were no elections and no resolutions. Those who remained were unsure of what to do. Montezuma wrote, "There being few delegates, things looked precarious. . . . One said: the Society is dead, let us go home." The present officers, including President Sloan, continued in office by default for another year. Despite this confusion, Montezuma said the conference was a success since the SAI was still on record as supporting the abolition of the Indian Office and continuing the fight for citizenship. Parker, learning of the events in Detroit, wrote to General Pratt, commenting on Sloan and Montezuma, and adding that "people with destructive programs always destroy everything they tackle and I am not surprised at the results."[39]

Between 1921 and 1922, the SAI more or less blended with the Tepee Order, which established an offshoot organization, the American Indian Association, the original name of the SAI. Publicity flyers were sent out under the byline "The American Indian Council of Tribes and the Society of American Indians," much of this orchestrated by Red Fox. He also had printed a brief autobiography that praised his many accomplishments for American Indians, listing his endorsements from prominent politicians to religious organizations. As the Tepee Order grew, Montezuma joined the Advisory Board, hoping to enlist them in his struggle against the Indian Office. Hertzberg, in her study of Pan-Indianism, pointed out that the rise of the Tepee Order coincided with the demise of the SAI. Several present and former SAI leaders also became involved with the Tepee Order. Reverend Coolidge worked with both organizations. He remained the chair of the SAI Advisory Board and was elected Great Incohnee of the Tepee Order. Others served on the Advisory Board, including Montezuma, Eastman, Bishop, Sloan, and James Irving, a former SAI vice president for education (1919–22). Some held offices in both organizations. As mentioned earlier, the new American Indian Association was open to Indian and non-Indian members. It sounded similar to the SAI in its desire to improve the condition of American Indians and its support for full citizenship, but there were major differences, specifically with the Association's racism and its xenophobic view of immigrants. With few exceptions, the American Indian Association and Teepee Order rarely took specific positions on Indian issues. As Hertzberg writes: "Clearly the organization was fraternal and social rather than political or reformist in its major interests." This haphazard merging says more about the demise of the SAI than the platforms and agendas of the Tepee Order and the American Indian Association. Neither survived the 1920s. Red Fox took advantage of the last chaotic days of the Society to try and enroll its remnants into his own organizations.[40]

Before the 1922 conference in Kansas City, Montezuma and Red Fox had a falling out when Red Fox decided to stop speaking out against the Indian Office. Montezuma wrote an angry editorial in *Wassaja*, indicating that "Red Fox Skiuhushu is either a slacker, a backslider, a hypocrite, a sham, or a fraud."[41] Since the SAI still supported abolishing the Indian Office, Montezuma went out of his way to publicize the Kansas City conference. He invited all to attend. He said he wanted to hear from various groups about local government mismanagement. He also restated the fact that the Society was not working for the government. In the September issue of *Wassaja*, he printed eight times, in bold type, "Go to Annual S. A. I. Meeting, Kansas City, Mo, October 9th to 14th."[42] The Kansas City conference was attended by most of the Society's leadership, including Sloan, Bishop, Reverend Coolidge, Father Gordon, Simon Redbird, Red Fox, and Montezuma, whose health was deteriorating. The conference program listed speakers, including the mayor of Kansas City, committee reports, business meetings, elections, and visits to local high schools and churches. With a new attempt to reach the public, President Sloan gave a radio address on contemporary Native issues. He focused on mismanagement, citizenship, and the Indians' desire for freedom from the Indian Office. As with recent conferences, the issues were citizenship and freedom, implying that citizenship meant freedom. Montezuma was the center of attention, thanks to the local press. They played up his background with a story "Sold as a Slave" and a photograph of him with the headline "Kidnapped." In a major address, he appealed for aid and moral support from churches and commercial and social organizations. He compared the SAI to the abolitionists, who fought to end slavery, and to those who fought in the American Revolution against taxation without representation.[43]

Although not well attended, with about twenty delegates, it was enough for a quorum. Several resolutions stating that the SAI should "wage an unrelenting campaign of propaganda and political activity directed toward abolishment of the bureau" and closing separate government Indian boarding schools were approved at the business meeting. The present officers were reelected. Montezuma later wrote that the conference was a disappointment. He was no longer happy with Sloan and Bishop, but he wrote that no one could do a better job. He was also upset that the conference was not held on the days it was advertised. Again, he blamed a lack of unity and too much energy being wasted on "fads," such as the promotion of Indian arts and industries. There should only be one effort: abolish the Indian Office. What disappointed him most was a discussion on how to reorganize the Indian Office, when all discussion should be its abolition. He wondered if this confused the public. The SAI was on record supporting the abolition of the Indian Office, yet they were discussing ways to reorganize it. A disgusted Montezuma left the conference. As disappointed as he was about the events in Kansas City, he still had hope for the future.[44]

The last issue of *Wassaja* appeared in November 1922. It is unclear if Montezuma intended for this to be the last issue, as he had been diagnosed with tuberculosis. He wrote a long piece assailing the Indian Office, calling it "the Indian Bureau—Slaughter House of Indian People." He assessed the SAI's missteps and lost opportunities, and was highly critical of those who did not support freedom and citizenship. He blamed many of the "friends of the Indian" groups, the churches, and missionaries for working with the Indian Office. He also blamed these groups for spreading false rumors about the SAI. He argued that the "churches are shy to defend the Indian cause. They are asleep; they have quenched the spirit of doing for the Indian race as they would do for themselves. They have turned away from the truth and shut their ears to the cry of the Indian people and they say 'not yet, not yet.'" He also blamed Sloan and Bishop. He wrote that Bishop was "a dirty creature" and Sloan "was not an Indian; he cheated the Indians. He ran for commissioner of Indian affairs, running for the very thing he opposed—shows his selfishness." He added that Sloan was a failure and thus the Society was no more. The only way to make the SAI powerful would be to have an executive team composed of fighting individuals—working loyally and unselfishly for "an agreed upon principle." He believed the attempt to better the lives of Indian people and the struggle for freedom was in the tradition of Red Jacket, Pontiac, Blackhawk, Logan, Tecumseh, Osceola, Sitting Bull, Hollow Horn Bear, Chief Joseph, Geronimo, and many others. He also criticized the SAI for not being single-minded in the struggle with the Indian Office. He wrote that "it is difficult to connect Indian art, Indian shows, and Indian this and that with freeing the Indians." He mentioned again the demise of the Society's magazine, lamenting that a publication was essential: "without it nobody would know if we existed or not." Despite his negative analysis, he ended with an optimistic note on the future and the possibility of the survival of the SAI. These are his last words published in *Wassaja*:

> Members of the Society of American Indians, if the world be against us, let us not be dismayed, let us not be discouraged, let us look up and go ahead, and fight on for freedom and citizenship of our people. If it means death, let us die on the pathway that leads to the emancipation of our race; keeping in our hearts that our children will pass over our graves to victory.[45]

After the Kansas City conference, Montezuma's health declined rapidly. That spring, he was greatly disappointed that the Indian Office denied his application for enrollment at the San Carlos Apache Reservation, but he continued to fight for land and water rights for the Yavapai on the Fort McDowell Reservation. He was also upset by the SAI's failure. He asked his attorney and longtime friend, Joseph W. Latimer, to write to another friend to explain that the SAI had failed to rejuvenate itself in Kansas City. With Montezuma's illness, Latimer continued working with the Indian Rights Association and the American Civil Liberties Union to pursue a bill in Congress for immediate citizenship. By late fall, Montezuma decided to spend his last days back home with the Yavapai. In December, he boarded a train from Chicago to Phoenix and onward to the Fort McDowell Reservation, where he died on January 31, 1923, at age fifty-six. Iverson wrote that he completed his life's circle, returning to the place of his birth to be with and die among his people. He is buried at Fort McDowell Yavapai Nation Cemetery. Upon his death, the SAI office in Washington issued a two-page pamphlet eulogizing him, with a poem and essay (unsigned) honoring his life and work. They wrote: "There probably has never lived a full-blooded Indian who so effectively demonstrated the capacities of the Indian race to high culture, and a life of real usefulness than Doctor Montezuma. . . . His voice was ever raised in defense of oppressed people of any race or color." Montezuma is still revered and honored by the Yavapai and other Native groups in Arizona. His commitment to the Yavapai in the struggle for land and water rights is unquestioned. In the 1980s, they built a new health facility and named it after him: the Wassaja Memorial Health Center. A bronze bust was commissioned to honor his memory and his role in helping establish the Fort McDowell Yavapai Reservation.[46]

Between the Kansas City and Chicago conferences, the few remaining SAI members and leaders were not very active. Sloan and Bishop were still using the SAI letterhead in limited correspondence relating to the Society. Parker, no longer involved with the SAI, as he had resigned from the Executive Committee, nevertheless took the opportunity to comment on its decline. His commentary was in response to a *Christian Science Monitor* article on the "Indian question." While challenging some points in the article, he analyzed the demise of the SAI, pointing to the long-standing controversy over Indian Office employees as SAI officers. He reaffirmed a point he made over the years that there was no connection between the SAI and the government, adding that Montezuma's intransigence over the issue led some members to resign. In hindsight, he pointed out that he realized the mistaken policy of bitter criticism and destructive action against the Indian Office all but destroyed the SAI. This certainly was a reference to Montezuma. He also pointed out Sloan's contradictory stances on the Indian Office, arguing for its abolition while campaigning to be commissioner, and in an additional reference to Sloan, he said that increased partisan politics had compromised SAI principles.[47]

## Chicago: The Last Gasp

By June 1923, plans were under way for what was to be the last SAI gathering. It was a last gasp, not a typical SAI conference. It was billed as the "American Indian Convention," with the SAI as one of the participating groups. The SAI had little to do with the planning. As far as can be ascertained, there were no Native Americans on the convention executive committee. The choice of Chicago had been recommended by Montezuma before his death. His friend, Augustina M. Stanley, executive secretary for the convention, helped with the plans. She contacted Arthur Parker for advice and invited him to attend. Anna Fitzgerald, secretary-treasurer, also invited Parker to be the banquet speaker, but he declined. However, they did invite Hubert Work, the new secretary of the interior, to give the convention's principal address. The event was planned by prominent Chicagoans and sponsored by the Chicago Historical Society, Field Museum of Natural History, Boy Scouts of America, Daughters of the American Revolution, Union League Club, and others. The only reference in their correspondence to the SAI was listing Thomas Sloan as honorary chairman. The convention was held at the Sherman House Hotel in downtown Chicago and an outdoor site at Deer Grove, a Cook County forest preserve in Palatine, Illinois. The hotel was used for speakers, banquets, and business meetings, and the outdoor site was an encampment for visiting Indians and for the public to come and view "war dances, native rites—all the beloved ceremonials," as one Chicago newspaper wrote. The events were timed to coincide with Indian Day festivities that had been celebrated in Chicago for several years. Big crowds were expected for a "glimpse of the past." Three days of outdoor activities were planned, as representatives of five tribes were to "present primitive life and customs in the tepee and around the council fire." Not everyone was supportive of these events. They were reminiscent of the old Wild West shows. The founders of the SAI would have been appalled by this spectacle. Even the present treasurer, William Madison (Ojibwe), told the press that the public was only interested in Indian dances and ancient ceremonies; they were not interested in Indians. He was right: thousands of people attended the outdoor events. He also decried the denial of citizenship. He said Indians "cannot become citizens without denying their own people and becoming beggars and roamers on the face of the land of their fathers."[48]

There was also an uproar and major confrontation at two of the events. The press reported that a group of local American Indians protested the exploitation implicit in the events at Deer Grove, which they believed reinforced stereotypes. The Chicago Friends of the American Indian sponsored an exclusive members-only banquet, inviting about sixty Indians, which they referred to as "warriors," who had performed at Deer Grove. A "Captain" R. D. Parker, head of a local Indian Fellowship League, walked in, uninvited, and took the floor. He told the Indians who were present that they were brought to Chicago under false pretenses. He was not allowed to finish his statement, as the police were called and he was escorted out. The following night at the annual SAI banquet, the uninvited "Captain" Parker appeared again and sat at the head table next to President Sloan. Words were exchanged, but two policemen in attendance kept the "peace." "Captain" Parker had attended the SAI conferences in St. Louis and Detroit and was attempting to establish a National or International Indian Fellowship League. He had written to Arthur Parker, asking him to join and come to the Chicago convention and help the SAI elect new leaders. It seems that "Captain" Parker also produced Indian shows and was upset at the group who planned the Deer Grove activities without him. In fact, he often bragged about putting on Indian shows across the country. Meanwhile, William Madison, the new SAI secretary, was drawing up a resolution to condemn the Indian Day activities, but it is unclear what happened to the resolution.[49] The few SAI members in Chicago went ahead and elected officers for 1924. Father Gordon was elected president and William Madison was elected secretary-treasurer. Also, Sloan went back to his old position as vice president for legislation. Unfortunately, little came of the election, as the SAI was all but defunct. Few members were left, and many others had joined new organizations that had emerged in the early 1920s. As mentioned previously, the American Indian Association was founded in 1922 as a supposedly reborn version of the SAI. As late as 1927, Red Fox claimed his organization was founded in 1911, implying it was still the Society of American Indians. In 1923, the Grand Council Fire of American Indians was established in Chicago. It functioned as a fraternal organization with elaborate titles for its leaders. It focused on education for Indian youth, advocating public schools. They also honored prominent American Indians, such as Henry Roe Cloud, Charles Eastman, and Arthur Parker. Several former SAI members joined, such as peyote community leaders Oliver Lamere and Asa Hill (Mohawk), both former members on the SAI Advisory Board.[50]

The events in Chicago, especially at Deer Grove, gave witness to Arthur Parker's insight into the American public's view of American Indians. Several years earlier, he wrote, "To the white man an Indian is only an Indian if dressed in feathers and buckskins. The white man is a queer mixture of inconsistencies and he likes to view men and things in the light of his preconceived notions. . . . Therefore, the vogue of the make believe 'wild' Indian." Hoxie referred to the same phenomena as the public's "imaginary Indians."[51] Dr. Eastman, who was in Chicago at the time of the convention, sent a letter to Commissioner Burke, commenting on the events and the demise of the SAI. He frowned upon almost all of the events. He pointed out that most of the Indians who were at Deer Grove were "show Indians, in other words 'floating' Indians. I found that there were no serious thinking Indian who holds the respect of his race and people, present." Concerning the SAI, he added that "the [news]papers spoke of the Society of American Indians also to have a meeting but I found no trace of such a meeting. It is possible that Thomas Sloan tried to revive the defunct society, but was not successful." The comments by Parker and Eastman on the fate of the Society were accurate assessments of its demise.

After a twelve-year history, the Society was defunct, but its principles of self-determination through citizenship and its political activism continued into the twentieth century, as did its contributions to American Indian intellectual history. Hoxie has written that they "created a tradition for Indian intellectuals who followed."[52] The same was true for many members who continued to attempt to shape federal Indian policy through writing and speaking, lobbying, joining other organizations, challenging public stereotypes, and participating in the Indian Office's Committee of One Hundred, which was formed in 1923 to make recommendations for reforming federal Indian policy. Seven of the one hundred had been SAI officers. The odds against the Society influencing Congress and the Department of the Interior were immense—almost an impossible task, an uphill struggle from the beginning—yet they persevered and helped establish a twentieth-century tradition of struggle, protest, and activism. Today, many of the SAI members are recognized for their efforts and contributions in trying to improve the lives of American Indians.

# CONCLUSION

## "We Are Still Here"

"**We are still here**, still telling stories, still singing whether it be in our native languages or in the 'enemy' tongue."

—Joy Harjo, 1997

"Look, ya tried to kill us all, and you couldn't. **We're still here**, waving the turkey leg in the face of evil."

—Sherman Alexie, 2017

"We were here before all others. . . . **We are still here**. . . . We will always be here."

—Jefferson Keel, National Congress of American Indians,
presidential address, February 12, 2018

An assessment of the legacy of the Society of American Indians must take into consideration its historic circumstances. The federal government, through the Office of Indian Affairs, was committed to assimilating the American Indian by reducing or eliminating tribal land and continuing its assault on Indigenous social and cultural practices. Could the SAI have done anything different to change the direction of federal policy at a time when Indian policy seemed to be set in stone? None of the administrations of Presidents Roosevelt, Taft, Wilson, or Harding had any interest in overhauling federal Indian policies. Even the Progressive movement, with its long litany of reform proposals, mostly turned a blind eye to American Indians. In addition, the government had the support of many missionary groups and "friends of the Indian" organizations that had their own agendas for supporting the government's assimilation policies. Many reservations were overrun by missionaries and government employees, all attempting to stifle Indigenous social and cultural practices. The sun dance had been outlawed, and sweat lodges, giveaways, traditional marriages, and praying with sacred pipes were discouraged, along with most traditional dancing. New holidays were introduced onto reservations. The Indian Office was adamant about introducing July 4th celebrations to replace Native gatherings. There was pressure to change one's name, clothing, hairstyle, and homemaking practices, and eliminate Indigenous languages. Individuals who would not cooperate were given the epithet "blanket Indian." The Indian Office encouraged reservation superintendents to initiate county fair–type events and award prizes for best livestock, best crops, best baked goods, and other homemaking prizes, as a way to encourage an Anglo lifestyle. They also sent field matrons to teach Indian women homemaking skills. In addition, there were government-run Indian boarding schools, as well as missionary schools, both attempting to shape children into an Anglo American mold. For some who received an allotment, a "ritual of citizenship" was performed, which was a symbolic rejection of the past—with parts of the ritual involving shooting an arrow into the air and hearing the words "You have shot your last arrow." The government was determined to abolish communal land tenure and was under extreme pressure from non-Indians for access to Indian land and natural resources. In hindsight, bringing about meaningful change in this environment would have been a herculean task.

It was not until the 1930s, with the new Franklin D. Roosevelt administration, that some of these policies were modified. If the SAI had more members, adequate finances, and less internal dissension, could they have influenced Congress and impacted federal Indian policy? It is highly doubtful. At this point in time, the federal bureaucracy, or "bureauism" as Montezuma called it, was determined to continue its assimilation programs, believing they were in the best interest of American Indians. In addition to these impediments, there were external forces that made success difficult at best. The social and political environment was not conducive to change. In addition to the impediments mentioned above, the attitudes and beliefs of the American public ranged from indifference to outright hostility, to racism, supported by continued stereotypes of Indians as a "vanishing race," a "backward race," incapable of adjusting to the modern world. During the last years of the Society, reservation conditions were appalling, poverty was endemic, food shortages were common, and health care facilities were underfunded, understaffed, and ill equipped. There was little that the SAI could have done to ameliorate everyday life on the reservations. For those living off the reservations in cities, life was little better. The racial climate was harsh, as reflected in the treatment of African Americans and Asian Americans, the solidifying of Jim Crow laws, lynching, the reemergence of the Ku Klux Klan, and anti-immigration sentiment.

Considering this harsh climate, how does one assess the impact and legacy of the Society? As noted in the introduction, Lucy Maddox has pointed out that one needs a wide lens to assess the SAI. She asserts that the reason some earlier scholars did not credit the SAI for having a positive impact or concrete accomplishments is that they had a narrow lens, looking for a specific effect on legislation or on policy shifts in the Office of Indian Affairs. She is correct. After almost a century since the SAI's demise, a wider lens is being used for reassessment. For example, the title of this conclusion, "We Are Still Here," is a phrase used since the 1990s. A 1992 exhibit of American Indian art in New York City was titled *We're Still Here*, poet Joy Harjo used it in her introduction to an anthology, and Peter Iverson used it for the title of his twentieth-century history of American Indians. Using a wide-lens perspective, the SAI can be credited with helping to initiate a century-long process of changing the public perception of a "vanishing race" to the contemporary Native American proclamation "We Are Still Here." By 1923, the last year of the SAI, the "vanishing Indian" myth was vanishing. It was obvious that American Indians were here to stay and not about to surrender their cultural heritage. The Society fought the Indian Office's attempt to erode that heritage and, in the process, helped establish a protest tradition that has continued into the twenty-first century.

In its brief existence, the SAI contributed to the slow but growing awareness of the American public that there was not only an "Indian problem" but a "government problem." An example is Montezuma's *Wassaja*, which hammered the Indian Office in every issue. While there was no public call for change, there was growing awareness among certain segments of the public concerning the reality of American Indian lives. One example is John Collier's American Indian Defense Association. I would credit the SAI, in part, for making this awareness possible. SAI members were outspoken, they were visible, they produced considerable writing, and they had media coverage. Their publications, such as *American Indian Magazine*, were distributed nationwide to libraries, museums, and universities. Their agendas appeared in the *New York Times*, *Washington Post*, and *Christian Science Monitor*, along with multiple news items in the cities where the conventions were held. For example, the SAI made it clear that government Indian schools were not only doing an inadequate job educating students; they were actually causing harm. They demanded quality education so Indian youth could compete in American society. The SAI was not successful in changing the quality of education, but they opened the discussion to a wider audience.

The SAI was also a forerunner in its attacks on federal policies that fostered dependency, criticizing the management of the trust fund system, the failure to live up to treaty obligations, and Indians' lack of access to the U.S. Court of Claims. On the question of individual identity and tribal affiliation, SAI members were clear that they were proud of their heritage and "their race" but wanted full participation in American society as U.S. citizens. Arthur Parker wrote that he was proud of his Iroquois heritage. This pride in one's heritage was shared by almost all SAI members. The assertion that the SAI and many of its members, especially its leaders, were assimilationists, as some have claimed in the past, is no longer tenable. It is clear from modern scholarship, particularly the recent biographies of SAI members and the research for this study, that they were determined to maintain and preserve an Indian identity. Two examples of SAI leaders who might fit an assimilationist mold are Dr. Carlos Montezuma and Henry Roe Cloud—one a medical doctor, the other an ordained Presbyterian minister, and both public intellectuals. From a superficial perspective, both lived an Anglo, middle-class lifestyle, yet they both remained "Indian" and expressed pride in their tribal identity.

A recent study, *Indigenous Intellectuals*, asserts that Montezuma fought "to attain equal rights promised by American citizenship while preserving tribally based traditions and practices." He was intent on inserting himself into the "system" in order to reform it. Montezuma, who referred to himself as an Apache, was a staunch advocate of birthright citizenship and abolishing the Office of Indian Affairs. Advertisements for his journal *Wassaja* stated it was edited by an "Apache Indian." He often spoke and wrote against what could be termed Indian interests. For example, he was publicly opposed to teaching Indian arts and crafts in boarding schools, opposed a national Indian Day, and opposed wearing traditional regalia at public events. These opinions could seem contrary to supporting Indian identity, but Montezuma believed these issues distracted from his two main concerns: abolishing the Indian Office and obtaining full citizenship, the latter not as an end in itself but as a tool to eliminate federal guardianship. Montezuma constantly criticized the SAI for spreading itself too thin. In reality, he was committed to supporting Indian cultures. He worked as a physician on several reservations and at the Carlisle Indian School. He opposed the reservation system and its paternalism, but he supported maintaining a land base for Indian communities. He supported the establishment of the San Carlos Reservation in 1903 and worked to ensure that the Yavapai living at Fort McDowell, Arizona, would not be evicted and that their water rights, along with the Pimas' water rights, would be protected. During his last days, when he was very ill, he chose to go "home" and die among his people. Also, throughout the last decades of his life, he was in regular correspondence with his relatives in Arizona (as indicated by the presence of letters found in the Montezuma Papers). In reality, he never gave up his Indian identity and used his education and influence to acquire and preserve the right to self-determination. He believed the best way to do this was through citizenship and abolishing the Indian Office. As a result, he is honored today by many Indian people in Arizona. Iverson concluded that Montezuma wanted American Indians to "adapt, survive and flourish."[1]

One could make a similar analysis of Henry Roe Cloud, part of the SAI leadership throughout most of its history. He participated in the founding of the SAI in 1911 and served in a variety of leadership positions until he left the Society in 1920 over policy disputes. Roe Cloud was born on the Winnebago Reservation in Nebraska. He attended a number of Indian boarding schools, eventually entering Yale University in 1906. As a freshman, he met Mary and Walter Roe, both missionaries, and as his parents had passed away, they informally adopted him. He was the first Native American to graduate from Yale, receiving his BA and MA, and a bachelor of divinity degree from Auburn Theological Seminary. He married Elizabeth Bender, an Ojibwa woman who worked with her husband on the behalf of Indian people. He joined the SAI and began a long activist career, struggling to help American Indians survive in the modern world. In 1912, for example, he led a Winnebago delegation to Washington to see President Taft. Earlier, he had assisted the Apaches in their land struggle with the government. In 1915, he founded Roe Institute (renamed American Indian Institute), a preparatory school for Indians. He was a lifelong advocate of higher education for Indians, committed to teaching youth about Indian culture. He was appointed to the Committee of One Hundred and was one of the authors of the *Meriam Report*, which called for a reform of the Indian Office. He later worked for the Indian Office in various capacities. According to Joel Pfister, his biographer, in *The Yale Indian*, Roe

Cloud used his education and social connections for the benefit of American Indians. He added that Roe Cloud, despite his professional appearance, clothing, and hairstyle, never stopped being a Winnebago and was never away from Indian communities for long. In another biography, Roe Cloud is described as battling settler colonialism in an effort to become U.S. citizens in order to fight for self-determination. It is clear, as with Montezuma, his identity as an Indian was central to his existence, as was his activism. As a result of Roe Cloud's long career (d. 1950) on behalf of American Indians, Yale University Press has established the Henry Roe Cloud Series on American Indians and Modernity. This is a very appropriate honor, as Roe Cloud's biographer has pointed out that he "learned that the with the acquisition of higher education and class he had more power to signify and contextualize Indianness as socially distinctive." His Indianness was an essential part of his years in the SAI.[2]

Other SAI leaders fit a similar paradigm. For example, Dr. Eastman spent his life attempting to infuse Indian values into American culture, including his writing on American Indian contributions to American art. He was committed to improving the lives of Indians on and off the reservation. His sense of identity as a Mdewakanton-Wahpeton Dakota Sioux is no longer questioned, although in the past he was labeled as a role model for assimilation. Any assertion that he followed an assimilationist agenda has been dispelled by recent scholars, and he is now seen as central to the American Indian intellectual tradition. He advocated education as a means to produce Indian leadership as a path to self-determination. He advocated Indian rights, rejected the "vanishing" rhetoric, and challenged stereotypes. Raymond Wilson, in a recent review of a film on Eastman, wrote: "Ohiyesa [Eastman] was not an assimilated Native American, but rather an acculturated one who did not abandon his Native cultural ideals." In his declining years, he moved to a cabin in the woods on the shore of Lake Huron. He believed he was a voice for those being pressured to assimilate. He proclaimed he was always an Indian but also an American.

Similarly, Arthur Parker worked most of his life on behalf of American Indians, such as defending the sovereignty of the Iroquois Six Nations and demanding an end to government paternalism. He supported the production of Indian arts and crafts, and in his later years, his sense of identity as a Seneca-Iroquois became more pronounced.

John Oskison, a short-story writer and essayist and World War I veteran, served in almost every SAI office. He wrote several novels on Indian life in Oklahoma and a biography of Tecumseh. His short story "The Problem of Old Harjo," published in 1907, defended Creek marriage and kinship traditions in the face of assimilationist forces. He argued for self-reliance and economic independence, claiming this was not assimilation, and that Indians had been independent and economically viable before as sovereign nations. Oskison maintained the same beliefs in his years with the SAI, working to provide agency, by way of citizenship, to protect peoples and cultures.

Thomas Sloan, attorney, longtime SAI leader and president, born on Winnebago Reservation, spent much of his life defending the Native American Church and its sacramental use of peyote. His views were controversial to many. He defended Peyotists in the courts and was an advocate for First Amendment protection for Native peoples. Hoxie credits him with being part of a long line of activists helping to construct the legal and political doctrines that made it possible for American Indians to survive into the twenty-first century.

Reverend Sherman Coolidge, Arapaho, missionary, and an SAI founder and president (1911–13, 1916), spent many years on the Wind River Reservation, working amid poverty, ill health, and food shortages. He attacked government paternalism and advocated major reforms in government policies. One could argue he lived an assimilationist lifestyle as a missionary, but he was secure in his identity. In public speaking, he always referred to his Arapaho origins, and he signed some of his letters "Arapaho."

Charles Carter (Chickasaw), one of the most popular SAI officials, was elected to the U.S. House of Representatives from Oklahoma, remained active in the SAI from 1911 to 1920, and served as the Society's vice president for legislation. In 1912, he introduced legislation to Congress to investigate and codify the legal status of American Indians. He advocated full citizenship as the path to self-determination.

Gertrude Bonnin's (Zitkala-Ša) reputation as a Yankton Dakota woman with a strong sense of identity is well established. She remained connected to the Yankton Sioux Reservation throughout her life as she fought to protect Indian rights. She continually encouraged American Indians, including the Yankton, to maintain a land base. Her literary career and political activism exemplified her determination to protect Native individuals and communities from being overwhelmed by federal policies.

William Kershaw, a Menominee attorney, served the SAI as chair of the finance committee and as vice president for legislation. As assistant attorney general of Wisconsin, he worked on behalf of Wisconsin Indians to protect treaty rights and a land base. He argued that in looking toward the future, one should never fail to look back to the past.

Laura M. Cornelius Kellogg, an SAI founder and vice president for education, was involved with the SAI for only a few years, but she had a significant impact, advocating for the protection of a Native land base under communal ownership, supported by local industry. Her Oneida identity is not questioned. Today she is highly respected by the Oneida.

Marie L. B. Baldwin (Ojibwe), activist and suffragette, a member of the original executive committee, served the SAI in many capacities, including as the treasurer for two years. As an attorney working in the Indian Office, she defended treaty rights of the Turtle Mountain Chippewa.

As one reviews the lives of the various SAI members, it is clear that a strong sense of Indian identity existed throughout the Society. Despite adjustments to twentieth-century America, such as language, dress, education, and career—whatever the outward trappings of modernity—these individuals fostered and protected their Native heritage. As Deloria has stated, while many appear to embody elements of assimilation, such as a professional lifestyle, nevertheless they "worked actively to preserve elements of Native culture and societies from destruction."[3]

The SAI was also a training ground for Indian intellectuals and activists, serving as a model for future national American Indian organizations. Many of the members joined and helped establish other organizations, such as the Tepee Order of America, the Indian Association of America, and Gertrude Bonnin's National Council of the American Indian. Historian Thomas Conger asserts that these organizations served as a link between the SAI and later organizations, such as the present-day National Congress of American Indians. The SAI was a bridge or springboard to later organizations, helping establish an activist/protest tradition. The SAI also played an essential role in the development of an American Indian intellectual tradition, or as David Martínez so aptly stated, the SAI was "indigenous thinkers taking a pro-active role in events around them setting an example for upcoming generations," particularly on the development of intellectual connections to political thought, as now studied by contemporary scholars.

A significant component of the SAI's legacy, as previously mentioned, was "talking back," demanding change, and seeking agency, with a goal of self-determination. Despite attempts by the federal government and secular and sectarian groups to force assimilation, American Indian identity and culture has not only survived but flourished. "Talking back" has continued into the twenty-first century, and the SAI must be given some credit for helping foster this legacy. Frederick Hoxie argues that the SAI laid the foundation for later cultural revivals. Even after its demise, many SAI leaders continued to work on behalf of American Indians, still using the SAI's early goals as their motivation. Lucy Maddox, in her assessment of the SAI, argued that the members knew who they were and should be given credit for introducing Indian issues into public discourse. They were determined to end dependency, improve health and wellness on reservations, and most importantly, ensure that the future of American Indians be determined by American Indians. They opposed all types of paternalism. They also supported the right of Native communities to continue their cultural traditions. They insisted that the government live up to its responsibilities and respect treaty rights and negotiated agreements. This refusal to accept the present situation provided a road map to the future.[4]

In the early 1920s, there was a slow but growing chorus for reform of federal Indian policies. John Collier, a social worker and future commissioner of Indian affairs, was part of that chorus. In 1923, he founded the American Indian Defense Association (AIDA), a group quite different from the "friends of the Indian" groups, as it called for an end to the allotment system, self-determination, and the protection of social and cultural traditions. Collier publicly criticized Charles Burke, the commissioner of Indian affairs, for attempting to curtail traditional dancing. The AIDA was founded specifically to oppose the 1922 Bursum bill in Congress, which would have transferred Pueblo land and water rights in New Mexico to "white squatters" and to corporate interests. With Pueblo protests and support from the AIDA, the bill failed. Encouraged, the AIDA established chapters in several states and called for broader reforms. With pressure from the growing call for policy changes, Hubert Work, the new secretary of the interior, called on Congress to increase its appropriations for reservations and proposed an advisory group to make recommendations for changes in federal Indian policies. He wrote to Arthur Parker, asking for his counsel and cooperation in establishing such a group.

Work appointed a Committee of One Hundred, requesting written recommendations. Out of this group of one hundred individuals, seven former and present SAI members were appointed: Henry Roe Cloud, Samuel Coolidge, Charles Eastman, Arthur Parker, Dennison Wheelock, Thomas Sloan, and Philip Gordon. Three of the seven were former SAI presidents. Several SAI Associate members were appointed to the committee, including Frederick Hodge, Reverend Moffett, Matthew Sniffen, George Latimer (Montezuma's lawyer), and Fayette McKenzie, who chaired the Resolutions Committee. Secretary Work appointed Arthur Parker to chair the full Committee of One Hundred. Meeting in December 1923, they produced a number of resolutions, calling to overhaul Indian boarding school education, send more Indian children to public schools, obtain funds for continuing education and better health care, and petition Congress to allow claims against the federal government to be admitted to the U.S. Court of Claims. These were all issues originally supported by the SAI; however, the committee did not approve a resolution calling for immediate citizenship, although Congress was discussing such a bill. Parker summarized the resolutions in a letter to the *New York Times*, encouraging the government to act on the resolutions, particularly regarding education. In an essay in *Southern Workman*, McKenzie wrote, "It would be interesting to compare the resolutions of the Committee [of One Hundred] with the positions taken in earlier years by the Society of American Indians. In general, it was a summation of those positions." In a letter to McKenzie, Parker expressed his disappointment that the secretary of the interior did not take their recommendations seriously, even though they were very moderate. They did not lead to any immediate changes; however, they added to the chorus of voices calling for changes in federal policies. The SAI had a significant voice on the committee, but unfortunately, the Indian Office was not ready to consider meaningful reform.[5]

John Collier continued the quest for reform. His disappointment at the slow pace of change convinced him a broader investigation of reservation conditions was needed. Secretary Work, responding to considerable pressure to investigate, agreed. They turned to a private organization, the Institute for Government Research (today's Brookings Institution), in 1926 to initiate a study on reservation conditions. Henry Roe Cloud and Fayette McKenzie were part of the investigative team. Roe Cloud was also one of the co-authors of the report. In 1928, they released the lengthy *Meriam Report*, calling for a major overhaul of federal Indian policies. Clearly, the SAI had directly influenced the Committee of One Hundred and at least certain aspects of the *Meriam Report*, dealing with health, legal issues, and calling for an end to federal Indian boarding schools. American Indian resistance to federal policies increased throughout the 1920s. The SAI helped lay the groundwork for this resistance.[6]

In June 1924, the U.S. Congress passed the Indian Citizenship Act, which the SAI had advocated since its founding. Although there were intense debates between those who called for a path to citizenship and those who called for birthright citizenship, nevertheless they issued a steady stream of publicity on the need for citizenship as the only way to solve the "Indian problem." The SAI helped keep the issue before the public in the years before and during the Great War. The SAI's demand for citizenship, participation in the war as soldiers, the patriotism of Native men and women supporting the war effort, the passage of the Nineteenth Amendment (women's suffrage), and pressure from various organizations, including the American Indian Defense Association, convinced Congress that the time had come for birthright citizenship, although not fully supported by several Indian nations, who feared it would compromise their inherent sovereignty. One scholar has stated that the SAI was "undoubtedly significant" in pressuring Congress to pass the citizenship bill. This is overstated. The SAI was just one voice—and a weak one in the years just before 1924—but they had kept the citizenship issue before Congress, the Indian Office, and the public throughout the previous decade. Unfortunately, citizenship did not solve the basic problem: a lack of self-determination for Indian people. That would come very slowly later in the twentieth century. In 1924, it was clear that citizenship did not alter federal guardianship over American Indians. However, the hope of the SAI throughout its history was that the acquisition of citizenship would open the door to full citizenship rights, including the waning of federal guardianship.[7]

Several scholars have recently argued that the SAI had a long-range impact on activism and protest. Professor Beth Piatote has written, "The legacies of the SAI are multiple, and the Society's contributions to contemporary political formations are only part of them," adding that the efforts of the Society have helped to bring forth the political agency of today. Philip Deloria made a similar comment that the "National Congress of American Indians [is] a latter-day descendant of the SAI."[8] In addition, the SAI had a number of short-term successes. Parker, as secretary-treasurer, assisted on local issues requested by individuals or groups living on reservations. As the word of a new organization spread, Parker received numerous requests for help, specifically asking the Society to intercede with the Department of the Interior, the Indian Office, members of Congress, or reservation superintendents. For example, Parker was asked by the heirs of two Sac and Fox Indians for help in resolving a complicated inheritance case. Parker wrote to the Indian Office and asked for assistance. The secretary of the interior agreed to look into the matter and reported back to Parker that it was resolved in favor of the heirs.[9] There were also many other requests, dealing with water rights, fencing, access to money in trust funds, receiving proper payment for the use or sale of leased or allotted land, and contesting arbitrary decisions by reservation superintendents. Sometimes individuals asked Parker to see that documents got into the right hands. On one occasion, the SAI contacted the War Department, requesting the release of Apache prisoners of war. However, most of these requests went unfulfilled, as the SAI had neither the staff nor the resources to offer legal assistance.

One significant factor that hindered the implementation of SAI objectives was inadequate financial resources. There were never enough funds to accomplish the Society's various goals. The Legal Aid Committee did not have the funds to function, and programs like Gertrude Bonnin's plan for Community Centers never came to fruition, except on one reservation where she and her husband worked. Membership fees, magazine subscriptions, donations, and sales of the Society's pamphlets were insufficient to offset costs. Postage took up much of the limited budget; in fact, some of the expenses were paid out of pocket by Arthur Parker. There were no travel funds and very little for salaries for those working in the Society's Washington office. Parker continually complained about the SAI's financial restraints.

The Society's leadership also had to deal with a variety of audiences with varying agendas: Active members with the vote, non-Indian Associate members with voice but no vote, reservation communities, a myriad of secular and sectarian organizations, and finally, the Office of Indian Affairs. Dealing with the latter was especially difficult, as some of the Active members had contrasting views on how to deal with the Indian Office. Parker represented a moderate approach, believing it was essential to cooperate while pressing for change. He wanted to convince the Indian Office to recommend citizenship to Congress. He did not believe this was possible by castigating them and advocating for their abolition. Montezuma wanted to abolish the Indian Office, arguing that in reality the Office was more interested in preserving its bureaucratic structure and budget and defending its policies, rather than actually helping those in need, as they were still appropriating Indian land and attacking cultural and social institutions on the reservations. The leadership vacillated on this issue, and the dispute on how to deal with the Indian Office could not be bridged. Years later, when planning for the National Congress of American Indians was underway, Parker was asked by Archie Phinney (Nez Perce) why the SAI did not survive. He said that the SAI's demise was the direct result of self-interest and poor leadership—particularly during the presidency of Thomas Sloan.[10]

Dealing with the SAI's Associate members could prove quite complicated at times. In the early years, the SAI leadership was convinced it needed non-Indian members—especially those with a public reputation. They were needed to increase membership and funds, but more importantly to give the SAI creditability. Having someone like General Pratt as a member would increase the Society's visibility and reputation among non-Indians. On occasion, the SAI published lists of its non-Indian supporters, claiming these endorsements boosted its reputation. For example, a 1914 pamphlet claimed that "the Society of American Indians is endorsed by the membership of such men and women." It listed five college presidents and several dozen prominent people with scholarly reputations. The problem with this dependence on non-Indian members was that most were avowed assimilationists, who believed the "Indian problem" could only be solved by surrendering one's cultural heritage and blending into American society. Several such members, such as General Pratt and Reverend Ketchum, threatened to withdraw their support when they disagreed with certain policies. By the late teens, when the SAI took more activist positions, such as advocating for the abolition of the Indian Office, some Associate members did not renew their memberships. The SAI leadership had to walk a tightrope to maintain its goals and strategies while not alienating the Associates. For example, Mathew Sniffen, an Associate member and secretary of the Indian Rights Association, supported the SAI's stand on citizenship but withdrew from the Society when it called for the closing of the Indian Office.

Another problem that affected the influence and impact of the SAI was the inability or unwillingness to connect with reservation communities. There were a number of reasons for this. The disconnect was partly the result of the SAI's focus on federal policy issues, lobbying, and raising public awareness.

On the other hand, Eastman and others argued that the SAI should focus on local involvement, to assist those on the reservations. There were not enough resources to do both. In the early years, as mentioned in the introduction, there was an intense debate over whether Native federal employees should be allowed to hold offices in the Society. In 1912, out of six thousand full-time employees in the Indian Office, about two thousand were American Indians, not including temporary employees. A large majority had ties to reservation communities and thus were potential SAI members. About one-third of the Indian employees were women. As Cathleen Cahill has pointed out, while federal non-Indian employees were committed to erasing Indian identity, the Indian employees were a force for resistance in "their fight for survival and sovereignty."[11] Dennison Wheelock warned Parker early on that it was a big mistake to deny government employees the right to hold SAI office, writing that "this was a direct slap to the most intelligent portion of society."[12] Several years later, Parker wrote that some of the ablest Indians were federal employees. The Society needed more members, but they were not forthcoming. Another dilemma was the debate over already-elected SAI office holders working for the Indian Office. Restricting the right to hold an office alienated some potential members, yet allowing Indian Office employees to become SAI officers (or vice versa) gave the perception that the government had control or at least an influence over the SAI. It was the same with Montezuma's quest to abolish the Indian Office. In 1918, at the Pierre, South Dakota conference, the SAI passed a resolution calling for the Indian Office's abolition. It alienated some individuals from local communities who needed their jobs with the Indian Office to support their families. These issues made it difficult for the SAI to confront problems with a unified front. Parker, writing to Rosa La Flesche, made it clear that the complexity of these issues prevented "working harmoniously."[13]

In addition, the locations chosen for the annual SAI conferences did not make sense to some who argued that they should be closer to reservation communities, rather than urban centers. Parker purposely chose urban and university settings, as he believed these locations added to the SAI's credibility and would increase public exposure. He hoped to attract non-Indian support for the SAI. In addition, the cost of travel to reservations was prohibitive. The SAI did not have the funds to cover these travel expenses. As early as 1914, Smithsonian ethnologist James Mooney criticized the SAI for not having closer ties to reservation communities. Marie Baldwin, acting as SAI secretary, wrote to Mooney and invited him to become a member. He declined, citing ill health, but added that the Society could become more effective if it "secured the cooperation of intelligent full-blood leadership."[14]

The Peyote controversy also affected relations with reservation communities, especially in Oklahoma and South Dakota, the home of many Peyotists. As the Peyote faith was spreading throughout western states, many individuals, including those who were not Peyotists, felt it was inappropriate for the SAI to officially support the government's efforts to criminalize the use and possession of Peyote. It seemed hypocritical and confusing to call for the closing of the Indian Office and yet support that office's efforts to suppress the Peyote faith. This seemed counterintuitive, since the Society's stated goal was to reduce federal control. More confusion arose when SAI President Thomas Sloan called for the closing of the Indian Office while seeking an appointment as commissioner of Indian affairs. Overall, the SAI needed to broaden its appeal, but several policy positions alienated certain individuals and groups.

In evaluating the long-term legacy of the SAI and its members, one must reference the massive body of writing they left for future generations. Their writings have influenced twentieth- and twenty-first-century scholarship, as well as on political and intellectual activism. Their writings appear regularly in anthologies. A full bibliography of SAI members, citing books, articles, essays, pamphlets, editorials, would be extensive.[15] The same would be true for newspaper accounts of the Society, especially if one considers the reporting on conferences and interviews with individuals. SAI members were prolific letter writers, with much of their work available on microfilm and more housed in archives and private collections. Many SAI members were also accomplished speakers, especially Carlos Montezuma, Sherman Coolidge, and Gertrude Bonnin, who traveled widely and spoke on behalf of American Indians. They gave hundreds, if not thousands, of talks to church groups and community organizations, and have left a vast body of material to study. The men and women of the SAI were complex individuals with varied lives—some with viewpoints that changed with time. What is certain is that whatever they wrote or said, they did not deny or repudiate their cultural heritage or their goal of self-determination. They had strong views on their Native identity. Iverson wrote that in this era of social and economic change, "the first two decades of the twentieth century had verified what Indians, regardless of their perspectives, had known all along. They were not going to disappear, and they would be Indians all of their lives."[16] What is clear today is that the mantra "We Are Still Here" is louder than ever, and the SAI played a role in this process. As the lives and writings of SAI members continue to be studied, scholars will be assessing and reassessing the intellectual, political, and cultural heritage of the Society of American Indians until its bicentennial in 2111—and beyond.

# Appendix A

*The Approval of a National Organization, 1911*

The following is a list of the individuals who approved of the establishment of a national organization and holding a conference in 1911, taken directly from reel 10 of the SAI Papers.

Mr. R.D. Agosa, Traverse City, Mich.
Mr. Joseph Bradley, Rosebush, Wis.
Mr. Walter Battice, Sac & Fox Agency, Okla.
Mr. Joseph R. Brown, Sesseton, S.D.
Mr. Alex Bewaw, Shawano, Wis.
Mr. Henry Roe Cloud, New Haven, Conn.
Mr. Chas. E. Degenette, Albuquerque, N.M.
Mr. R. Reginald DeFoe, Lawrence, Kan.
Mr. Howard Gansworth, Buffalo, N.Y.
Mr. James Hill, St. Xavier, Mont.
Rev. John Jacobs, Omena, Mich.
Mr. Aug. A Breuninger, Neopit, Wis.
Mr. Roy D. Stabler, Winnebago, Wis.
Rev. F. K. Wright, Dallas, Texas.
Mr. Dennison Wheelock, West DePere, Wis.
Mr. C. H. Kealear, Arapahoe, Wyo.
Mr. W. H. Hudson, LaPush, Wash.

Mr. Thomas W. Tuttle, Crow Creek, South Dakota.
Dr. Carlos Montezuma, Chicago Il.
Mr. J. M. Oskison, (Collier's) New York, N.Y.
Mr. Peter Paquette, Ft. Defiance, Ariz.
Mr. Simon Redbird, Genoa, Nebr.
Mr. Thomas L. Sloan, Pender, Nebr.
Dr. E. F. Smith, Milwaukee, Wis.
Senator Charles Curtis, Washington, D.C.

# Appendix B

*The Constitution of the Society of American Indians*

The following excerpt is the full 1916 SAI pamphlet titled *Constitution and Bylaws of the Society of American Indians* (Society of American Indians: Washington, D.C., 1916).

---

ARTICLE I: SECTION 1: The organization shall be known as The Society of American Indians.

ARTICLE II: SECTION 1: The purpose of this Society shall be:

First. To promote co-operate with all efforts looking to the advancement of the Indian in enlightenment which leaves him free as a man to develop according to the natural laws of social evolution.

Second. To provide, through our open conference, the means for a free discussion on all subjects bearing on the welfare of the race.

Third. To present in a just light a true history of the race, to preserve its records and to emulate its distinguishing virtues.

Fourth. To promote citizenship among Indians and to obtain the rights thereof.

Fifth. To establish a legal department to investigate Indian problems, and to suggest and obtain remedies.

Sixth. To exercise the right to oppose any movement which may be detrimental to the race.

Seventh. To direct its energies exclusively to general principles and universal interest, and not allow itself to be used for any personal or private interest.

"The honor of the race and the good of the country will always be paramount."

Article III: Section 1: The membership of this organization shall be divided into five classes, namely:

Active, Indian-Associate, Associate, Junior, and Honorary.

Active members and Indian-Associates shall be adult persons of Indian blood only and they only may vote and hold office, but Indian-Associates may only vote upon questions relating to their own tribal interests.

Junior members shall be Indians under the age of twenty-one years.

Associate members shall be persons of non-Indian blood interested in Indian welfare.

Honorary members shall be such persons of distinguished attainment as the society may choose to elect.

Section 2: The officers of this society shall be a President, a First Vice-President, a Secretary, a Treasurer, and three Vice-Presidents of Divisions. These officers shall constitute the Executive Council.

Section 3: No officer, except the Secretary, the Treasurer, and the President, may hold the same elective office more than two successive years, and the President, may not be from the same state as his predecessor.

Section 4: Only active members in good standing shall be eligible to hold office in this Society, either elective or appointive.

ARTICLE IV: SECTION 1: For the execution of its purposes the Society shall be divided into different lines of work, namely: Membership, Legislation, and Education. Each line of work thus specified shall be known as a division and a vice president, except the First Vice-President, shall be a chairman of the division.

SECTION 2: If any vacancy occurs in the office of the Society, the President, with the consent of the Council, shall fill it by temporary appointment.

SECTION 3: There shall be an Advisory Board elected consisting of fifteen Active members. The function of this Board shall be purely advisory.

ARTICLE V: SECTION 1: Amendments to this Constitution shall be submitted in writing at a session of a regular or special convention, but shall not be adopted except by a majority of two-thirds of the members registered at a special constitutional conference, held within one year of the date when the proposed amendment or amendments are made.

*Revised, 1916*

# Appendix C

*A List of Active SAI Members in Attendance at the 1912 Conference*

The following is a list of SAI members who attended the 1912 conference, derived from the *Quarterly Journal of the Society of American Indians* 1, no. 1 (1913): 247–49.

Marie L. B. Baldwin, The Clayborne, Washington, D.C.
Miss Ella L. Brewer, Salem School, Chemawa, Ore.
Geo. W. Brown, Hampton Institute, Hampton, Va.
Henry Roe Cloud, Auburn Seminary, Auburn, N.Y.
Mrs. Chas. H. Conley, 665 Girard Ave., Marion, Okla.
Rev. Sherman Coolidge, Faribault, Minn.
Miss Angel De Cora Dietz, U.S. Indian School, Carlisle, Pa.
Mr. Chas. E. Dagenett, The Congressional, Washington, D.C.
Mrs. Minnie B. Dell, 1115 Mt. Pleasant Ave., Columbus, Ohio
Daisy May Dell, 1115 Mt. Pleasant Ave., Columbus, Ohio
Mrs. Nellie R. Denny, Indian School, Carlisle, Pa.
Elsie Elm, Syracuse, N.Y., R.D. No. 5
Horton C. Elm, Syracuse, N.Y., R.F.D. No. 5
Rev. Jos. K. Griffis (Tahan), 9604 Wade Park Ave., Cleveland, Ohio
William J. Gardner, care of University (Otterbein), Westerville, Ohio
Miss Anna Hauser, Indian School, Carlisle, Pa.
Asa R. Hill, care of University (Dennison), Granville, Ohio

Burges Hunt, Anadarko, Okla.
Chief J. S. Johnson, Ohsweken, Ontario, Canada, S.N.C.
Stephen S. Jones, Santee, Nebr.
Chas. H. Kealear, Arapahoe, Wyo.
Mr. Francis LaFlesche, Pawhuska, Okla.
Mrs. Rosa B. LaFlesche, U.S. Indian School, Carlisle, Pa.
Oliver LaMere, Winnebago, Neb.
Victor M. Locke, Antlers, Okla.
Dr. Carlos Montezuma, 7 W. Madison St., Chicago, Ill.
Dr. Roland A. Nichols, Hiram, Ohio
S. J. Nori, U.S. Indian School, Carlisle, Pa.
J. M. Oskison, *Collier's Weekly*, New York, N.Y.
David Owl, Hampton Institute, Hampton Va.
Arthur C. Parker, Education Bldg., Albany, N.Y.
Frederick E. Parker, corner of Lee and Putnam Aves., White Plains, N.Y.
Miss Jeanetta Pappin, Indian School, Carlisle, Pa.
Bertha A. Parker, 742 Clinton Ave., Albany, N.Y.
Harriet Rouillard, Santee, Nebr.
Thomas S. Sloan, Pender, Nebr.
Tahan (Joseph K. Griffis), 1660 E. 79th St., Cleveland, Ohio
John Tatuim, Anadarko, Okla.
Eunice Vail, Denison University, Granville, Ohio
Miss Leila Waterman, Indian School, Carlisle, Pa.
Michael V. Wolf, Hampton Institute, Hampton, Va.
Dennison Wheelock, West DePere, Wis.
Miss Agnes C. Wright, Detroit

# Appendix D

## *A List of Annual Conferences*

The following is a list of annual SAI conferences, taken directly from John W. Larner, ed., *Guide to the Scholarly Microfilm Edition of the Papers of the Society of American Indians* (Wilmington, Del.: Scholarly Resources, 1987), 9.

Ohio State University and Hartman Hotel, Columbus, Ohio, October 12–15, 1911

Ohio State University and Hotel Columbus, Columbus, Ohio, October 2–6, 1912

Albany Hotel, Denver, Colorado, October 14–20, 1913

University of Wisconsin, State Historical Society and New Park Hotel, Madison, Wisconsin, October 6–11, 1914

University of Kansas, Lawrence, Kansas, September 28–October 6, 1915

Coe College, Majestic Theatre and Hotel Montrose, Cedar Rapids, Iowa, September 26–October 1, 1916

University of Oklahoma, Norman, Oklahoma, October 9–13, 1917, canceled

St. Charles Hotel, Pierre, South Dakota, September 25–28, 1918

St. James Hotel, Minneapolis, Minnesota, October 2–4, 1919

Planter's Hotel and Missouri Historical Society, St. Louis, Missouri, November 15–19, 1920

YMCA Auditorium and Lincoln Hotel, Detroit, Michigan, October 25–29, 1921
The Coates House, Kansas City, Missouri, October 17–20, 1922
Hotel Sherman and Chicago Historical Society, Chicago, Illinois, September 27–30, 1923

# NOTES

## Introduction

1. Arthur Parker, Editor's Viewpoint, *Quarterly Journal of the Society of American Indians*, henceforth *QJ* 2, no. 1 (1914): 13–23; Arthur Parker, "Sherman Coolidge: A Study in the Complexities of an Indian's Legal Status," *QJ* 3, no. 3 (1915): 220–23; Fayette McKenzie, "Lo! The Poor Indian," 1912, Papers of the Society of American Indians, Reel 9, henceforth SAI Papers.
2. K. Tsianina Lomawaima, "The Mutuality of Citizenship and Sovereignty: The Society of American Indians and the Battle to Inherit America," in *The Society of American Indians and Its Legacies*, ed. Chadwick Allen and Beth Piatote, *Studies in American Indian Literatures* (*SAIL*) 25, no. 2 (2013), and *American Indian Quarterly* (*AIQ*) 37, no. 3 (2013): 333–51; Paul C. Rosier, "Surviving the Twentieth Century, 1890–1960," in *The Oxford Handbook of American Indian History*, ed. Frederick E. Hoxie (New York: Oxford University Press, 2016), 111.
3. Second Annual Conference, *QJ* 1, no. 1 (1913): 69, 71–74, covers issues discussed at the conference; Executive Committee, Statement of Purpose, November 1911, Reel 7, SAI Papers. The term "citizens clothing" was used by the Indian Office in its reservation census to indicate the numbers of Indians wearing Anglo American–style clothing.
4. Rosier, "Surviving the Twentieth Century, 1890–1960," 117; Beth Piatote, *Domestic Subjects: Gender, Citizenship, and Law in Native American Literature* (New Haven: Yale University Press, 2013), 2–9, 173; Michael D. McNally, "The Indian Passion Play: Contesting the Real Indian in 'Song of Hiawatha' Pageants, 1901–1965," *American Indian Quarterly* 59, no. 1 (2006): 105–36; Michelle Wick Patterson, "'Real' Indian Songs: The Society of American Indians," *American Indian Quarterly* 26, no. 1 (2002): 22–44; Linda McNenly, *Native Performers in Wild West Shows* (Norman: University of Oklahoma Press, 2012), 3–14.

5. Kiara M. Vigil, *Indigenous Intellectuals: Sovereignty, Citizenship, and the American Imagination 1880–1930* (New York: Cambridge University Press, 2015), 57–59, 310–11, 317. Vigil incorrectly states that the SAI disbanded in the 1930s; C. Daniel Richmond, "The Sartorial Indian: Zitkala-Ša, Clothing, and Resistance to Colonization," *Studies in American Indian Literatures* 28, no. 3 (2016): 52–82. Note that Gertrude Bonnin was Dakota but she chose a Lakota name.
6. Arthur Parker, "Editor's Viewpoint," *QJ* 2, no. 1 (1914): 13–23; Arthur Parker, "Sherman Coolidge: A Study in the Complexities of an Indian's Legal Status," *QJ* 3, no. 3 (1915): 220–23; "General Statement of the SAI: Our Beliefs," 1913, Reel 10, SAI Papers.
7. Bradley G. Shreve, *Red Power Rising: The National Indian Youth Council and the Origins of Native Activism* (Norman: University of Oklahoma Press, 2011), 3, 19, 35.
8. http://www.niyc-alb.com, accessed May 4, 2017; Thomas W. Conger, *The National Congress of American Indians* (Lincoln: University of Nebraska Press, 1999), chapter 2. For the continuity of these historic themes, note the Annual State of Indian Nations address by President Jefferson Keel (Chickasaw) at the National Congress of American Indians annual meeting (February 12, 2018). He addressed historic themes such as the "right to determine our destinies." He also reiterated the common refrain "we are still here," http://www.ncai.org, accessed March 28, 2018; Daniel Cobb and Loretta Fowler, eds., *Beyond Red Power: American Indian Politics and Activism Since 1900* (Santa Fe: School for Advanced Research, 2006), iii; Daniel Cobb, ed., *Say We Are Nations: Documents of Politics and Protest In Indigenous America Since 1887* (Chapel Hill: University of North Carolina Press, 2015), 3; Vigil, *Indigenous Intellectuals*, 304, 310.
9. Hazel Hertzberg, *The Search for an American Indian Identity: Modern Pan-Indian Movements* (Syracuse: Syracuse University Press, 1971); Lucy Maddox, *Citizen Indians: Native American Intellectuals, Race, and Reform* (Ithaca: Cornell University Press, 2004), 121–25, 166; David Martínez, ed., *The American Indian Intellectual Tradition* (Ithaca: Cornell University Press, 2011), 106; Joy Porter, *To Be Indian: The Life of Iroquois-Seneca Arthur Caswell Parker* (Norman: University of Oklahoma Press, 2001), 92; Society of American Indians, *Report of the Executive Council on the Proceedings of the Annual Conference of the Society of American Indians* (Washington, D.C.: 1912), 2–5, henceforth, *Proceedings*; Kenneth W. Townsend and Mark A. Nicholas, *First Americans: A History of Native Peoples* (Upper Saddle River, N.J.: Pearson, 2013); Leon Speroff, *Carlos Montezuma, M.D., A Yavapai Hero* (Portland, Ore.: Arnica Publishers, 2005), 451, 459; Frederick E. Hoxie, *This Indian Country: American Indian Political Activism and the Place They Made* (New York: Penguin, 2012), 219, 362; Robert Allen Warrior, *Tribal Secrets: Recovering American Indian Intellectual Traditions* (Minneapolis: University of Minnesota Press, 1995), 4–6, 129n14; Robert Allen Warrior, "The SAI and the End(s) of Intellectual History," in *Society of American Indians*, 221–35.

10. Deloria, "Four Thousand Invitations," in *Society of American Indians*, 26; Martínez, *American Indian Intellectual Tradition*; Hoxie, *Indian Country*, 219, 362; *Proceedings*, 4.
11. Frederick E. Hoxie, ed., *Talking Back to Civilization: Indian Voices from the Progressive Era* (New York: Bedford / St. Martins, 2001); Martínez, *American Indian Intellectual Tradition*; Cobb, ed., *Say We Are Nations*, 9–11, 27–35.
12. James Howard, "The Pan Indian Culture of Oklahoma," *Scientific Monthly* 18, no. 5 (1955): 215–20; Philip J. Deloria, *Playing Indian* (New Haven: Yale University Press, 1998), 124; D. Anthony Tyeeme Clark, "At the Headwaters of the Twentieth Century 'Indian' Political Agenda: Rethinking the Origins of the Society of American Indians," in Cobb and Fowler, *Beyond Red Power*, 85; http://www.ncai.org, accessed May 4, 2017.
13. Hoxie, *Talking Back*, 4–5. Norman J. Wilson, *History in Crisis: Recent Directions in Historiography* (Upper Saddle River, N.J.: Pearson Prentice Hall, 2005), 140–45.
14. The SAI Papers were collected from thirty-five repositories. The Montezuma Papers were collected from forty-five repositories. Publication was partially funded by the National Historical and Records Commission.
15. Peter Iverson, *Carlos Montezuma and the Changing World of American Indians* (Albuquerque: University of New Mexico Press, 1982); Tadeusz Lewandowski, *Red Bird, Red Power: The Life and Legacy of Zitkala-Ša* (Norman: University of Oklahoma Press, 2016); David Martínez, *Dakota Philosopher: Charles Eastman and American Indian Thought* (St. Paul: Minnesota Historical Society, 2009); Joel Pfister, *The Yale Indian: The Education of Henry Roe Cloud* (Durham, N.C.: Duke University Press, 2009); Porter, *To Be Indian*; Speroff, *Carlos Montezuma*; Linda M. Waggoner, *Firelight: The Life of Angel De Cora, Winnebago Artist* (Norman: University of Oklahoma Press, 2008); Raymond Wilson, *Ohiyesa: Charles Eastman: Santee Sioux* (Urbana: University of Illinois Press, 1983); Renya K. Ramirez, *Standing Up to Colonial Power: The Lives of Henry Roe and Elizabeth Bender Cloud* (Lincoln: University of Nebraska Press, 2018).

## Chapter 1

1. Hoxie, *Talking Back*. The cover photo is "Blackfoot Indians Talking with Dr. Dixon at Flag Raising Ceremony, September 13, 1913, Blackfoot Reservation." Dixon was well-known for his "vanishing" Indian rhetoric. More on him below. "General Statement of the Society of American Indians" (1913), Reel 10, SAI Papers.
2. *Proceedings*, 4; Tom Holm, *The Great Confusion in Indian Affairs: Native Americans and Whites in the Progressive Era* (Austin: University of Texas Press, 2005), xv–xvi; see also chapter 7, "The 'Great Confusion' in Indian Affairs."
3. The federal agency in charge of American Indians has used several names in the past. The official name was the Office of Indian Affairs, but Indian Office, Indian Bureau, and Indian Service were also used. In 1947, the Bureau of Indian Affairs (BIA) became the official name. For an excellent analysis of the BIA, see Donald Fixico, *Bureau of Indian Affairs* (Santa Barbara, Calif.: Greenwood, 2012), and

Cathleen D. Cahill, *Federal Fathers & Mothers* (Chapel Hill: University of North Carolina Press, 2011).

4. Charles Eastman, *The Indian To-Day* (New York: Doubleday: 1915), 105–6.
5. Pokegon's speech is reprinted in Hoxie, *Talking Back*, 31–35; Eastman, *Indian To-Day*, 130–31; Proceedings of the Fourth Annual Conference, 1914, Reel 10, SAI Papers. In describing the origins of the Society, McKenzie mentioned the meeting between Eastman and Coolidge in Washington.
6. General Richard Pratt to Carlos Montezuma, July 1, 1901, Reel 1, *Carlos Montezuma Papers*, henceforth CM Papers; Eastman to Montezuma, June 16, 1903, Reel 1, CM Papers; Iverson, *Carlos Montezuma*, 37.
7. Clark, "At the Headwaters of a Twentieth-Century 'Indian' Political Agenda," 70–85; Eastman, *Indian To-Day*, 130–31.
8. Omer Stewart, *Peyote Religion: A History* (Norman: University of Oklahoma Press, 1987), 65–66.
9. Fayette McKenzie, "Pledge," Reel 10, SAI Papers.
10. McKenzie to W. E. B. Du Bois, January 9, 1904, Du Bois to McKenzie, January 16, 1904, in *The Correspondence of W. E. B. Du Bois*, vol. 1, ed. Herbert Aptheker (Amherst: University of Massachusetts Press, 1973), 71–72; "The Talented Tenth," in *The Negro Problem: A Series of Articles by Representative American Negroes To-Day* (Miami: Mnemosyne, 1969; reprint), 33–75, (1903); Pratt to Parker, August 10, 1915, Reel 9, SAI Papers. Pratt wrote that in reviewing past correspondence, he found a letter from McKenzie written ten and a half years earlier. He forwarded a copy of the original to Parker without commenting on its content. Copies of this correspondence are not in the SAI Papers; *Crisis* 8, no. 4 (August 1914), comments on Zitkala-Ša's *Sun Dance Opera*, describing it as "a representation of America's aboriginal life . . . by a highly educated Sioux woman," 164; "Gabe Parker," *Crisis* 6, no. 5 (1913).
11. Fayette McKenzie, "The American Indian of Today and Tomorrow," *Journal of Race Development* 3, no. 2 (1912): 140–50.
12. Charles H. Kealear to Parker, May 5, 1912; Parker to Kealear, May 8, 1912; Kealear to Parker, September 25, 1912; Kealear to Parker, November, 15, 1912, Reel 4, SAI Papers.
13. E. O. Randall, "The Indian Conference," *Ohio Archeology and Historical Society*, 21 (1912): 487–88; Fayette McKenzie, "The Indian Conference," *Kit Kat Club Magazine*, September 1912, 147–50; *Ohio State Journal*, November 4, 13, 18, 1908; *Columbus Dispatch*, November 11, 14, 17, 1908; *Columbus Citizen*, November 17, 21, 1908.
14. Walter Battice to Montezuma, June 6, 30, July 15, 17, 1909; Thomas Saul to Montezuma, May 25, 1909, Reel 2, CM Papers; McKenzie to Valentine, September 15, 1909, McKenzie to Valentine, April 12, 1910, Reel 8, SAI Papers; Clark, "Headwaters," 76–80.
15. Dagenett to Valentine, November 13, 1909, Reel 8, SAI Papers; Dagenett to McKenzie, January 13, 1910, Reel 8, SAI Papers.

16. Valentine to Charles Norton, February 17, 1911, Reel 7, SAI Papers; McKenzie to Valentine, February 28, 1910; Valentine to McKenzie April 4, 1910; McKenzie to Valentine, April 12, 1910; Valentine to McKenzie, April 30, 1910; Valentine, "Memorandum: Regarding Proposed Conference of Progressive Indians," n.d., Reel 7, SAI Papers; McKenzie to Progressive Indians, March 10, 1910, Reel 8, SAI Papers; see Reel 10, SAI Papers, for the list of twenty-five who sent approval.
17. Parker to McKenzie, April 1, 1911, Reel 1, SAI Papers; Dagenett to Parker, April 26, 1911, Reel 2, SAI Papers; Minutes: First Meeting of the Americans Indians to Consider a General Indian Convention, April, 3–4, 1911, Reel 10, SAI Papers; Temporary Executive Committee to Pratt, April 4, 1911; Temporary Executive Committee to Mayor et al., April 4, 1911, Reel 8, SAI Papers. For purposes of clarity, I have chosen to capitalize *Active* and *Associate* as the official categories of membership.
18. *Proceedings*, 7–8.
19. McKenzie to President Thompson, April 6, 1911, Reel 8, SAI Papers; The Hilles-Thompson correspondence is cited in Chadwick Allen, "Introduction: Locating the Society of American Indians," in *Society of American Indians*, 3–22.
20. Executive Committee to Dear Fellow Indian, July 11, 1911, Reel 7, SAI Papers; Minutes: Second Committee Meeting of the American Indian Association, June 20, 1911, SAI Papers, Reel 7. The minutes are also printed in the *Proceedings*, 12–17.
21. Pamphlet: First National Conference of the American Indian Association, October 12–15, 1911, Reel 8, SAI Papers.
22. Minutes: Second Committee Meeting, June 20, 1911, Reel 7, SAI Papers.
23. McKenzie to Parker, May 22, 1911, Reel 4 SAI Papers; Minutes: Local Committee, July 18, 1911, September 8, 1911, Reel 7, SAI Papers.
24. McKenzie to Lawrence Abbott, August 18, 1911; Valentine to Roosevelt, August 22, 1911, Reel 8, SAI Papers.
25. Iverson, *Montezuma*, 3–5, 32; Speroff, *Montezuma*, chapters 1 and 2, includes details of his early life in Arizona, college, and medical school, 92–98.
26. Iverson, *Montezuma*, xiv, 11–13, 41, 177; Montezuma to Pratt, December 25, October 1, 10, 1901, Reel 1, CM Papers; Speroff, *Montezuma*, chapter 3.
27. La Flesche to McKenzie, August 19, 1911, Reel 8, SAI Papers; Montezuma to Pratt, October 16, 1899, Reel 1, CM Papers.
28. April 9, 1905, quoted by Iverson, *Montezuma*, 67
29. Montezuma to Pratt, June 2, 1911, Reel 2, CM Papers; Montezuma to Dagenett, September 25, 1911, Reel 5, SAI Papers; Executive Committee to Montezuma, October 11, 1911, Reel 3, CM Papers; McKenzie, "The Indian Conference," 149; Iverson, *Montezuma*, 73–74.
30. Porter, *Parker*, 4–5; *Albany Argus*, June 14, 1911, quoted in Chip Colwell-Chanthaphonh, *Inheriting the Past: The Making of Arthur C. Parker* (Tucson: University of Arizona Press, 2009), 96–99, 142–43. This biography of Parker focuses on his career as an archeologist and does not include much on his role in the SAI. Parker wrote a biography of his great-uncle: *The Life of General Ely S.*

*Parker* (Buffalo: Buffalo Historical Society, 1919). Ely Parker was the first Native American to serve as commissioner of Indian affairs, from 1869 to 1871.

31. Both papers are reprinted in *Papers on Inter-Racial Problems, The First Universal Races Congress*, ed. Gustav Spiller (London: P. S. King, 1911, reprint, Charleston: Biblio Life, 2011), xiii, 348–76; Wilson, *Charles Eastman*, 152–53. Dr. Eastman's scheduled paper was not reprinted in the SAI *Proceedings*. A second Universal Races Congress scheduled for 1914 was canceled due to the outbreak of World War I. In an editorial, Du Bois claimed the Congress was the greatest event of the twentieth century so far. *Crisis* published a photo of several hundred delegates in front of the University of London and an individual photo of Eastman, *Crisis* 2:5 (September 1911): 198–209.
32. Rosa La Flesche to Parker, June 29, July 25, 1911, Reel 4, SAI Papers.

## Chapter 2

1. *Proceedings*, 8–9; *Ohio State Journal*, October 8, October 13, 1911; *Columbus Dispatch*, October 12, 1911; *Columbus Citizen*, October 11, 1911.
2. *Proceedings*, 23–28.
3. *Proceedings*, 28–42. The Indian Office established a farmer program and a field matron program to teach reservation residents about farming and homemaking skills. This was part of the government's assimilation policy of imposing Anglo values. Cahill, *Federal Fathers and Mothers*, 45–50.
4. Kellogg, "Industrial Organization for the Indian," *Proceedings*, 43–55, reprinted in Peyer, *American Indian Non-Fiction*, 308–16.
5. *Ohio State Journal*, October 15, 1911; and *Proceedings*, 43–55. For Kellogg's plan on industrial villages, see Patricia Stovey, "Opportunities at Home: Laura Cornelius Kellogg and Village Industrialization," in *Oneida Voices in the Age of Allotment*, ed. L. M. Hauptman and L. G. McLester (Norman: University of Oklahoma Press, 2006), 143–75.
6. *Proceedings*, 81; Kellogg, "Some Facts and Figures On Indian Education," *QJ* 1, no. 1 (1913): 36–46. For analyses of Kellogg's long and varied career, see Christiana Stanciu, "An Indian Woman of Many Hats: Laura Cornelius Kellogg's Embattled Search for an Indigenous Voice," and Kristina Ackley, "Laura Cornelius Kellogg, Lolomi, and Modern Oneida Placemaking," in *Society of American Indians*, 87–115, 117–38; Kristina Ackley, "Renewing Haudenosaunee Ties: Laura Cornelius Kellogg and the Idea of Unity in the Oneida Land Claims," *American Indian Culture and Research Journal* 32, no. 1 (2008): 57–81.
7. Marie Baldwin, "Modern Home-Making and the Indian Woman," *Proceedings*, 58–67; Cathleen D. Cahill, "Marie Louise Bottineau Baldwin: Indigenizing the Federal Indian Service," in *Society of American Indians*, 65–86. Baldwin also wrote an essay on ethnologist John Hewitt (Tuscarora), an SAI member, praising his writings on Iroquois history and Indigenous languages: "John H. B. Hewitt, Ethnologist," *QJ* 2, no. 2 (1914): 146–50.
8. Parker, "The Philosophy of Indian Education," *Proceedings*, 68–76, Parker's paper was intended for a wider audience, as he had it reprinted as a pamphlet; Porter,

*Arthur Parker*, 98–100; *NYT*, September 12, November 18, 1912. See Colwell-Chanthaphonh, *Inheriting the Past*, on the development of Parker's ideas on anthropology and archeology and his professional career in museum work.

9. *Proceedings*, 82–87, 101; Waggoner, *Fire Light: Angel De Cora*, 128–52, 155, 191–95; Francis Leupp was commissioner of Indian affairs. He appointed De Cora to the position and had the department named after himself. For more on Dietz's career and his role in the controversial naming of the Boston and Washington Redskins, see C. Richard King, *Redskins: Insult and Brand* (Lincoln: University of Nebraska Press, 2016), 21–22. Dietz was an assistant coach with Pop Warner at Carlisle, 1912–1915, and went on to coach college teams for nineteen years. He was elected to the College Football Hall of Fame in 2012. Waggoner also questioned Dietz's Lakota heritage and pointed out that he was indicted on two charges by a federal grand jury in 1918 for claiming he was a noncitizen and falsifying his draft registration information. He pleaded "no contest" in a second trial and sentenced to thirty days in jail. For details on the trial, see Tom Benjey, *Keep A-Goin': The Life of Lone Star Dietz* (Carlisle, Pa.: Tuxedo Press, 2006), 185–206. For more on De Cora's career at Carlisle, see Anne R. Gere, "The Art of Survivance: Angel De Cora at Carlisle," *American Indian Quarterly* 28, no. 3–4 (2004): 649–84.
10. Dr. Hartman was an avid art collector. His daughter married Frederick Schumacher, and they donated part of their art collection to Capital University in Columbus to establish the Schumacher Gallery.
11. *Proceedings*, 110–11.
12. *Columbus Citizen*, October 13, 1911. At the time, almost all American Indian baseball players were called "chief." After baseball, Bender coached the U.S. Naval Academy and the Chicago White Sox. See Jeffery Powers-Beck, "'Chief': The American Indian Integration of Baseball, 1897–1945," *American Indian Quarterly* 25, no. 4 (2001): 508–38. "Chief" was typically used in a mocking way, accompanied by war whoops and other derogatory epithets.
13. *Proceedings*, 112–21. Sloan graduated from Hampton, as did several other SAI members. See Hoxie, *Indian Country*, 225–76, for an analysis of Sloan's career.
14. *Proceedings*, 149. Eastman's comment on voting was in response to stories in the local press about voter fraud.
15. Wilson, *Eastman*, 152–53, 156.
16. *Ohio State Journal*, October 16, 1911; *Columbus Dispatch*, October 15, 1911. The *Dispatch* published this photograph with the name of each member under their picture. It became an iconic photo for the SAI. It was published in the 1912 *Proceedings* and reprinted for the 2011 SAI centennial conference at The Ohio State University.
17. *Proceedings*, 156; J. M. P. Hewitt to Parker, September 11, 1912, Reel 3, SAI Papers. Hewitt insisted that it be called an eagle. He was an SAI member and worked for the Bureau of American Ethnology.
18. *QJ* 1, no. 3 (1913): 304–5; Parker to Emblem Committee, n.d., Reel 7, SAI Papers; Parker to Angel De Cora Dietz, October 23, November 23, 1911, Reel 4, SAI

Papers; Hewitt to Parker, September 11, 1912, Reel 3, SAI Papers; Frederick W. Hodge, ed., *Handbook of North American Indians* (Washington, D.C.: GPO, 1907), part 1: 346; Waggoner, *Fire Light: Angel De Cora*, 202–3.

19. *Proceedings*, 161–62, reprints a copy of the bill; Parker to Sloan, October 31, 1911, Reel 4, SAI Papers.
20. *Proceedings*, 161; Parker to McKenzie, December 29, 1911, Reel 4, SAI Papers.
21. *Columbus Citizen*, October 17, 1911; *Columbus Dispatch*, October 17, 1911; Parker to Luther Standing Bear, November 6, 1911, Reel 6; Parker to Emma P. Johnson, November 8, 1911; Parker to McKenzie, November 8, 1911, Reel 4, SAI Papers; Hertzberg, *Search*, 216–18; Armand S. La Potin, ed., *Native American Voluntary Organizations* (New York: Greenwood Press, 1987), 67, 83. John Converse, the president of the Improved Order of Red Men, became an Associate member of the SAI.
22. "Delegates Sing 'America' on Prehistoric Mound Near City," *Ohio State Journal*, October 17, 1911; *Proceedings*, McKenzie, 177; Rae Norris, "Excavation of the Toepfner Mound," *Archaeology of Eastern North America* 13 (1985): 128–37; Marti L. Chaatsmith, "Singing at the Center of the Indian World: The SAI and the Ohio Earthworks," in *Society of American Indians*, 181–98, is based on the assumption that the SAI delegates visited the Newark Earthworks. Warrior made the same assumption in "The SAI and the End(s) of Intellectual History," in *Society of American Indians*, 224.
23. Emma Johnson to Parker, November 20, 1911, Reel 4, SAI Papers; Parker to McKenzie, December 6, 1911, Reel 4, SAI Papers.
24. Parker to Dagenett, December 22, 1911, Reel 2, SAI Papers; Parker to Roe Cloud, January 23, 1912, Reel 6, SAI Papers.
25. Sloan to Parker, November 10, 1911, Reel 6, SAI Papers; Parker to Sloan, November 20, Reel 6; Parker to Coolidge, November 20, 1911, Reel 2; La Flesche to Parker, November 25, 1911, Reel 4; Parker to Dagenett, December 4, 1911, Reel 2; Parker to Coolidge, September 12, 1912, Reel 2. This lengthy correspondence reflects the complicated nature of these issues.
26. Wheelock to Parker, February 24, 1912, Reel 7, SAI Papers.
27. Lawrence Hauptman, "From Carlisle to Carnegie Hall: The Musical Career of Dennison Wheelock," in *Oneida Voices*, ed. Laurence Hauptman, 112–38; Kellogg to Montezuma, September 14, 1912, Reel 3, CM Papers. Wheelock conducted the U.S. Indian Band at Carnegie Hall in 1900.
28. *QJ* 1, no. 2 (1913): 230–32; Parker to Hewitt, November 9, 1911, Reel 8; Hewitt to Parker, December 20, 1911, Reel 3; Parker to Eastman, January 21, 1912, Reel 3, Eastman to Parker, February 2, 1912, Reel 3; Parker to Hewitt, September 9, 1912, Reel 3, SAI Papers. Copies of the *Proceedings* were sent to several libraries and museums.
29. Parker to Wheelock, March 5, 1912, Reel 7, SAI Papers; Fayette A. McKenzie, *The Indian and Citizenship* (Washington, D.C.: Society of American Indians, 1912).

30. Edward S. Curtis, *The North American Indian* (Cambridge, Mass.: Harvard University Press, 1907), vol. 1; L. G. Moses, *Wild West Shows and the Images of American Indians, 1888–1933* (Albuquerque: University of New Mexico Press, 1996); Timothy Egan, *Short Nights of the Shadow Catcher: The Epic Life of Edward Curtis* (New York: Houghton Mifflin Harcourt, 2012), 146–47, 207–8, photograph, 156; E. D. Soden, "The Indian at the Olympic Games," *Baseball Magazine* (Fall 1912). For analysis of American Indians in professional and amateur sports, see Philip J. Deloria, *Indians in Unexpected Places* (Lawrence: University Press of Kansas, 2004), 125–33; McNenly, *Native Performers*, 192–96, examines the motives of those who joined the Wild West shows.
31. Kathleen Woodward and Irene Beatlieu, *Tribute to a Vanishing Race* (Pawhuska, Okla.: n.p., 1913); Joseph K. Dixon, *The Vanishing Race: The Last Great Indian Council* (New York: Doubleday, 1913); La Potin, *Native American Organizations*, 112–13.
32. For a thorough discussion of Dixon, Wanamaker, and the memorial, see Maddox, *Citizen Indians*, 33–47; Frederick E. Hoxie, *A Final Promise: The Campaign to Assimilate the Indians, 1880–1920* (Lincoln: University of Nebraska Press, 1984), 102–3; Alan Trachtenberg, *Shades of Hiawatha* (New York: Hill & Wang, 2004), 256–66, includes an artist's rendering of the proposed memorial.
33. Warren Moorehead, *The American Indian in the United States* (Andover, Mass.: Andover Press, 1914); Brian W. Dippie, *The Vanishing American: White Attitudes and U.S. Indian Policy* (Lawrence: University Press of Kansas, 1982), 218–20; Hoxie, *Final Promise*, 93–94; Trachtenberg, *Shades of Hiawatha*, 245–46. James Fraser also designed the Indian-head nickel.
34. Theodora Kroeber, *Ishi of Two Worlds: A Biography of the Last Wild Indian* (Berkeley: University of California Press, 1962); Orin Starn, *Ishi's Brain: In Search of America's Last "Wild" Indian* (New York: W. W. Norton, 2005).
35. Parker, Letter to the Editor, *NYT*, September 12, 1912.
36. Pratt to Montezuma, May 22, 1909; Montezuma to Thomas Saul, May 25, 1909; Battice to Montezuma, June 30, 1909; McKenzie to Montezuma, September 14, 1909, Reel 2, CM Papers; Clark, "Headwaters of a Twentieth Century," 76–80; Hoxie, *This Indian Country*, 255.
37. Aug. A. Breuninger to Montezuma, January 22, February 4, 1912, Reel 3, CM Papers. Breuninger (Menominee) tried to convince Montezuma to join the Brotherhood. His letterhead claims he is the "Washington Representative of All Tribes." Copy of the Brotherhood Constitution, Reel 3, CM Papers. Clark, "Headwaters of a Twentieth Century," 80–84. Richard Adams authored five books on Delaware history and legends. He fought to protect mineral rights on Delaware land in Oklahoma.
38. Parker to McKenzie, January 20, 1912, Reel 4, SAI Papers; Editorial, *QJ* 1, no. 1 (1913): 74; La Flesche to Parker, November 23, 1911, Reel 4, SAI Papers; Parker to La Flesche, November 23, 1911, Reel 4, SAI Papers; La Flesche to Parker, November 25, 1911, Reel 4, SAI Papers; La Flesche to Parker, December 15, 1911,

Reel 4, SAI Papers; Hertzberg, *Search*, 103; Steven Crum, "Almost Invisible: The Brotherhood of North American Indians (1911) and the League of North American Indians," *Wicazo Sa Review* 21, no. 1 (2006): 43–49; Clark, "Headwaters of a Twentieth Century," 80–84.

39. Parker to Albert Hensley, March 5, April 2, 1912, Reel 3, SAI Papers; Parker to Montezuma, March 4, 1912, Reel 3, CM Papers. Parker to McKenzie, March 27, 1912, Reel 4, SAI Papers; Parker to Dear Fellow Members, May 27, 1912, Reel 3, CM Papers; Henry Roe Cloud to My Dear Friend, May 24, 1912, Reel 3, CM Papers.
40. *Columbus Dispatch*, October 1, 1912; McKenzie to Parker, September 2, 7, 1912, Reel 4, SAI Papers. Thorpe's medals were confiscated when it was discovered he played minor league baseball for two summers, 1909, 1910, thus negating his amateur status. In 1987, after years of protest, the U.S. Olympic Committee returned the gold medals to his family.
41. Washington Gladden, "The Race Awakening," *QJ* 1, no. 1 (1913): 13–19.
42. Photo in *QJ* 1, no. 2 (1912): 116; Charles Dagenett, "Address," *Ohio Archaeological and Historical Society* 22 (1912): 288–94.
43. Coolidge, *QJ* 1, no. 2 (1913):117–18; Coolidge, *QJ* 1, no. 1 (1913): 20–24; Parker, "Aims and Purposes of the Conference," *QJ* 1, no. 2 (1913): 140–44.
44. Business Meeting Minutes, *QJ* 1, no. 2 (1913): 208–29 includes the constitution and bylaws; Platform and Resolutions, *QJ* 1, no. 1 (1913):71–74; Eastman, *Indian To-Day*, 133.
45. Coolidge, *QJ* 1, no. 1 (1913): 20–24.
46. Montezuma, "Light on the Indian Situation," *QJ* 1, no. 1 (1913): 50–55; Speroff, *Montezuma*, 341–42.
47. *QJ* 1, no. 1 (1913): 64.
48. Pratt, "The Solution of the Indian Problem," *QJ* 1, no. 2 (1913): 197–204; Pratt, "American Indians: Chained and Unchained," (Philadelphia: n.p., 1912); Wheelock, *QJ* 1, no. 2 (1913): 291; Ketchum, *QJ* 1, no. 2 (1913): 193–95.
49. Parker to Montezuma, November 25, 1912, Reel 5, SAI Papers. Parker wrote to Montezuma, describing his meeting with the president.
50. Parker, Editorial, *QJ* 1, no. 1 (1913): 1–12.
51. *Columbus Citizen*, October 7, 1912.
52. *QJ* 1, no. 2 (1913): 243–55; Parker to Montezuma, September 4, 1913, Reel 5, SAI Papers.

## Chapter 3

1. Parker to Dear Fellow Member, November 5, 19, 1912; Dagenett to Members, January 2, 1913, Reel 3, CM Papers.
2. Chauncey Yellow Robe to Montezuma, March 27, 1913, Reel 3, CM Papers.
3. Denver Convention Association to SAI, February 24, 1913, Reel 1, SAI Papers; Governor Ammons to Parker, February 25, 1913, Reel 1, SAI Papers; J. B. Maling to Parker, March 22, 1913, Reel 4, SAI Papers; Parker to Ammons, March 28, 1913, Reel 1, SAI Papers; Maddox, *Citizen Indians*, 47–50.

4. *Denver Republican*, April 24, 1913, Reel 3, CM Papers; Pratt to Montezuma, Pratt to Parker, Pratt to Lane, all May 7, 1913; Pratt to Dagenett, May 13, 1913, Coolidge to Montezuma, May 20, 1913, Reel 3, CM Papers. The language used by Denver officials to describe the planned pageant is similar to today's rationalizations justifying sports mascots and stereotypes.
5. Parker to McKenzie, June 24, 1913, Reel 4, SAI Papers.
6. Coolidge to Montezuma, May 20, 1913, Reel 3, CM Papers; Parker to Montezuma August 14, 1913, Reel 3, CM Papers; Porter, *Arthur Parker*, 112–13.
7. Maddox, *Citizen Indians*, 47–49; Susan A. Krouse, *North American Indians in the Great War* (Lincoln: University Nebraska Press, 2007), 9–11, reviews Dixon's three expeditions.
8. Parker to Franklin K. Lane, January 2, 1913, Reel 4, SAI Papers; Dipple, *Vanishing American*, 212–21; Trachtenberg, *Shades of Hiawatha*, 211–77; Krouse, *North American Indians*, 66; Maddox, *Citizen Indians*, 33–42. Dixon's trip lasted six months. He visited 169 reservations, taking 11,000 photos and 50 miles of film; meanwhile, his book *The Vanishing Race* was published.
9. Hodge, ed. *Handbook*, passim; Marie L. Baldwin, "John N. B. Hewitt, Ethnologist," *QJ* 1, no. 2 (1914): 146–50.
10. Hewitt, "Teaching Elementary Ethnology In Indian Schools," *QJ* 1, no. 1 (1913): 30–35.
11. Hewitt to Parker, August 25, 1913, Reel 3, SAI Papers.
12. Parker to Hewitt, August 30, 1913, Reel 3, SAI Papers.
13. Parker to Fellow Members, August 21, 1913, Reel 7, SAI Papers; Parker to Montezuma, September 4, 1913, Reel 3, CM Papers.
14. Parker to Sells, January 12, 1914, Reel 6, SAI Papers; Parker, Editorial Comment, *QJ* 1, no. 3 (1913): 259–77.
15. *QJ* 1, no. 4 (1913): 413–14, for a list of attendees; Matthew K. Sniffen, "Conditions Among the Indians of the Southwest," *QJ* 2, no. 1 (1914): 55. On the role of the Indian Rights Association and similar groups in advocating assimilation, see Hoxie, *Final Promise*, 1–39; Cahill, *Federal Fathers and Mothers*, chapters 3 and 4. On the role of Anglo women in assimilation campaigns, see Valerie Sherer Mathes, ed., *The Women's National Indian Association* (Albuquerque: University of New Mexico Press, 2015).
16. Jacquelyn Kilpatrick, *Celluloid Indians: Native Americans and Film* (Lincoln: University of Nebraska Press, 1999), 19–22; Yellow Robe, "The Indian and The Wild West Show," *QJ* 2, no. 1 (1914): 39–40; "Sioux Fullblood Scores Cody," *Denver Republican*, October 17, 1913; Moses, *Wild West Shows*, 229–45; Deloria, *Indians in Unexpected Places*, 52–74; *NYT*, April 19, June 3, 1914; McNenly, *Native Performers*, 37, 205n61. A print of the film *The Indian Wars* does not exist today, but still photographs of the filming are extant, as are many contemporary reviews. Also see Dippie, *Vanishing American*, 209–15, for a discussion of early films with a vanishing theme.
17. "An Appeal to the Nation," *QJ* 1, no. 4 (1913): 351–60. The National Congress of American Indians lobbied extensively to have Congress establish the Indian

Claims Commission in 1946. John Hall Stephens from Texas was also instrumental in removing funding for Indian students to attend Hampton Institute. He was an ardent segregationist who believed Indian and African American students should not be educated together, Maddox, *Citizen Indians*, 74.

18. Montezuma, "The Indian Reservation System," *QJ* 1, no. 4 (1913): 359–60; Oliver Lamere, "The Indian Culture of the Future," *QJ* 1, no. 4 (1913): 361–63. Some authors use La Mere. He signed all his letters Lamere.
19. Henry Roman Nose, "How to Settle the Problem," *QJ* 2, no. 1 (1914): 78; Stewart, *Peyote Religion*, 103–4. Roman Nose's brief talk is printed in the *Quarterly*, but it is not listed in the table of contents.
20. Parker, Current Comments, Editor's Viewpoint, *QJ* 1, no. 4 (1913): 329–50; *Denver Platform* 1, no. 4 (1913): 411–12; William Johnson to Parker, December 3, 1913, Reel 4, SAI Papers; Hertzberg, *Search*, 111–18; *QJ* 1:4 (1913): 413–14, lists all the attendees in Denver.
21. Goulette to Parker, October 24; Parker to Goulette, December 11, 1913, Reel 3, SAI Papers; Hertzberg, *Search*, 111–18; William Kershaw, "Looking Backward," *QJ* 2, no. 1 (1913): 36–38. Kershaw was a prominent public speaker whose talks emphasized that when looking to the future, one cannot forget to look back. The SAI was governed by an Executive Council of elected officers and a General Committee, renamed the Advisory Board after 1912.
22. Parker to Dear Friend, November 10, 1913, Reel 3, CM Papers; Dagenett to Montezuma, January 14, 1914, Reel 3, CM Papers. Stewart, *Peyote Religion*, 133–47. "Pussyfoot" Johnson was an ardent prohibitionist, appointed by President Roosevelt to enforce the prohibition of alcohol on reservations.
23. Dagenett to Parker, April 30, 1914, Reel 2, SAI Papers.
24. Father Ketchum to Parker, February 2; Parker to Ketchum, February 5; Parker to Ketchum, February 6; Ketchum to Parker, February 7, 1914, Reel 4, SAI Papers.
25. Parker, "Quaker City Conference," *QJ* 2, no. 1 (1914): 56–59; Montezuma, "The Reservation is Fatal to the Development of Citizenship," *QJ* 2, no. 1 (1914): 69–74; Frank Speck to Parker, February 19, 1914; Parker to Speck, February 25, 1914, Reel 6, SAI Papers; Speck, "Educating the White Man Up to the Indian," *QJ* 2, no. 1 (1914): 64–68. See photograph of the banquet, 56.
26. Parker to Kershaw, January 10, 1914, Reel 4, SAI Papers; Parker to Montezuma, April 18, 1914, Reel 3, CM Papers; Receipts and Disbursements, September 30, 1914, Reel 7, SAI Papers.
27. Henry Roe Cloud to Mrs. Mary W. Roe, June 6, 1914, Reel 9, SAI Papers; Dagenett to Montezuma, September 29, 1914, Reel 3, CM Papers.
28. Kellogg to Montezuma, September 15, October 1, 1914, Reel 3, CM Papers. Kellogg's new organization had little support and some outright hostility. For example, the Prohibitionist newspaper the *New Republic* (May 30, 1913) wrote that there is a "fake Grand Council gotten up by a gang of politicians and grafters to further their own political schemes."
29. Sells to Montezuma, September 22, 1914, Reel 3, CM Papers.

30. Parker to Every Member, September 1, 1914, Reel 3, CM Papers; Parker to McKenzie, September 26, 1914, Reel 5, SAI Papers; Parker, Editorial, *QJ* 2, no. 2 (1914): 95–108. World War I provided an opportunity to close Carlisle, with dwindling enrollment and a slow trend away from off-reservation boarding schools. Commissioner Sells transferred Carlisle to the War Department, which established a U.S. Army hospital. Today it is the U.S. Army War College, which has maintained the cemetery where Indian students are interred.
31. Yellow Robe, "The Menace of The Wild West Shows," *QJ* 2, no. 3 (1914): 224–25. *Indian Wars* was filmed on the Pine Ridge Reservation, the home of Yellow Robe, and produced by the William F. Cody (Buffalo Bill) Historical Film Company. Cody and General Nelson Miles are in the cast, although neither was at Wounded Knee in 1890.
32. Parker, Editorial Comment, *QJ* 2, no. 3 (1914): 174–76. Sixty-three people registered for the conference: forty-four Active, fifteen Associate members, and four nonmembers.
33. Platform: Madison Conference, *QJ* 2, no. 3 (1914): 231–32; Parker to Montezuma, October 22, 1914, Reel 5, SAI Papers.
34. *QJ* 2, no. 4 (1914): 270–71. The entire petition is reprinted, with italics in the original.
35. Kershaw, "The Red Man's Appeal," *QJ* 2, no. 4 (1914): 275–76; Parker, "The Awakened American Indian," *QJ* 2, no. 4 (1914): 269–79, includes a list of attendees. Parker to Secretary Lane, January 23, 1915; Parker to Senator Gronna et al., January 25, 1915, Reel 9, SAI Papers. Cato Sells, the commissioner of Indian affairs, was the keynote speaker at the banquet. In 2014, the University of Wisconsin held a conference in recognition of the hundredth anniversary of the 1914 SAI meeting in Madison. It was organized by Professor Larry Nester, Department of Anthropology.
36. Thomas Moffett to Parker, November 17, 1911, Reel 5, SAI Papers; Parker to Dagenett, December 4, 1911; Dagenett to Parker, December 22, 1911; Parker to Coolidge, September 12, 1912, Reel 2, SAI Papers.
37. For in-depth studies on Peyotism, see Stewart, *Peyote Religion*; Thomas C. Maroukis, *The Peyote Road: Religious Freedom and the Native American Church* (Norman: University of Oklahoma Press, 2010); Edward F. Anderson, *Peyote: The Divine Cactus*, 2nd ed. (Tucson: University of Arizona Press, 1996); Beatrice C. Labate and Clancy Cavanar, eds. *Peyote: History, Tradition, Politics and Conservation* (Santa Barbara, Cali.: Praeger, 2016). Note that references to the *Peyote faith, Peyotism,* and *Peyotists* are capitalized, just as one would capitalize references to the *Christian faith* and *Christians.*
38. William (Pussyfoot) Johnson, Address, *QJ* 1, no. 2 (1913): 207; Stewart, *Peyote Religion*, 133, 146; James Mooney, "Peyote," *Handbook* 2:237; Thomas C. Maroukis, "The Peyote Controversy and the Demise of The Society of American Indians," in *Society of American Indians*, 161–80; Maroukis, *Peyote Road*, 39–41.
39. Lamere, "Indian Culture of the Future," *QJ* 1, no. 4 (1913): 361–63. For studies on Peyote art, see Daniel C. Swan, *Peyote Religious Art* (Jackson: University of Mississippi Press, 1999), and Maroukis, *Peyote Road*, chapter 5.

40. Parker to Samuel Brosius, June 16, 23, 1913, Reel 1, SAI Papers; Parker to A. L. Riggs, April 12, October 19, 1912, Reel 6, SAI Papers; Henry Roe Cloud to Mary W. Roe, April 8, 1914, Reel 9, SAI Papers.
41. J. K. Griffis to Parker, September 17, 1912, Reel 3, SAI Papers.
42. Parker to Lamere, September 24, 1913, Reel 4, SAI Papers.
43. Porter, *Parker,* 118.
44. Parker to Franklin Lane, May 6, July 3, 1913, Reel 4, SAI Papers; Department of the Interior to Parker, June 13, 1913, Reel 8, SAI Papers; Parker to George Masquequa, October 31, 1914, Reel 4, SAI Papers; Parker to Senator Harry Lane, July 3, 1913, Reel 4, SAI Papers; Stewart, *Peyote Religion,* 213–15; Maroukis, *Peyote Road,* 49–50.
45. Parker, "Drug-Induced Religion," *QJ* 2, no. 2 (1914): 99–101.
46. Parker, Editorial Comment, *QJ* 3, no. 1 (1915): 1–2.

## Chapter 4

1. Parker to Lane, April 14, 1915, Reel 4, SAI Papers.
2. Parker to Pratt, September 10, 1915, Reel 5, SAI Papers.
3. Parker, "Certain Important Elements of the Indian Problem," *QJ* 3, no. 1 (1915): 24–28.
4. Parker to Montezuma, March 9, 1915, Reel 5; Parker to Sloan, May 16, 1915, Reel 6, SAI Papers.
5. Parker to Sells, April 10, 1915; Sells to Parker, April 21, 1915; Parker to Lane, August 17, 1915 Reel 6, SAI Papers.
6. McKenzie to Parker, April 29, 1915, Reel 5; Hewitt to Parker, September 27, 1915, Reel 3, SAI Papers.
7. Parker to Bonnin, August 10; Bonnin to Parker, August 18; Parker to Bonnin, August 23, 1915, Reel 1, SAI Papers; Zitkala-Ša, *American Indian Stories* (Washington, D.C.: Hayworth, 1921, reprint, Lincoln: University of Nebraska Press, 1985); *Old Indian Legends* (Boston: Ginn, 1901, reprint, Lincoln: University of Nebraska Press, 1985); Stewart, *Peyote Religion,* 228–29; Stewart, "Gertrude Simmons Bonnin," *Institute of American Indian Studies,* 1981; Maroukis, *Peyote Road,* 116–17; Lewandowski, *Red Bird,* chapters 1–3. I have chosen to use Gertrude Bonnin (neé Simmons) throughout the text. She chose the name Zitkala-Ša (Red Bird) as a nom de plume in 1900 as her short stories were published. In her personal correspondence during her SAI years, she signed her name as Gertrude Bonnin, Gertrude B., or G. B. As editor of *American Indian Magazine,* she used Gertrude Bonnin. It was the same on SAI letterheads. During the 1918 congressional hearings, she used Gertrude Bonnin, as she did at home on the Yankton Reservation, where she was sometimes called Gertie. There are some exceptions. In her early correspondence with Carlos Montezuma, she signed her name Zitkala. Lewandowski argues that he uses Zitkala-Ša, since she would have preferred that name as part of her legacy. However, he cites no evidence. I disagree with his assertion, since she mostly used Gertrude Bonnin, except in

her creative writing (200n28). See pp. 192–95 on the comparison of Bonnin with later activists. See also Speroff, *Montezuma*, 246.

8. Wheelock to Parker, May 24, 1915, June 5, 1915, Reel 7, SAI Papers; Parker to Wheelock, June 7, 1915, Reel 7, SAI Papers; Wheelock to Pratt, October 14, 1914, SAI Papers, Reel 9; Laurence M. Hauptman, "From Carlisle to Carnegie Hall: The Musical Career of Dennison Wheelock," in *Oneida Voices*, 112–38; Wheelock served on the Executive Council, as vice president for legislation, on the Advisory Board, and as a contributing editor to the *Quarterly*.
9. *QJ* 3, no. 2 (1915): 126–27.
10. Editorial, *QJ* 3, no. 3 (1915): 148; Parker, Editorial Viewpoint, *AIM* 3, no. 3 (1915): 159, 165–67.
11. Lane to Parker, September 24, 1915, Reel 9, SAI Papers; *AIM* 4, no. 1 (1916): 37, 49.
12. President Wilson to Parker, September 24, 1915, Reel 9, SAI Papers; Bulletin Board, *QJ* 3, no. 4 (1915): 274; "A Christmas Letter from Zit-kal-a-sa [*sic*]," *QJ* 3, no. 4 (1915): 322–25. On her experience at the Community Center, see Gertrude Bonnin, "A Year's Experience in Community Service Work among the Ute Tribe of Indians," *AIM* 4, no. 4 (1916): 307–10.
13. *QJ* 3, no. 4 (1915): 304–16.
14. Montezuma, "Let My People Go," Reel 8, SAI Papers; Reel 6, CM Papers (both contain the full speech). The full speech is also reprinted in Speroff, *Montezuma*, 347–54; see p. 357 for more the details on the pamphlet. Montezuma photo: *AIM* 7, no. 1 (1919): 9.
15. Iverson, *Montezuma*, 178; the extract is in *AIM* 4, no. 1 (1916): 32–33; Parker to Montezuma, October 11, 1915, Reel 5, SAI Papers; Parker to Pratt, October 26, 1915, Reel 9, SAI Papers; Julianne Newmark, "A Prescription for Freedom: Carlos Montezuma, *Wassaja*, and the Society of American Indians," in *Society of American Indians*, 140. Parker explained to Pratt, who was not at the conference, why there was opposition to Montezuma's speech. Montezuma to Pratt, October 4, 1915, Reel 4, CM Papers, also explains the opposition to his speech.
16. Lawrence Conference Platform, *QJ* 3, no. 4 (1915): 283–87.
17. Resolutions, *QJ* 3, no. 4 (1915): 289–90.
18. Editorial Board, *QJ* 3, no. 4 (1915): 283.
19. *QJ* 3, no. 4 (1915): 275–77; Parker to Philips, July 1, October 11, 1915, Reel 5, SAI Papers.
20. Parker to Pratt, November 3, 1915, Reel 9, SAI Papers; *AIM* 4, no. 2 (1916): 113.
21. Parker to Representative Carl Hayden et al., March 27, 1916, Reel 6, SAI Papers.
22. Sloan to McKenzie, March 31, 1916, Reel 6, SAI Papers.
23. McKenzie to Parker, June 11, 1912, Reel 4, SAI Papers; 1912 Platform, *QJ* 1, no. 1 (1913): 71–74; Sherman Coolidge et al. to the President of the United States, December 14, 1914, Reel 6, SAI Papers; Red Fox to Mr. President [Wilson], December 17, 1914, Reel 6, SAI Papers; "Holiday for Indians Urged on Nation," *NYT*, May 7, 1916. As the date for first Indian Day approached, the *NYT* reported the story of Red Fox and reprinted the SAI proclamation of an Indian Day.

24. Parker to Dr. Finley, n.d. [1916], Reel 6, SAI Papers; Memorandum, n.d. [1916], Reel 10, SAI Papers; La Potin, *Native American Organizations*, 154–55.
25. American Indian Day, Pamphlet, Reel 9, SAI Papers; Parker, "A New Sort Of American Day," *AIM* 4, no. 1 (1916): 60–65; Parker, Editorial Comment, "American Indian Day," *AIM* 4, no. 2 (1916): 118–20; "An Indian Holiday," *NYT*, October 5, 1915; Proclamation, May 3, 1916, Reel 10, SAI Papers.
26. Parker, "American Indian Day," *AIM* 4, no. 2 (1916): 118–20; Porter, *Parker*, 105–6; Dagenett to Parker, January 22, 1914, Reel 2, SAI Papers. In 1898, the Indian Office instituted an Indian Citizenship Day in all of its schools; however, it was not to celebrate Native America life and culture. It was part of the Bureau's assimilation agenda to imbue Native youth with the responsibilities of citizenship.

    Illinois and Washington also enacted an Indian day in 1919. The Indian Council Fire celebrated American Indian Day in Chicago in 1928. The first federal recognition was in 1976, when President Gerald Ford announced a week in October as Native American Awareness Week, followed by Congress authorizing President Ronald Reagan in 1986 to declare a week in November as American Indian Week, later changed in 1988 to National American Indian Heritage Week. In 1990, President George H. W. Bush proclaimed National American Indian Heritage Month each November (renamed National Native American Heritage Month). In 2009, President Obama and Congress declared the Friday after Thanksgiving as Native American Heritage Day. Since 1994, all U.S. presidents have made an official proclamation of the month-long observance, reaffirmed each year by Presidents Obama and Trump. See http://www.bia.gov/DocumentLibrary/Heritage; www.nativeamericanheritagemonth.gov; www.whitehouse.gov, accessed January 19, 2019, and November 10, 2019. On October 31, 2019, President Trump proclaimed November as National American History and Founders Month. Some commentators saw this as an attempt to downplay National Native American Heritage Month. For a more detailed analysis of the early history of American Indian Day, see Thomas Grillot, *First Americans: U.S. Patriotism in Indian Country after World War I* (New Haven: Yale University Press, 2018), 40–49. In 1926, Dr. Carter G. Woodson and the Association for the Study of Negro Life and History established Negro History Week.
27. *Wassaja* (henceforth *WJ*, which is not paginated) 1, no. 1 (April 1916); Montezuma, "Changing Is Not Vanishing," *WJ* 1, no. 3 (July 1916); Parker, "Dr. Montezuma's *Wassaja*," *AIM* 4, no. 2 (1916): 170–71; Julianne Newmark, "A Prescription for Freedom: Carlos Montezuma, *Wassaja*, and the Society of American Indians," in *Society of American Indians*, 139–55; Rochelle Zuck, "'Yours in the Cause': Readers, Correspondents, and the Editorial Politics of Carlos Montezuma's *Wassaja*," *American Periodicals* 22, no. 1 (2012): 73–81; Iverson, *Montezuma*, 106–7. In 1916, Parker removed Montezuma as a contributing editor to *AIM*.
28. *Cedar Rapids Daily Republican*, September 23, 1916, Reel 10, SAI Papers; Sixth Annual Conference Program, Reel 8, SAI Papers; Parker, "Our Office Work," *AIM* 4, no. 2 (1916): 167–68.

29. Parker, "A Conference on Race Progress," *AIM* 4, no. 2 (1916): 219.
30. Coolidge, "Opening Address," 227–28; "Open Debate," *AIM* 4, no. 3 (1916): 252–56.
31. Montezuma, Address, *AIM* 4, no. 3 (1916): 260–62; "Attacks on Bureau System Stirs Blood," *Cedar Rapids Evening Gazette*, September 28, 1916, Reel 10, SAI Papers; "Tribal War Averted," *Tomahawk* (White Earth, Minn.), October 5, 1916, Reel 10, SAI Papers; Open Debate, *AIM* 4, no. 3 (1916): 252–56. Montezuma's remarks on serving God and the devil were not reported in *AIM*. Local reporters wrote about the controversies. One must conclude that Parker edited some of the floor debate for publication, recalling that he did not reprint the full version of Montezuma's "Let My People Go" speech. The SAI employed a stenographic service and a news clipping service for its conferences. The latter are found in the SAI Papers, Reel 10.
32. Parker to Coolidge, n.d. [early 1916], Reel 7, SAI Papers; Parker to Henry Roman Nose, June 16, 1915, Reel 6, SAI Papers; Stewart, *Peyote Religion*, 103–4.
33. George Gibbs to Parker, July 2, 1915, Reel 3, SAI Papers.
34. Fifth Annual Conference Platform, October 2, 1915, Reel 9, SAI Papers; Parker to Dagenett, November 4, 1915, Reel 2, SAI Papers; Editorial, *QJ* 3, no. 4 (1915): 324.
35. *AIM* 4, no. 2 (1916): 160–63, original in *Survey* 34, no. 7 (1916): 181–83; Seymour to Parker, April 12, 1916; Parker to Seymour, April 22, 1916, Reel 6, SAI Papers.
36. *Deadwood Daily Pioneer-Times*, September 8, 1916, reprint *AIM* 4, no. 4 (1916): 345–46.
37. "Indian Woman Has Accomplished Much," *Cedar Rapids Evening Gazette*, September 29, 1916; Lewandowski, *Red Bird*, 111–13, explores Bonnin's pivotal role at Cedar Rapids and credits her with the passage of the anti-peyote resolution. Also see Hertzberg, *Search*, 146–54.
38. Henry A. Larson, "The Indian and His Liquor Problem," *AIM* 4, no. 3 (1916): 234–36; Pratt, "Remarks and Motion," *AIM* 4, no. 3 (1916): 237–38.
39. Delos Lone Wolf, "How to Solve the Problem," *AIM* 4, no. 3 (1916): 257–59; "Whiskey Is Being Replaced by Drug," "Traffic in Drug Among Indians," *Cedar Rapids Evening Gazette*, September 28, 29, 1916; *Tomahawk*, October 5, 12, 1916, Reel 10, SAI Papers.
40. Bonnin to Parker, November 11, 1916, Reel 1, SAI Papers.
41. Brosius, "Ravages of Peyote," *Annual Report of Indian Rights Association* 34 (1916): 37–41; Stewart, *Peyote Religion*, 198; Maroukis, *Peyote Road*, 116.
42. Brosius, "Ravages of Peyote," 37–41; Bonnin to Parker, November 11, 1916, Reel 1, SAI Papers. Figure 14 is probably a photo from one of Zitkala-Ša's short stories, published early in the century and later included in her 1921 short-story collection, *American Indian Stories*.
43. "Parker Heads Indian Society," *Cedar Rapids Evening Gazette*, September 30, 1916, Reel 10, SAI Papers; Sixth Annual Conference, *AIM* 4, no. 3 (1916): 216–24. Also see Hertzberg, *Search*, 146–54, on the Cedar Rapids Conference.

## Chapter 5

1. Dorcas J. Spencer, "Indians And Prohibition," *AIM* 4, no. 4 (1916): 311–14.
2. Parker to Members of the United States Congress, December 1, 1916, *AIM* 4, no. 4 (1916): 282–84; Parker to Father Gordon, March 23, 1917, Reel 9, SAI Papers.
3. Porter, *Parker*, 130. Porter was probably making a comment on Parker's depressed mood; it was not a clinical diagnosis of depression.
4. Parker to Bonnin, March 2, 1917, Reel 1, SAI Papers; Baldwin to Parker, June 2, 1917 Reel 1; Bonnin to Parker, June 2, 1917, Reel 1; Bonnin to Parker, June 6, 1917, Reel 1; Moffett to Parker, July 10, 1917, Reel 5; Parker to Reverend and Mrs. Coolidge, February 6, 1918, Reel 2, SAI Papers.
5. Parker, "Problems of Race Assimilation in America, with Special Reference to American Indians," *AIM* 4, no. 4 (1916): 285–304. For further analyses of Parker's article, see Hertzberg, *Search*, 156–66. She offered a psychological evaluation that the article is more about Parker and his identity issues. Baldwin to Parker, September 6, 1912, Reel 3, SAI Papers; Maddox, *Citizen Indians*, 75–77. From the mid-1920s onward, Parker expressed racist views, using faulty theories of eugenics that associated physical traits, mental capacity, and the ability of civilization building, Porter, *Parker*, 137–38, 215–16.
6. Indian Office Questionnaire, Reel 9, SAI Papers; Grillot, *First Americans*, 1–10; Krouse, *North American Indians in the Great War* (Lincoln: University of Nebraska Press, 2007) concludes that patriotism was one of the driving forces behind participation in the war.
7. His speech, "Making Democracy Safe for the Indians," was delivered to the Federated Conference of the Friends of the Indians, quoted in Porter, *Parker*, 132; Editorial Comment, *AIM* 5, no. 1 (1917): 5–8.
8. Sells to Marie Humphrey, President, American Indian League, February 19, 1918, Reel 6, SAI Papers; Iverson, *"We Are Still Here,"* 49–52; "10,000 Navajos," "Cherokees Are Loyal," *AIM* 6, no. 1 (1918): 63; Valeria Red-Horse et al., "Choctaw Code Talkers" (Lincoln: Neb.: Vision Maker Video, 2010); "Played Joke on Huns," *AIM* 7, no. 2 (1919); Grillot, *First Americans*, 6, 35; on American Indians and World War I, see Krouse, *North American Indians in the Great War*; Thomas A. Britten, *American Indians In World War I: At Home and Abroad* (Albuquerque: University of New Mexico Press, 1996), chapters 5–7; Russell Barsh, "American Indians In the Great War," *Ethnohistory* 7, no. 3 (1991): 276–303. Barsh estimates that 20–30 percent of adult Indian men served in the military.
9. Montezuma, "Drafting Indians and Justice," *WJ* 2, no. 7 (October 1917); Speroff, *Montezuma*, 417.
10. Montezuma, *WJ* 2, no. 3 (June 1917), 2:9 (December 1917), Reel 5, CM Papers. For full analysis on the investigation, see Speroff, *Montezuma*, 416–17, 424–27; David Martínez, "Carlos Montezuma's Fight against 'Bureauism,'" in *Society of American Indians*, 311–30.
11. Provost Marshal, "Indians of New York You Must Register," Poster, Reel 10, SAI Papers; Porter, *Parker*, 131.

12. Parker to Walter Kennedy, August 5, 1918, Reel 4, SAI Papers; Grillot, *First Americans*, 171.
13. Bonnin to Parker, November 23, 1917, Reel 1, SAI Papers.
14. Parker, "The American Indian's Part In The World War," *AIM* 5, no. 3 (1917): 146–49; Parker to Newton D. Baker, Secretary of War, July 17, 1917, Reel 1, SAI Papers; Sells to Henry Tidwell, Superintendent, Pine Ridge Reservation, February 4, 1918, Reel 6, SAI Papers; Sells to Ives Humphrey, President, American Indian League, February 19, 1918, Reel 6, SAI Papers; Sells to Coolidge (n.d., 1917), Reel 9, SAI Papers; Michael L. Tate, "From Scout to Doughboy: The National Debate Over Integrating American Indians Into the Military, 1891–1918," *Western Historical Quarterly* 27, no. 4 (1986): 424–25; Grillot, *First Americans*, 22. Lewandowski argues that Sells supported segregated units, but Sells's correspondence clearly indicates the opposite; see Lewandowski, *Red Bird*, 124–26. See Holm, *Great Confusion*, 146–47, on the Indian Office using the war to advance its assimilation agenda.
15. Bonnin to Parker, August 6, 1917, June 20, 1917, Reel 1, SAI Papers; Britten, *American Indians in World War I*, 44–47; Grillot, *First Americans*, 13, 22; Krouse, *American Indians in the Great War*, 11–12, 133, 163, 176. After the war, Joseph Dixon began a project to interview as many American Indian veterans as possible. He received interview questionnaires from 2,846 veterans. SAI members Thomas Sloan and Reverend Philip Gordon assisted Dixon.
16. Eric Foner, "The Civil War, Reconstruction and the Origins of Birthright Citizenship," *Marquette Lawyer* (Summer 2012): 32–42; Francis P. Prucha, *Great Father*, 682–83. Section 2 of the Fourteenth Amendment reinforced this, stating that "Indians not taxed" be excluded from purposes of congressional apportionment.
17. Prucha, *Great Father*, 879–84, for a detailed analysis of the Competency Commissions; Hoxie, *Final Promise*, 176–77.
18. Anne W, Lane and Louise H. Wall, eds., *The Letters of Franklin K. Lane* (New York: Houghton Mifflin, 1922), 208–10.
19. Parker, Editorial Comment, *AIM* 5, no. 2 (1917): 72.
20. Parker, "A Bill Conferring Citizenship," *AIM* 5, no. 3 (1917): 138–40; Eastman, "A Review of the Citizenship Bills," *AIM* 6, no. 4 (1918): 181–83; Holm, *Great Confusion*, 178–81; Hoxie, *Final Promise*, 231–36; Hoxie, *Indian Country*, 225–76.
21. Parker to Bonnin, March 7, March 27, 1917, Reel 1, SAI Papers; Parker, Conference Postponed, *AIM* 5, no. 3 (1917): 137–38.
22. Parker, Editorial Comment, *AIM* 5, no. 4 (1917): 213–15. This is the "Special Sioux Issue" of *AIM*.
23. Parker "Charles A. Eastman (Ohiyesa)," *AIM* 5, no. 4 (1917): 269–70.
24. Parker, "Philadelphia Conference," *AIM* 6, no. 1 (1918): 12–14; "Indian Progress Delayed by U.S. Control Method," *Philadelphia Press*, January 22, 1918, Reel 10, SAI Papers; "Charges Indians Are Being Drugged," *Public Ledger* (Philadelphia), January 22, 1918, Reel 10, SAI Papers; "Report of the Meeting of Friends of the Indian," January 21–22, 1918, Reel 9, SAI Papers.

25. Program: SAI Conference, February 8–9, 1918, Reel 8, SAI Papers; Parker, "Washington Conference," *AIM* 6, no. 1 (1918): 41–42. The content of the presentations are not in the SAI Papers or the *American Indian Magazine*.
26. Parker to Bonnin, February 12, 1918; Parker to Bonnin, April 8, 1918, Bonnin to Parker, July 18, Reel 1, SAI Papers; *WJ* 3, no. 4 and *WJ* 3, no. 5 (1918).
27. Bonnin to Parker, April 20, 1918, Reel 1; Parker to Moffett, June 20, 1918, Reel 5, SAI Papers.
28. Parker, "Stand by Your Country's Flag," *AIM* 6, no. 1 (1918): 5–6, 18.
29. "Society of American Indians Meets in City," September 25, 1918, *Pierre Capitol-Journal*; "Indian Society Is Welcomed to the City," *Pierre Capitol-Journal*, September 26, 1918, Reel 10, SAI Papers.
30. "Sessions of Great Interest at St. Charles," *Pierre Capitol-Journal*, September 27, 1918, Reel 10, SAI Papers; Grillot, *First Americans*, 171–79, examines the relationship between patriotism and citizenship in the SAI's struggle for citizenship. See Krouse, *North American Indians*, for many personal stories of valor and sacrifice by American Indian veterans.
31. "At The Indian Convention," *Pierre Capitol-Journal*, September 28, 1918, Reel 10, SAI Papers.
32. The speech is reprinted in "Abolish the Indian Bureau," *AIM* 7, no. 1 (1919): 9–20, and Reel 6, CM Papers.
33. "Pierre Platform and Resolutions," *AIM* 6, no. 3 (1918): 138–40.
34. Bonnin's first editorial after Pierre conference can be found in *AIM* 6, no. 3 (1918): 113; *WJ* 3, no. 7 (October 1918).
35. Bonnin to Parker, October 3, 1918; Parker to Bonnin, October 14, 1918, Reel 1, SAI Papers.
36. Moffett and Sniffen to Parker, September 28, 1918, Reel 5, SAI Papers.
37. Herbert Welsh, *Peyote—An Insidious Evil* (Philadelphia: Indian Rights Association, 1915); Reports of the Thirty-Third, Thirty-Fourth, Thirty-Fifth Lake Mohonk Conference, 1914–1916; Parker, "The Perils of Peyote Poison," *AIM* 5, no. 1 (1917): 12–13.
38. Gertrude Seymour, "Peyote Worship," *Survey* 34 (May 13, 1916): 181–84; Stewart, *Peyote Religion*, 217–18; Maroukis, *Peyote Road*, 103–30, on the federal, state, and sectarian assaults on Peyotism.
39. Parker to Bonnin, January 2, 1917; Bonnin to Parker, January 10, 12, 1917, Reel 1, SAI Papers; Hertzberg, *Search*, 133–34; Stewart, *Peyote Religion*, 198–200.
40. Bonnin to Parker, June 13, 1917, Reel 1, SAI Papers; Parker, "Perils of Peyote Poison," *AIM* 5, no. 1 (1917): 12–13; Stewart, *Peyote Religion*, 217–18.
41. *Peyote: Hearings Before a Subcommittee of the Committee of Indian Affairs on H.R. 2614, 65th Congress, 2nd Session, 1918* (Washington, D.C.: GPO, 1918), 5–14 (henceforth *Peyote Hearings*). For the most part, Montezuma stayed out of the peyote debate.
42. *Peyote Hearings*, 14–22. Walter Roe died in 1913; nevertheless, an article written by him was submitted to the committee. Several samples of peyote buttons

were brought to the hearings. Some of these samples, which I saw, are still in the National Archives. They were shown to me by one of the staff.

43. James Mooney to Baldwin, December 8, 1914, Reel 5, SAI Papers.
44. *Peyote Hearings,* 60–79, 145–47; Hertzberg, *Search,* 264–66; L. G. Moses, *Indian Man: A Biography of James Mooney* (Urbana: University of Illinois Press, 1984), 57–60, 182–84, 200–203; Stewart, *Peyote Religion,* 219–21; Lewandowski, *Red Bird,* 138–141, is very harsh on Mooney, using terms to describe him an ethnocentric, racist, and making boorish and ad hominin remarks. History has proven Mooney correct, as the Native American Church has full constitutional protection as well as legal protection for the sacramental use of peyote.
45. Bonnin to Parker, March 2, 1917, Reel 1, SAI Papers; *Peyote Hearings,* 123–36; 165–66; Hertzberg, *Search,* 262–63; Bonnin to Parker, February 23, 1918, Reel 1, SAI Papers; Deborah Welch, "Zitkala-Ša: An American Indian Leader, 1876–1938" (PhD diss., University of Wyoming, 1985), 84–85, 133–44, 148; Bonnin admitted in her testimony that she did not attend Carlisle.
46. *Peyote Hearings,* 139–42; Hertzberg, *Search,* 263–64; Maroukis, *Peyote Road,* 50–56; Wilson, *Eastman,* 160.
47. *Peyote Hearings,* 141–47.
48. *Peyote Hearings,* 74–77, 186–89.
49. *Peyote Hearings,* 80–84, 100–3, 149–59.
50. *Prohibition of the Use of Peyote,* U.S. Congress, Documents and Reports, 65th Congress, 2nd sess., May 13, 1918; Hertzberg, *Search,* 259–71; Stewart, *Peyote Religion,* 218–22; Maroukis, *Peyote Road,* 53–57.
51. Bonnin to President Wilson, June 22, 1918; Bonnin to Sells June 29, 1918, Reel 9, SAI Papers; Zitkala-Ša, "The Menace of Peyote," reprinted in Zitkala-Ša, *American Indian Stories, Legends, and Other Writings,* ed. Cathy M. Davidson and Ada Norris (New York: Penguin, 2003), 239–41; the original is in the Brigham Young University Special Collections; Lewandowski, *Red Bird,* 136–49; Maroukis, *Peyote Road,* 54–58; Maroukis, "Peyote Controversy," 71–74.
52. Mooney to Parker, October 21, 1918, Reel 9, SAI Papers.
53. Moses, *Indian Man,* 203–7; Hertzberg, *Search,* 272; Stewart, *Peyote Religion,* 222–25. Delos Lone Wolf is the nephew of Kiowa chief Lone Wolf, of *Lone Wolf v. Hitchcock,* 1903. He was also a Carlisle graduate and played on the Carlisle football team, 1894–1897.
54. Bonnin to Pratt, January 29, 1919, Reel 9, SAI Papers; Moses, *Indian Man,* 205–10; Maroukis, *Peyote Road,* 56–58.

## Chapter 6

1. Eastman to Friends, January 11, 1919, Reel 9, SAI Papers.
2. Harvey Wiley, "Peyote," *AIM* 7, no. 1 (1919): 37–42; Theodore D. Sargent, *The Life of Elaine Goodale Eastman* (Lincoln: University of Nebraska Press, 2005), analyzes her life and influence on her husband Charles. In addition to general

editing work, she wrote several book reviews for *AIM*. She and Gertrude Bonnin were lifelong friends.

3. Bonnin, Editorial Comment, *AIM* 6, no. 4 (1919): 161–62; Eastman, "The Indian's Plea For Freedom," *AIM* 6, no. 4 (1919): 162–65; Martínez, *Dakota Philosopher, Charles Eastman*, 103–5. American Indians did not have a representative at the Paris Peace Conference. African Americans were represented by W. E. B. Du Bois and Robert R. Moton, president of the Tuskegee Institute.
4. "Indians' War Record Is Citizenship Plea," January 23, 1919; "Citizenship Rights for Indians Urged," January 24, 1919, *Public Ledger*; "Damaging Drug, Rum Substitute, Menace to Indian," *Philadelphia Press*, January 23, 1919, Reel 10, SAI Papers.
5. *WJ* 4, no. 2 (May 1919), Reel 5, CM Papers; Editorial, *AIM* 7, no. 2 (1919): 62–63.
6. Bonnin to My Dear Fellow-Indian, August 22, 1920, Reel 1, SAI Papers; "Indian Convention Opens Tomorrow," *Minneapolis Journal*, October 1, 1919; "300 Indians Gather for Council in City," *Minneapolis Morning Tribune*, October 2, 1919, Reel 10, SAI Papers.
7. *AIM* 7, no. 3 (1919): 145–56; Lewandowski, *Red Bird*, 154–56.
8. "Citizenship for Indian, Keynote of Convention," *Minneapolis Journal*, October 2, 1919, Reel 10, SAI Papers; Coolidge, *AIM* 7, no. 3 (1919): 157–59; Eastman, *AIM* 7, no. 3 (1919): 159–60.
9. See *AIM* 7, no. 3 (1919): 163–74, for speeches; "Indian Reservation System Condemned in Convention Here," *Minneapolis Journal*, October 3, 1919, Reel 10, SAI Papers; Eastman, "A Review of Indian Citizenship Bills," *AIM* 6, no. 4 (1918): 181–83; Martínez, *Dakota Philosopher, Charles Eastman*, 106–7.
10. "Indians Propose Legal War on the U.S. to Escape Bonds of Ward System," October 4, 1919; "Indian Convention Adopts Resolution to End U.S. Bureau," *Minneapolis Journal*, October 5, 1919; "Indians for Race Extinction If U.S. [Indian] Bureau Is Continued," *Minneapolis Morning Tribune*, October 5, 1919, Reel 10, SAI Papers.
11. Elaine Eastman, "In Memoriam: Angel De Cora Dietz," *AIM* 7, no. 1 (1919): 51–52; Waggoner, *Fire Light: The Life of Angel De Cora*, 248–51, 258–59; Benjey, *Lone Star Dietz*, 176–77 and 185–206, for a detailed account of Deitz's two trials. For Carlisle football, see David Wallace Adams, "More Than a Game: The Carlisle Indians Take to the Gridiron, 1893?–1917," *Western Historical Quarterly* 31, no. 1 (2001): 25–53.
12. "Pageant for Indians' Plea for Citizenship," *Minneapolis Morning Tribune*, October 4, 1919, Reel 10, SAI Papers; Bonnin, "Letter to Chiefs and Headmen," *AIM* 7, no. 4 (1919): 196–97. Bonnin, now editor, put her good friend Charles Eastman's photo on the cover. Also, for Indians playing Indians, see Deloria, *Playing Indian*; Redmon, "Sartorial Indian," 52–80.
13. Election Results, *AIM* 7, no. 3 (1919): 179–81 (the last issue edited by Bonnin); Hertzberg, *Search*, 184–89; Lewandowski, *Red Bird*, 150–57; Hoxie, *Indian Country*, 264–66.

14. Rochelle Zuck, "'Yours in The Cause': Readers, Correspondence, and Editorial Politics of Carlos Montezuma's *Wassaja*," *American Periodicals* 22, no. 1 (2012): 72–93, 91–92n19, includes a partial mailing list for *Wassaja*; Newmark, "A Prescription for Freedom," 139–58; *WJ* 5, no. 4 (July 1920); *WJ* 5, no. 8 (November 1920); *WJ* 5, no. 9 (December 1920), Reel 5, CM Papers; Leicester Davis to General Hugh Scott, June 25, 1920, Reel 9, SAI Papers. Davis was the business manager; he sent this letter describing the new format of the magazine. Bishop to Parker, March 13, 1920, Reel 1, SAI Papers.
15. Davis, "Thomas L. Sloan, American Indian," *AIM* 7, no. 4 (1919): 39–41; Sloan to Pratt June 5, June 29, Reel 9, SAI Papers. Volume 7, no. 5 was announced, but it never appeared.
16. Irving to Parker, January 14, 1920, Reel 4; Sloan to CIA, February 10, February 13, 1920, Reel 9, SAI Papers.
17. Parker to Irving, February 20, 1920, Reel 4; Wheelock to Parker, April 9, 1920, Reel 7, SAI Papers.
18. *WJ* 4, no. 10 (January 1920); *WJ* 4, no. 11 (February 1920); *WJ* 5, no. 1 (April 1920), Reel 5, CM Papers.
19. "Republicans Favor Quick Tax Revision . . . Indians to Aid Harding," *NYT*, August 4, 1920; "Harding Would Assist Indians," August 19, 1920, *Ohio State Journal*, Reel 10, SAI Papers; Bishop to DeWitt Hare, September 11, 1920, Reel 9, SAI Papers; *WJ* 5, no. 5 (August 1920), Reel 5, CM Papers. The Associated Press reported Harding's words a little differently: the United States should "bestow democracy and idealism on the nation's native race rather than to waste American lives trying to make sure of that bestowal thousands of miles across the sea." Sloan to Burke, October 4, 1921, Reel 9, SAI Papers. The day before the visit with Harding, Sloan visited Governor Cox of Ohio, the 1920 Democratic nominee for president. Montezuma attended the Republican National Convention in Chicago.
20. Carter to Bishop, September 30, 1920; Pratt to Sloan September 1, 1920, Reel 9, SAI Papers.
21. Roe Cloud to Bishop, October 11, 1920, Reel 9, SAI Papers; *WJ* 5, no. 4 (July 1920); *WJ* 5, no. 6 (September 1920), Reel 5, CM Papers; Hoxie, *Indian Country*, 267–68; Pfister, *Yale Indian*, 205, n. 188.
22. "Quarter-Blood Chippewa Wears War Bonnet of Late Chief Hollow Horn Bear, Pictured on Old $5 Bills," *St. Louis Globe—Democrat*, November 16, 1920, Reel 10, SAI Papers.
23. "300 Delegates Here for Convention," November 15, 1920; "War Bonnets at Meeting of American Indians," "Editorial," November 16, 1920, *St. Louis Globe—Democrat*, Reel 10, SAI Papers.
24. "Indian Is Real Asset to U.S. Says Gen. Pratt," *St. Louis Globe—Democrat*, November 17, 1920, Reel 10, SAI Papers; *WJ* 5, no. 8 (November 1920), Reel 5, CM Papers; Editorial, "Americanize Him by Giving Him Citizenship," *St. Louis Post-Dispatch*, November 21, 1920, Reel 10, SAI Papers; La Potin, *Native American Organizations*, 154–55; Hertzberg, *Search*, 213–22.

25. "Indians Urge Women to Help Them Obtain the Privilege of Voting," *St. Louis Globe—Democrat,* November 17, 1920, Reel 10, SAI Papers.
26. "Minister [Red Fox] Makes Citizenship Plea for the Indians," *St. Louis Globe—Democrat,* November 17, 1920; "Calls War Dance Mild Compared to Shimmy Shakin," *St. Louis Times,* November 17, 1920, Reel 10, SAI Papers.
27. "Indians Soon Expect Full Emancipation," *St. Louis Globe—Democrat,* November 18, 1920; "Indians Want to Be Placed under Laws of the States," *St. Louis Globe—Democrat,* November 18, 1920, Reel 10, SAI Papers.
28. *WJ* 5, no. 9 (December 1920), Reel 5, CM Papers (reprints of the resolutions); "Resolution States the Continuation of the Indian Office Spells for the American Indian Misery, Misrule and Cruel Oppression"; "Indian Convention Here Closes with Varied Program," *St. Louis Globe—Democrat,* November 19, 1920, Reel 10, SAI Papers.
29. Program: Ninth Annual Conference, St. Louis, November, 15–19, 1920, Reel 10, SAI Papers; *WJ* 5, no. 9 (December 1920), Reel 5, CM Papers; Deloria, *Indians in Unexpected Places,* 210–23; also see discussion of the stereotypic term "princess" for Native female singers.
30. "Indians Dance on Ancestors' Mound," *St. Louis Globe—Democrat,* November 19, 1920, Reel 10, SAI Papers.
31. "Indians Will Meet Here Again in 1921," *St. Louis Post-Dispatch,* November 20, 1920; "Conference Here Opens New Era for Indian, President Sloan Says," *St. Louis Globe—Democrat,* November 20, 1920, Reel 10, SAI Papers; *WJ* 5, no. 10 (January 1921); Montezuma encouraged his readers to write to Congress and to influential people they knew.
32. Program: Opening of the Tepee Order of America, 1915, Reel 3, SAI Papers. *American Indian Tepee,* published from 1920 to 1928, was more of a newsletter and difficult to ascertain its circulation. It went under several titles: *American Indian Tipi, Indian Tepee,* and *American Indian Advocate.* Hertzberg, *Search,* 213–20, 350; La Potin, *Native American Organizations,* 154–55. For Eastman's approach to American youth, see his *Indian Scout Talks: A Book for Boys Scouts and Camp Fire Girls* (Boston: Little, Brown, 1914); Martínez, *Dakota Philosopher, Charles Eastman,* 156.
33. Petition Protesting Appointment Application of Sloan to Secretary of the Interior, n.d. (1921), Reel 9, SAI Papers; *WJ* 5, no. 9 (December 1920); *WJ* 5, no. 10 (January 1921); *WJ* 5, no. 11 (February 1921); *WJ* 5, no. 12 (March 1921); *WJ* 6, no. 1 (April 1921), Reel 5, CM Papers; Hoxie, *Indian Country,* 266–68. Montezuma believed Sloan's involvement with the peyote community precluded any serious consideration for the appointment.
34. *WJ* 6, no. 4 (July 1921), Reel 5, CM Papers.
35. Bishop to Burke, October 4, 1921, Reel 9, SAI Papers. Hoxie, *Indian Country,* 266–68. Meritt was very unpopular. He refused to curb several superintendents and helped facilitate the further alienation of Indian land.
36. *WJ* 7, no. 10 (October 1921), Reel 5, CM Papers.

37. "International Convention of the American Indian," *American Indian Tepee* 2, no. 3 (1921), Reel 10, SAI Papers; *WJ* 7, no. 9 (September 1921), Reel 5, CM Papers.
38. *American Indian Tepee* 2, no. 4 (Winter 1921), Reel 10, SAI Papers, carried some of the proceedings of the conference and the entertainment program; "Lo Tells How U.S. Fails Him," *Detroit Free Press*, October 26, 1921; "Red Men Rebel at 'Wild' Title," *Detroit Free Press*, November 27, 1921, Reel 10, SAI Papers. Many of these pseudo-Indian groups are discussed in Deloria, *Playing Indian*, chapter 4; Hertzberg, *Search*, 219–22.
39. *WJ* 7, no. 11 (November 1921), Reel 5, CM Papers; Parker to Pratt, January 21, 1922, Reel 9, SAI Papers.
40. American Indian Council of Tribes, "Red Fox Skiuhushu," Reel 10, SAI Papers; Hertzberg, *Search*, 219–22; La Potin, *Native American Organizations*, 21–22, 154–55.
41. *WJ* 8, no. 3 (March 1922), Reel 5, CM Papers.
42. *WJ* 8, no. 18 [*sic*] (August 1922); *WJ* 8, no. 19 (September 1922), Reel 5, CM Papers. For an inexplicable reason, *Wassaja* jumped from issue 8, no. 5 (May 1922) to 8, no. 16 (June 1922).
43. "Scores the White Father," *Kansas City Times*, October 19, 1922; "Sold as a Slave, Wassaja Says," *Kansas City Journal*, October 18, 1922; "Indians Appeal for Aid," *Kansas City Times*, October 19, 1922, Reel 10, SAI Papers.
44. "Fight on Indian Bureau," *Kansas City Times*, October 20, 1922, Reel 10, SAI Papers; *WJ* 8, no. 20 (October 1922), Reel 5, CM Papers.
45. *WJ* 8, no. 21 (November 1922), Reel 5, CM Papers.
46. Joseph W. Latimer to Roger S. Baldwin, October 30, 1922, Reel 9, SAI Papers; Iverson, *Montezuma*, 173; see Speroff, *Montezuma*, 439–50, for a description of his illness, death, and funeral; "To the Memory of Dr. Montezuma," Reel 8, CM Papers. The health center is owned and operated by the Fort McDowell Yavapai Nation. In recent years, Montezuma has been honored. In 2003, the Yavapai Nation commemorated the centennial of the establishment of their reservation and celebrated the life and works of Montezuma, praising him as the "father of American Indian journalism." In 2016, the University of Illinois named a dormitory complex "Wassaja Hall," honoring Montezuma as their first American Indian graduate. The university requested permission from the Yavapai Tribal Council to use his birth name.
47. Parker to Editor, *Christian Science Monitor*, April 13, 1923, Reel 2, SAI Papers.
48. "Indians to Give Cook County a Glimpse of the Past," *Chicago Tribune*, September 23, 1923; "City Honors Indians Starting To-morrow," *Daily News* (Chicago), September 26, 1923; "Indians Thrill with Dances at Palatine Park," *Chicago Tribune*, September 30, 1923, Reel 10, SAI Papers. The events at Deer Grove were similar to the portrayal of American Indians at the Chicago World's Columbian Exposition of 1893.
49. "Pipe of Peace Nearly Out at Paleface Feast," *Daily News* (Chicago), September 29, 1923, Reel 10, SAI Papers; R. D. Parker to Parker, n.d. (1922), Reel 5, SAI Papers.

50. La Potin, *Native American Organizations*, 79–80; see Hertzberg, *Search*, 221–33, for a discussion of the organizations that emerged in the 1920s.
51. Quoted in Porter, *Parker*, 142; Hoxie, *Indian Country*, 271.
52. Eastman to Burke, October 9, 1923, Reel 9, SAI Papers; Hoxie, "*Talking Back*," 25.

## Conclusion

1. Vigil, *Indigenous Intellectuals*, 102–4; Brooks, "Intellectual History," 527; Iverson, *Montezuma*, 186.
2. Pfister, *Yale Indian*, 56–59, 99, 163; Ramirez, *Standing Up to Colonial Power*, 3, 72–80, 234–35; Elizabeth Bender was the sister of Baseball Hall of Fame pitcher Henry "Chief" Bender. She met her husband at the 1914 SAI conference in Wisconsin. In recent years, Roe Cloud has been honored by Yale, with the establishment of the Roe Cloud Alumni Award and the hosting of several academic conferences on his career.
3. Vigil, *Indigenous Intellectuals*, 83–84; Piatote, *Domestic Subjects*, 38–47; Angela Calcaterra, "A 'Second Look' at Charles Alexander Eastman," *Studies in American Indian Literatures* 27, no. 4 (2015): 1–36; Martínez, *Eastman*, xi, 75, 97, 153–55; Raymond Wilson, review of "The Soul of An Indian," *American Indian Culture and Research Journal* 42, no. 1 (2018): 151–53; on reevaluating the career of Oskison, see Lionel Larré, "John Milton Oskison and Assimilation," *American Indian Quarterly* 37, no. 1 (2013): 3–33; Hoxie, *Indian Country*, 5–7; Cahill, "Marie Baldwin," 65–83; Deloria, "Four Thousand Invitations," 26.
4. Conger, *National Congress of American Indians*, 18–19; Martínez, *American Indian Intellectual Tradition*, xvi; Brooks, "Intellectual History," 515; Maddox, *Citizen Indians*, 124–25.
5. Work to Parker, May 10, 1923, Reel 7, SAI Papers; *Southern Workman* 53, no. 3 (1924): 96–99, quoted in Hertzberg, *Search*, 204; Parker to McKenzie, March 8, 1924, Reel 5, SAI Papers; Parker, Letter to the Editor, *NYT*, January 19, 1924, Reel 5, SAI Papers. In 1924, the Committee of One Hundred issued these recommendations in a document, "The Indian Problem." For more on the committee, see Prucha, *Great Father*, 806–7. He concluded that it accomplished little or nothing. The official name of the Committee of One-Hundred was the Advisory Council on Indian Affairs. The singer Tsianina was on the committee, although it was unclear if she was an SAI member.
6. Lewis Meriam et al., *The Problem of Indian Administration* (Baltimore: Johns Hopkins, 1928); Ramirez, *Standing Up to Colonial Power*, 18–19, 122–126. Roe Cloud also helped draft the Indian Reorganization Act of 1934.
7. Hoxie, *Final Promise*, 236; Steven Sabol, "In Search of Citizenship: The Society of American Indians and the First World War," *Oregon Historical Quarterly* 118, no. 2 (2017): 268–71; Krouse, *North American Indians in the Great War*, focuses on the relationship between patriotism and the struggle for citizenship. From 1921 onward, the SAI was not a functioning organization. Individuals such as

Thomas Sloan, Arthur Parker, and Carlos Montezuma (through *Wassaja*, up until 1922) continued to lobby. In addition, the SAI ceased publication of its journal in 1920. It did not have a significant voice after 1920.

8. Beth H. Piatote, "The Indian/Agent Aporia," in *Society of American Indians*, 58; Deloria, "Four Thousand Invitations," 29.
9. Sells to Parker, December 22, 1913, Reel 5, SAI Papers.
10. Archie Phinney to Parker, August 28 1942, Parker to Phinney, September 1, 1942, quoted in Conger, *National Congress of American Indians*, 32, 169n7.
11. Cahill, *Federal Fathers and Mothers*, 2, 113; see pp. 45–50 on the role of the field matrons on reservations.
12. Wheelock to Parker, September 10, 1913, Reel 7, SAI Papers.
13. Parker to La Flesche, April 25, 1916, Reel 4, SAI Papers; Hertzberg, *Search*, 135, argued that the demand to abolish the Indian Office was the leading cause of the Society's demise.
14. Mooney to Marie Baldwin, December 8, 1914, Reel 5, SAI Papers.
15. For a full bibliography of articles and books by and about Sherman Coolidge, Charles Eastman, Carlos Montezuma, Arthur Parker, Henry Roe Cloud, Dennison Wheelock, and Zitkala-Ša, see Martínez, *American Indian Intellectual Tradition*.
16. Cobb, ed., *Say We Are Nations*, includes Parker, Montezuma, and Roe Cloud; Iverson, *"We Are Still Here,"* 52.

# BIBLIOGRAPHY


## Primary Sources

*First National Conference of the American Indian Association, October 12–15, 1911 on the Campus of The Ohio State University*. Columbus, Ohio: Stoneman Press, 1911.

Larner, John W., Jr. *Guide and Index to the Microfilm Edition of the Papers of Carlos Montezuma, M.D., 1871–1952*. Woodbridge, Conn.: Gale Centage Learning, 2004.

Larner, John W., Jr. *Guide to the Scholarly Resources Microfilm Edition of the Papers of the Society of American Indians*. Wilmington, Del.: Scholarly Resources, 1987.

Larner, John W., Jr. *The Papers of Carlos Montezuma, M.D.*, Microfilm, 9 Reels. Wilmington, Del.: Scholarly Resources, 1984.

Larner, John W., Jr., ed. *The Papers of the Society of American Indians, 1906–1946*. Microfilm, 10 reels. Wilmington, Del.: Scholarly Resources, 1986.

*Peyote: Hearings Before a Subcommittee of the Committee on Indian Affairs of the House of Representatives on H.R. 2614*, 65th Cong., 2nd sess. Washington, D.C.: Government Printing Office, 1918.

*Prohibition of the Use of Peyote*, U.S. Congress, Documents and Reports, 65th Cong., 2nd sess., May 13, 1918. Washington, D.C.: Government Printing Office, 1918.

Society of American Indians. *Constitution and Bylaws of the Society of American Indians*. Washington, D.C.: Society of American Indians, 1916.

Society of American Indians. *Report of the Executive Council on the Proceedings of the Annual Conference of the Society of American Indians*. Washington, D.C.: Society of American Indians, 1912.

## Secondary Sources

### *Books*

Allen, Chadwick, and Beth H. Piatote, eds. *The Society of American Indians and Its Legacies: A Special Combined Issue of* Studies in American Indian Literatures

*25:2 (2013) and* American Indian Quarterly *37:3 (2013).* Lincoln: University of Nebraska Press, 2013.

Anderson, Edward F. *Peyote: The Divine Cactus.* 2nd ed. Tucson: University of Arizona Press, 1996.

Aptheker, Herbert, ed. *Correspondence of W. E. B. Du Bois.* Vol. 1. Amherst: University of Massachusetts Press, 1973.

Baker, Lee D. *Anthropology and the Racial Politics of Culture.* Durham, N.C.: Duke University Press, 2010.

Benjey, Tom. *Keep A-Goin': The Life of Lone Star Dietz.* Carlisle, Pa.: Tuxedo Press, 2016.

Britten, Thomas A. *American Indians in World War I: At Home and Abroad.* Albuquerque: University of New Mexico Press, 1997.

Cahill, Cathleen D. *Federal Fathers and Mothers: A Social History of the United States Indian Service, 1869–1933.* Chapel Hill: University of North Carolina Press, 2011.

Cobb, Daniel M., ed. *Say We Are Nations: Documents of Politics and Protest in Indigenous America Since 1887.* Chapel Hill: University of North Carolina Press, 2015.

Cobb, Daniel M., and Loretta Fowler eds. *Beyond Red Power: American Indian Politics and Activism Since 1900.* Santa Fe: School for Advanced Research, 2007.

Colwell-Chanthaphonh, Chip. *Inheriting the Past: The Making of Arthur C. Parker and Indigenous Archaeology.* Tucson: University of Arizona Press, 2009.

Conger, Thomas W. *The National Congress of American Indians: The Founding Years.* Lincoln: University of Nebraska Press, 1999.

Coolidge, Grace. *Teepee Neighbors.* Boston: Four Seas, 1917. Reprint, Norman: University of Oklahoma Press, 1984.

Curtis, Edward S. *The North American Indian,* 20 vols. Cambridge, Mass.: Harvard University Press, 1907–9 (vols. 1–5); Norwood, Conn.: Plimpton Press, 1911–30 (vols. 6–20).

Deloria, Philip J. *Indians in Unexpected Places.* Lawrence: University Press of Kansas, 2004.

Deloria, Philip, J. *Playing Indian.* New Haven: Yale University Press, 1998.

Dippie, Brian W. *The Vanishing American: White Attitudes and U.S. Indian Policy.* Lawrence: University Press of Kansas, 1982.

Dixon, Joseph K. *The Vanishing Race: The Last Great Indian Council.* New York: Doubleday, 1913.

Du Bois, W. E. B. *The Souls of Black Folks.* New York: Bedford/St. Martin's, 1997 (1903).

Eastman, Charles. *From the Deep Woods to Civilization.* 1916. Reprint, Lincoln: University of Nebraska Press, 1977.

Eastman, Charles. *The Indian To-Day: The Past and Future of the First American.* New York: Doubleday, 1915.

Eastman, Charles. *The Soul of an Indian and Other Writings from Ohiyesa.* 1911. Reprint, New York: New World Library, 1993.

Egan, Timothy. *Short Nights of the Shadow Catcher: The Epic Life and Immortal Photographs of Edward Curtis.* New York: Houghton Mifflin Harcourt, 2012.

Fixico, Donald F. *Bureau of Indian Affairs*. Santa Barbara, Calif.: Greenwood, 2012.

Grillot, Thomas. *First Americans: U.S. Patriotism in Indian Country after World War I*. New Haven: Yale University Press, 2018. Originally published in France as *Après la grande guerre: Comment les Amérindiens des États-Unis sont devenus patriotes (1917–1947)*, 2014.

Hagan, William. *The Indian Rights Association: The Herbert Welsh Years*. Tucson: University of Arizona, 1985.

Harjo, Joy, and Gloria Bird, eds. *Reinventing the Enemy's Language: Contemporary Native Women's Writing of North America*. New York: Norton, 1998.

Hertzberg, Hazel. *The Search for an American Indian Identity: Modern Pan-Indian Movements*. Syracuse: Syracuse University Press, 1971.

Hodge, Frederick W., ed. *Handbook of American Indians North of Mexico*. 2 vols. Washington, D.C.: Government Printing Office, 1907–1910.

Holm, Tom. *The Great Confusion in Indian Affairs: Native Americans and Whites in the Progressive Era*. Austin: University of Texas Press, 2005.

Hoxie, Frederick E. *A Final Promise: The Campaign to Assimilate the Indians, 1880–1920*. Lincoln: University of Nebraska Press, 1984.

Hoxie, Frederick E. ed. *The Oxford Handbook of American Indian History*. New York: Oxford University Press, 2016.

Hoxie, Frederick E. ed. *Talking Back to Civilization: Indian Voices from the Progressive Era*. Boston: Bedford, 2001.

Hoxie, Frederick E. *This Indian Country: American Indian Activists and the Place They Made*. New York: Penguin, 2012.

Iverson, Peter. *Carlos Montezuma and the Changing World of American Indians*. Albuquerque: University of New Mexico Press, 1982.

Iverson, Peter. *"We Are Still Here": American Indians in the Twentieth Century*. Wheeling, Ill.: Harlan Davidson, 1998.

Kilpatrick, Jacqueline. *Celluloid Indians: Native Americans and Film*. Lincoln: University of Nebraska Press, 1999.

King, C. Richard. *Redskins: Insult and Brand*. Lincoln: University of Nebraska Press, 2016.

Kroeber, Theodora. *Ishi of Two Worlds: A Biography of the Last Wild Indian of North America*. Berkeley: University of California Press, 1961.

Krouse, Susan Applegate. *North American Indians in the Great War*. Lincoln: University of Nebraska Press, 2007.

Labate, Beatriz C., and Clancy Cavanar, eds. *Peyote: History, Tradition, Politics, and Conservation*. Santa Barbara, Calif.: Praeger, 2016.

Lane, Anne W., and Louise H. Wall, eds. *The Letters of Franklin K. Lane*. New York: Houghton Mifflin, 1922.

La Potin, Armand, ed. *Native American Voluntary Organizations*. New York: Greenwood, 1987.

Lewandowski, Tadeusz. *Red Bird, Red Power: The Life and Legacy of Zitkala-Ša*. Norman: University of Oklahoma Press, 2016.

Liberty, Margot, ed. *American Indian Intellectuals of the Nineteenth and Early Twentieth Century*. Norman: University of Oklahoma Press, 2002.

Maddox, Lucy. *Citizen Indians: Native American Intellectuals, Race and Reform*. Ithaca, N.Y.: Cornell University Press, 2004.

Maroukis, Thomas C. *The Peyote Road: Religious Freedom and the Native American Church*. Norman: University of Oklahoma Press, 2010.

Maroukis, Thomas C. *Peyote and The Yankton Sioux: The Life and Times of Sam Necklace*. Norman: University of Oklahoma Press, 2004.

Martínez, David. ed. *The American Indian Intellectual Tradition: An Anthology from 1772 to 1972*. Ithaca, N.Y.: Cornell University Press, 2011.

Martínez, David. *Dakota Philosopher: Charles Eastman and American Indian Thought*. St. Paul: Minnesota Historical Society, 2009.

Mathes, Valerie S., ed. *The Women's National Indian Association: A History*. Albuquerque: University of New Mexico Press, 2015.

McDonnell, Janet A. *The Dispossession of the American Indian, 1887–1934*. Bloomington: Indiana University Press, 1991.

McKenzie, Fayette A. *The Indian and Citizenship*. Washington, D.C.: Society of American Indians, 1912.

McKenzie, Fayette A. *"Lo! The Poor Indian": Calls for the Attention of the American Public*. Washington, D.C.: Society of American Indians, 1912.

McNenly, Linda S. *Native Performers in Wild West Shows: From Buffalo Bill to Euro Disney*. Norman: University of Oklahoma Press, 2012.

Merian, Lewis, et al. *The Problem of Indian Administration*. Baltimore: Johns Hopkins, 1928.

Moorehead, Warren C. *The American Indian In the United States*, Andover, Mass: Andover Press, 1914.

Moses, L. G. *Indian Man: A Biography of James Mooney*. Urbana: University of Illinois Press, 1984.

Moses, L. G. *Wild West Shows and the Images of American Indians, 1883–1933*. Albuquerque: University of New Mexico, 1996.

Parker, Robert D. ed., *Changing Is Not Vanishing: A Collection of American Indian Poetry to 1930*. Philadelphia: University of Pennsylvania Press, 2011.

Peyer, Bernd C. ed. *American Indian Non-fiction: An Anthology of Writings, 1760s–1930s*. Norman: University of Oklahoma Press, 2007.

Pfister, Joel. *The Yale Indian: The Education of Henry Roe Cloud*. Durham, N.C.: Duke University Press, 2009.

Piatote, Beth H. *Domestic Subjects: Gender, Citizenship, and Law in Native American Literature*. New Haven: Yale University Press, 2013.

Porter, Joy. *To Be Indian: The Life of Iroquois-Seneca Arthur Caswell Parker*. Norman: University of Oklahoma Press, 2001.

Prucha, Francis Paul. *The Great Father: The United States Government and the American Indian*. Lincoln: University of Nebraska Press, 1984. Unabridged ed., 1 vol., 1995.

Ramirez, Renya K. *Standing Up to Colonial Power: The Lives of Henry Roe and Elizabeth Bender Cloud.* Lincoln: University of Nebraska Press, 2018.

Red-Horse, Valeria, et al. *Choctaw Code Talkers.* Lincoln, Neb.: Vision Maker Video, 2010.

Sargent, Theodore D. *The Life of Elaine Goodale Eastman.* Lincoln: University of Nebraska Press, 2005.

Shreve, Bradley G. *Red Power Rising: The National Indian Youth Council and the Origins of Native Activism.* Norman: University of Oklahoma Press, 2011.

Smith, Paul Chaat, and Robert Allen Warrior. *Like a Hurricane: The Indian American Movement from Alcatraz to Wounded Knee.* New York: New Press, 1996.

Speroff, Leon. *Carlos Montezuma, M.D., A Yavapai American Hero: The Life and Times of an American Indian, 1866–1923.* Portland, Ore.: Arnica Publishers, 2005.

Spiller, Gustave, ed. *Papers on Inter-racial Problems, Communicated to the First Universal Races Congress.* London: P. S. King, 1911.

Starn, Orin. *Ishi's Brain: In Search of America's Last "Wild" Indian.* New York: Norton, 2005.

Stewart, Omer C. *Peyote Religion: A History.* Norman: University of Oklahoma Press, 1987.

Swan, Daniel C. *Peyote Religious Art: Symbols of Faith and Belief.* Jackson: University of Mississippi Press, 1999.

Townsend, Kenneth W., and Mark A. Nicholas. *First Americans: A History of Native Peoples.* New York: Pearson, 2013.

Trachtenberg, Alan. *Shades of Hiawatha: Staging Indians, Making Americans, 1880–1930.* New York: Hill & Wang, 2004.

Waggoner, Linda M. *Fire Light: The Life of Angel De Cora, Winnebago Artist.* Norman: University of Oklahoma Press, 2008.

Warrior, Robert Allen. *Tribal Secrets: Recovering American Indian Intellectual Traditions.* Minneapolis: University of Minnesota Press, 1995.

Welsh, Herbert B. *Peyote: An Insidious Evil.* Philadelphia: Indian Rights Association, 1915.

Wilson, Norman J. *History in Crisis: Recent Directions in Historiography.* Upper Saddle River, N.J.: Pearson Prentice Hall, 2005.

Wilson, Raymond. *Ohiyesa: Charles Eastman, Santee Sioux.* Urbana: University of Illinois Press, 1983.

Woodward, Kathleen, and Irene C. F. Beatlieu. *Tribute to A Vanishing Race.* Pawhuska, Okla.: 1913.

Zitkala-Ša. *American Indian Stories.* Washington, D.C.: Hayworth, 1921. Reprint, Lincoln: University of Nebraska Press, 1985.

Zitkala-Ša. "*The Menace of Peyote.* Pamphlet, 1916." In *American Indian Stories,* edited by Cathy N. Davidson and Ada Norris, 239–41. 1921. Reprint, New York: Penguin, 2003.

Zitkala-Ša. *Old Indian Legends.* Boston: Ginn, 1901. Reprint, Lincoln: University of Nebraska Press, 1985.

## *Articles*


Ackley, Kristina. "Laura Cornelius Kellogg, Lolomi, and Modern Oneida Placemaking." In *The Society of American Indians and Its Legacies: A Special Combined Issue of* Studies in American Indian Literatures *25:2 (2013) and* American Indian Quarterly *37:3 (2013),* edited by Chadwick Allen and Beth H. Piatote, 117–38. Lincoln: University of Nebraska Press, 2013.

Ackley, Kristina. "Renewing Haudenosaunee Ties: Laura Cornelius Kellogg and the Idea of Unity in the Oneida Land Claim." *American Indian Culture and Research Journal* 32, no. 1 (2008): 57–81.

Adams, David Wallace. "More Than a Game: The Carlisle Indians Take to the Gridiron, 1893–1917." *Western Historical Quarterly* 32, no. 1 (2001): 25–53.

Allen, Chadwick. "Introduction: Locating the Society of American Indians." In *The Society of American Indians and Its Legacies: A Special Combined Issue of* Studies in American Indian Literatures *25:2 (2013) and* American Indian Quarterly *37:3 (2013),* edited by Chadwick Allen and Beth H. Piatote, 3–22. Lincoln: University of Nebraska Press, 2013.

Berg, S. Carol. "Arthur C. Parker and the Society of the American Indian, 1911–1916." *New York History* 81 (2000): 237–46.

Brooks, Lisa. "Intellectual History." In *The Oxford Handbook of American Indian History,* edited by Frederick E. Hoxie, 513–37. New York: Oxford University Press, 2016.

Brosius, Samuel. "Ravages of Peyote." *Annual Report of the IRA* 34 (1916): 37–41.

Cahill, Cathleen D. "Marie Louise Bottineau Baldwin: Indigenizing the Federal Indian Service." In *The Society of American Indians and Its Legacies: A Special Combined Issue of* Studies in American Indian Literatures *25:2 (2013) and* American Indian Quarterly *37:3 (2013),* edited by Chadwick Allen and Beth H. Piatote, 65–86. Lincoln: University of Nebraska Press, 2013.

Carpenter, Cari. "Detecting Indianness: Gertrude Bonnin's Investigation of Native American Identity." *Wicazo Sa Review* 20, no. 1 (2005): 139–59.

Chaatsmith, Marti L. "Singing at the Center of the Indian World: The SAI and the Ohio Earthworks." In *The Society of American Indians and Its Legacies: A Special Combined Issue of* Studies in American Indian Literatures *25:2 (2013) and* American Indian Quarterly *37:3 (2013),* edited by Chadwick Allen and Beth H. Piatote, 181–98. Lincoln: University of Nebraska Press, 2013.

Clark, D. Anthony Tyeeme. "At the Headwaters of a Twentieth Century 'Indian' Political Agenda: Rethinking the Origins of the Society of American Indians." In *Beyond Red Power: American Indian Politics and Activism Since 1900,* edited by Daniel Cobb and Loretta Fowler, 70–90. Santa Fe: School for Advanced Research, 2007.

Crum, Steven. "Almost Invisible: The Brotherhood of North American Indians (1911) and the League of North American Indians." *Wicazo Sa Review* 21, no. 1 (2006): 43–59.

Crum, Steven. "Henry Roe Cloud: Winnebago Indian Reformer: His Quest for American Indian Higher Education." *Kansas History* 11 (1988): 171–84.

Deloria, Philip J. "American Master Narratives and the Problem of Indian Citizenship in the Gilded Age and Progressive Era." *Journal of the Gilded Age and Progressive Era* 15 (2015): 3–12.

Deloria, Philip J. "Four Thousand Invitations." In *The Society of American Indians and Its Legacies: A Special Combined Issue of* Studies in American Indian Literatures *25:2 (2013) and* American Indian Quarterly *37:3 (2013)*, edited by Chadwick Allen and Beth H. Piatote, 25–43. Lincoln: University of Nebraska Press, 2013.

Foner, Eric. "The Civil War, Reconstruction and the Origins of Birthright Citizenship." *Marquette Lawyer* (Summer 2012): 32–42.

Gere, Anne Ruggles. "The Art of Survivance: Angel DeCora at Carlisle." *American Indian Quarterly* 28, no. 3–4 (2004): 649–84.

Hafen, P. Jane. "'Help Indians Help Themselves': Gertrude Bonnin, the SAI, and the NCAI." In *The Society of American Indians and Its Legacies: A Special Combined Issue of* Studies in American Indian Literatures *25:2 (2013) and* American Indian Quarterly *37:3 (2013)*, edited by Chadwick Allen and Beth H. Piatote, 199–218. Lincoln: University of Nebraska Press, 2013.

Hafen, P. Jane. "Zitkala-Ša: Sentimentality and Sovereignty." *Wicazo Sa Review* 12, no. 2 (1997): 31–41.

Hauptman, Laurence M. "From Carlisle to Carnegie Hall: The Musical Career of Dennison Wheelock." In *Oneida Voices in the Age of Allotment, 1860–1920*, edited by L. M. Hauptman and L.G. McLester, 112–38. Norman: University of Oklahoma Press, 2006.

Hertzberg, Hazel. "Arthur C. Parker, Seneca, 1881–1951." In *American Indian Intellectuals of the Nineteenth and Twentieth Centuries*, edited by Margot Liberty, 29–40. Norman: University of Oklahoma Press, 1978.

Howard, James. "The Pan Indian Culture of Oklahoma." *Scientific Monthly* 18, no. 5 (1955): 215–20.

Hutchinson, Elizabeth. "Modern Native American Art: Angel De Cora's Transcultural Aesthetic." *Art Bulletin* 83, no. 4 (2001): 740–56.

Larner, John W. "Society of American Indians." In *Native America in the Twentieth Century: An Encyclopedia*, edited by Mary B. Davis, 603–4. New York: Garland, 1994.

Larré, Lionel. "John Milton Oskison and Assimilation." *American Indian Quarterly* 37, no. 1–2 (2013): 3–33.

Lomawaima, K. Tsianina. "The Mutuality of *Citizenship* and *Sovereignty*: The Society of American Indians and The Battle to Inherit America." In *The Society of American Indians and Its Legacies: A Special Combined Issue of* Studies in American Indian Literatures *25:2 (2013) and* American Indian Quarterly *37:3 (2013)*, edited by Chadwick Allen and Beth H. Piatote, 333–51. Lincoln: University of Nebraska Press, 2013.

Maroukis, Thomas C. "The Founding of the Society of American Indians in Columbus, Ohio, October 12–17, 1911." Unpublished paper presented at the Ohio Academy of History conference, Denison University, Granville, Ohio, April 2011.

Maroukis, Thomas C. "The Peyote Controversy and The Demise of The Society of American Indians." In *The Society of American Indians and Its Legacies: A Special Combined Issue of* Studies in American Indian Literatures *25:2 (2013) and* American Indian Quarterly *37:3 (2013)*, edited by Chadwick Allen and Beth H. Piatote, 161–80. Lincoln: University of Nebraska Press, 2013.

Martínez, David. "Carlos Montezuma's Fight against 'Bureauism': An Unexpected Pima Hero." In *The Society of American Indians and Its Legacies: A Special Combined Issue of* Studies in American Indian Literatures *25:2 (2013) and* American Indian Quarterly *37:3 (2013)*, edited by Chadwick Allen and Beth H. Piatote, 311–30. Lincoln: University of Nebraska Press, 2013.

Mays, Kyle T. "Transnational Progressivism: African Americans, Native Americans, and the Universal Races Congress of 1911." In *The Society of American Indians and Its Legacies: A Special Combined Issue of* Studies in American Indian Literatures *25:2 (2013) and* American Indian Quarterly *37:3 (2013)*, edited by Chadwick Allen and Beth H. Piatote, 243–61. Lincoln: University of Nebraska Press, 2013.

McKenzie, Fayette A. "The American Indian Conference." *The Red Man* 4, no. 1 (1911): 3–8.

McKenzie, Fayette A. "The American Indian of Today and Tomorrow." *Journal of Race Development* 3, no. 2 (1912): 135–55.

McKenzie, Fayette A. "The Assimilation of the American Indian." *Publications of the American Sociological Association* 8 (1913): 37–48.

McKenzie, Fayette A. "The First National Conference of Indians." *Report of the Executive Council on the Proceedings of the First Annual Conference of the Society of American Indians*. Washington, D.C.: Society of American Indians, 1912, 171–78.

McKenzie, Fayette A. "The Indian Conference." *Kit Kat Club Magazine*, September 1912, 147–50.

McKenzie, Fayette A. "My People: The Indian's Contribution to the Art of America." *Red Man* 7 (December 1914): 133–40.

McNally, Michael D. "The Indian Passion Play: Contesting the Real Indian in 'Song of Hiawatha' Pageants, 1901–1965." *American Indian Quarterly* 28, no. 1 (2006): 105–36.

Newmark, Julianne. "A Prescription for Freedom: Carlos Montezuma, *Wassaja*, and the Society of American Indians." In *The Society of American Indians and Its Legacies: A Special Combined Issue of* Studies in American Indian Literatures *25:2 (2013) and* American Indian Quarterly *37:3 (2013)*, edited by Chadwick Allen and Beth H. Piatote, 139–58. Lincoln: University of Nebraska Press, 2013.

Newmark, Julianne. "Pluralism, Place, and Gertrude Bonnin's Counternativism from Utah to Washington, D.C." *American Indian Quarterly* 36, no. 3 (2012): 318–47.

Parker, Arthur. "The Social Elements of the Indian Problem." *American Journal of Sociology* 22, no. 2 (1916): 252–67.

Patterson, Michelle Wick. "'Real' Indian Songs: The Society of American Indians and the Use of Native American Culture as a Means of Reform." *American Indian Quarterly* 26, no. 1 (2002): 44–66.

Piatote, Beth H. "The Indian/Agent Aporia." In *The Society of American Indians and Its Legacies: A Special Combined Issue of* Studies in American Indian Literatures *25:2 (2013) and* American Indian Quarterly *37:3 (2013)*, edited by Chadwick Allen and Beth H. Piatote, 45–62. Lincoln: University of Nebraska Press, 2013.

Randall, E. O. "The Indian Conference." *Ohio State Archeological and Historical Society* 21 (1912): 487–88.

Redmond, C. Daniel. "The Sartorial Indian: Zitkala-Ša, Clothing, and Resistance to Colonization." *Studies in American Indian Literatures* 28, no. 3 (2016): 52–80.

Rosier. Paul C. "Surviving the Twentieth Century, 1890–1960." In *Oxford Handbook of American Indian History*, edited by Frederick E. Hoxie, 111–27. New York: Oxford University Press, 2016.

Sabol, Steven. "In Search of Citizenship: The Society of American Indians and the First World War." *Oregon Historical Quarterly* 118, no. 2 (2017): 268–71.

Seymour, Gertrude. "Peyote Worship: An Indian Cult and a Powerful Drug." *Survey* 34 (May 13, 1916): 181–84.

Smith, Michael T. "The History of Indian Citizenship." *Great Plains Journal* 10 (1970): 25–35.

Smith, Sherry. "Native Americans and Indian Policy in the Progressive Era." *Journal of the Gilded Age and Progressive Era* 9, no. 4 (2010): 503–7.

Stewart, Omer. "Gertrude Simmons Bonnin." *Bulletin of the Institute of the American Indian Studies: University of South Dakota* 87 (1981).

Stovey, Patricia. "Opportunities at Home: Laura Cornelius Kellogg and Village Industrialization." In *Oneida Voices: The Age of Allotment, 1860–1920*, edited by L. M. Hauptman and L. G. McLester, 143–75. Norman: University of Oklahoma Press, 2006.

Tate, Michael L. "From Scout to Doughboy: The National Debate over Integrating American Indians into the Military, 1891–1918." *Western Historical Quarterly* 27, no. 4 (1986): 417–37.

Warrior, Robert. "The SAI and the End(s) of Intellectual History." In *The Society of American Indians and Its Legacies: A Special Combined Issue of* Studies in American Indian Literatures *25:2 (2013) and* American Indian Quarterly *37:3 (2013)*, edited by Chadwick Allen and Beth H. Piatote, 221–35. Lincoln: University of Nebraska Press, 2013.

Washburn, Wilcomb E. "The Society of American Indians." *Indian Historian* 3 (1970): 21–23.

Willard, William. "Zitkala-Ša: A Woman Who Would Be Heard!" *Wicazo Sa Review* 1, no. 1 (1985): 11–16.

Zuck, Rochelle R. "'Yours in the Cause': Readers, Correspondents, and the Editorial Politics of Carlos Montezuma's *Wassaja*." *American Periodicals: A Journal of History, Criticism and Bibliography* 22, no. 1 (2012): 72–93.

## *Journals*

*American Indian Magazine*
*American Indian Quarterly*

*Crisis: A Record of the Darker Races* (National Association for the Advancement of Colored People)
*Quarterly Journal of the Society of American Indians*
*Studies in American Indian Literatures*
*Wassaja: Freedom's Signal for the Indians*

## *Dissertations*

Clark, David A. Tyeeme. "Representing Indians: Indigenous Fugitives and the Society of American Indians in the Making of a Common Culture." PhD diss., University of Kansas, 2004.

Dominguez, Susan Rose. "The Gertrude Bonnin Story: From Yankton Destiny into American History, 1876–1938." PhD diss., Michigan State University, 2005.

Furnish, Patricia L. "'Aboriginally Yours': The Society of American Indians and U.S. Citizenship, 1890–1924." PhD diss., University of Oklahoma, 2005.

Lisa, Laurie O'Dell. "The Life Story of Zitkala-Ša/Gertrude Simmons Bonnin: Writing and Creating a Public Image." PhD diss., Arizona State University, 1996.

McKenzie, Fayette. "The Indian in Relation to the White Population of the United States." PhD diss., University of Pennsylvania, 1908.

Welsh, Deborah S. "Zitkala-Ša: An American Indian Leader, 1876–1938." PhD diss., University of Wyoming, 1985.

# INDEX

Page numbers in *italics* refer to illustrations.

# ABOUT THE AUTHOR

**Thomas Constantine Maroukis** is professor emeritus in the Department of History at Capital University in Columbus, Ohio. He is the author of *The Peyote Road: Religious Freedom and the Native American Church* and *Peyote and the Yankton Sioux*.